STAGES OF FAITH AND RELIGIOUS DEVELOPMENT

Stages of Faith
and Religious Development:

Implications for
Church, Education and Society

edited by

James W. Fowler, Karl Ernst Nipkow and Friedrich Schweitzer

SCM PRESS

Copyright © 1991 by Center for Research in Faith and Moral
Development, Candler School of Theology, Emory University

British Library Cataloguing in Publication Data

Stages of faith and religious development :
implications for Church, education and society.
I. Fowler, James W.   II. Nipkow, Karl Ernst
III. Schweitzer, Friedrich
200.1

ISBN 0334 025206

First published in Britain 1992
by SCM Press Ltd
26-30 Tottenham Road London N1 4BZ

Typeset and printed in the United States of America

Contents

Preface

THE CHAPTERS OF this book focus on the two major theories of faith development to emerge out of the cognitive developmental tradition pioneered by
Jean Piaget. James Fowler and his associates, first at Harvard and now at
Emory University, have generated a structural developmental theory focused
on the operations of knowing, valuing, and committing that underlie persons'
ways of finding and making meaning. Faith, for Fowler, includes but is not
restricted to religious faith. His theory of seven developmental stages has
exerted wide influence in North America. Now its influence is being felt in
Europe, Africa, Latin America, and Asia, with translations of his writings
appearing in Korean, Danish, German, Portuguese, Swedish, and an Indone-
sian dialect.

Fritz Oser, of Fribourg University in Switzerland, heads a Piagetian
research enterprise that has sought to establish structural-developmental
stages of religious knowing. Adhering closely to the model of Lawrence
Kohlberg, by whom both he and Fowler are influenced, Oser has worked
vigorously to establish an empirical grounding for a stage theory of religious
reasoning. He has looked for universal structures of thought underlying the
human ways of dealing with such issues as evil and God's involvement in historical events, the suffering of innocents, the limits of human knowledge, the
meaning of death, and questions of life after death, as well as questions of
cosmic justice and fairness. The work of Oser and his associates is exerting
wide influence in education in Europe and will soon be available in English
translations. His chapter in this volume offers one of the first extensive
presentation of his work in English.

In this collection of essays the structural developmental theories of Fowler
and Oser are subjected to interpretation and critique by a carefully selected
group of North American, British, and European authors. In a substantive
introduction, Karl Ernst Nipkow, Friedrich Schweitzer, and James Fowler,
editors of this volume, provide an initial tracing of the issues that arise in the
crossfire of subsequent chapters.

We then turn to Part 1, where James Fowler examines the theological
underpinnings of faith development theory. He traces the evolution of his
work in practical theology and explores the relationship between practical

theology and faith development theory. Throughout, he argues for both the
social scientific integrity of faith development theory and the theological
origins and relevance of this theory against those who wish to restrict its
utility to one or the other sphere of inquiry.

Fritz Oser, in the second chapter, tells how he and his Swiss colleagues
use religious dilemmas to provoke religious judgments and reasoning on the
part of subjects, much as Kohlberg used moral dilemmas to probe moral
reasoning. A stage theory of religious judgment has emerged from analysis
of subject responses to these dilemmas, a theory parallel to Piaget's analysis
of cognitive development and to Kohlberg's work with moral development.
In this chapter, Oser summarizes the theory, describes the development of
religious judgment as portrayed in his interpretation of research interviews,
and responds to critics. The chapter provides a concise introduction to this
theory of religious development, exploring both its formulation and many of
its perceived limitations.

After the introductory essays by Fowler and Oser in Part 1, Friedrich
Schweitzer and Karl Ernst Nipkow, both of Tübingen University, place
developmental theories in historical and theological contexts. In chapter 3
Schweitzer traces some of the early history of perspectives on children's
religious understanding, briefly discussing the views of such figures as M.
Luther, J. A. Comenius, A. H. Francke, F. Schleiermacher, J. Paul, J. J.
Rousseau, G. Herbert, and T. Ziller. He uses this framework to note that the
awareness of religious development is not a product of this century and that
current theories of religious development—notably stage theories—have
historical antecedents. Indeed, modern theories share both strengths and
weaknesses with these earlier formulations. Schweitzer argues that this
historical perspective may assist theorists in avoiding previous errors, such
as devaluing childhood religiosity, emphasizing unidirectional progress in
development, and scheduling development too tightly.

In chapter 4 Karl Ernst Nipkow wrestles with problems that arise in
developing an appropriate relationship between faith development theory
and religious education. In doing so, he challenges both the practices of
education and the current formulations of faith development theory, noting
the inadequacies of each. For example, Nipkow criticizes education practitioners for too often failing to take the active role of the learner seriously.
Regarding faith development theory, one of his challenges involves the
contrast between faith development as the evolution of increasingly complex
patterns of meaning making and faith development as a matter of increasing
strength of attachment. The thrust of the chapter is to further the dialogue
between faith development theory and the theory and practice of religious
education.

In Part 3 our authors locate Fowler and Oser's work in relation to their
critics and the larger context of current debates on theories of human

development. Sharon Parks, in chapter 5, examines five prominent categories of criticism of Fowler's faith development theory that have arisen in its North American context: criticisms of the definition of faith; concerns regarding the characterization of the Universalizing Stage; particular denominational perspectives on the theory; perceptions that the theory truncates a full accounting of the dynamics of faith experience; sociopolitical critiques and the question of gender inclusiveness or bias. She uses the North American context and these criticisms to propose a view of the theory that recognizes its role in fostering theological discussion and interdisciplinary dialogue.

The relationship between stage theories purporting to map various psychological domains is a topic that has aroused considerable controversy. Clark Power, author of chapter 6, is a former student of and joint author with Lawrence Kohlberg. From the standpoint of Piagetian and Kohlbergian theory he assesses the theoretical rigor and status of the work of Fowler and Oser. He categorizes the structure of stages in the work of Piaget and Kohlberg as "hard stages," while designating those of Oser and Fowler as "soft stages." The distinction differentiates between theories that employ the rigorous logical structures of Piaget and those that do not. Power makes a case for distinguishing between these two types of stage theories while arguing for the integrity of each.

In chapter 7, Nicola Slee presents work on the development of religious thinking that has been done in the United Kingdom, work that may not be as well known in North America. In particular, she examines the Piagetian research of Ronald Goldman and of those who have continued his efforts. Goldman began his research because of dissatisfaction with religious education in English schools. He used interviews with children, in which he employed three biblical stories and three pictures, to analyze religious development. Slee analyzes the state of this research while briefly reporting on current work in England with Fowler's and Oser and Gmünder's theories as well.

Part 4 of the book builds around four critiques of developmental theories. In chapter 8, Gabriel Moran probes deeply the dangerous associations carried in our time by the metaphor "development." He offers alternative models for imaging the life of personal and communal faith, and makes a plea for intergenerational interaction in the awareness that human existence is not so much linear progress toward greater perfection but a circling movement around the deep center of life.

Sociologist Reiner Döbert, employing critical social theory, questions in chapter 9 whether structural developmental theories of religious reasoning and faith have really tapped "deep structures" in human cognition, or whether they merely reflect ideological cultural *content*. Döbert's particular concern has to do with stage 3 (the "Conventional" stage) in Oser and Gmünder's theory. He suggests that Oser's descriptions have captured

surface phenomena, mere ripples of the deep structure. The definition of
stage 3 lacks the logical seeds of future development and interacts with
modern culture in a way that seems to result in developmental stagnation.
The scope of the chapter extends beyond this somewhat limited focus to
reflect on the larger realm of cognitive developmental theories in general.
He argues that theories of moral, ego, and faith development have yet to tap
the deep structures underlying development.

In chapter 10, Günther Bittner, a psychoanalyst, argues that cognitively
oriented approaches to the religious or faith domain fail to engage the real
wellsprings of meaning making, which he sees as nonrational, imaginal, and
unconscious. He suggests that religious experience emerges primarily from
aesthetic, nonrational, noncognitive sources. As a result, he has serious
doubts about the ability of cognitive theories to explore this domain. His
chapter raises important questions about the nature of faith and the limits
of cognitively based theories.

Building in a similar direction in chapter 11, Heinz-Gunther Heimbrock
points to the indispensability of studying ritual processes if we would understand the dynamics of faith and religious knowing. Heimbrock explores the
place of ritual in developmental theories, particularly in Oser and Gmünder's
theory of religious judgment. He argues that ritual can be too easily relegated to the realm of immaturity in such frameworks. The insights of Erik
Erikson regarding the developmental significance of ritual, and those of
other social scientists who caution against the modern tendency to devalue
ritual, may both serve as important correctives. Heimbrock concludes by
calling for an expansion of developmental theories to address more adequately ritual across the stages, suggesting that such efforts may enable us
to expand our understanding of the nature of Christian education.

In Part 5 John M. Hull and Gloria Durka examine the developmental
theories of Fowler and Oser in light of critiques of late capitalist societies,
movements for feminist liberation, and patterns of secularization and ecclesial response in the United Kingdom and the United States. In chapter 12,
Hull applies a sociopolitical critique to stage development theories generally
and with particular reference to faith development theories. He argues that
such theories are enmeshed with the values and forces that have driven and
sustained modern Western capitalist societies. If this is granted, he argues,
they run the risk of sanctioning, even sanctifying, the status quo. Hull offers
some suggestions of ways in which these theories may mitigate some of the
more damaging aspects of this hazard and may indeed yet help point beyond
modernity.

In chapter 13, Gloria Durka presents a broad overview of emerging
American feminist perspectives on human experience. This overview provides a context for feminist reflection on religious development and education. She offers some concrete suggestions as to the implications of feminist

thought for religious education, that is, emphasizing "connection over separation, understanding and acceptance over assessment, and collaboration over debate." Durka focuses most heavily on the questions raised by the feminist movement regarding religious development and education, calling for further research on women's experience and increased inclusion of women's voices in the theoretical conversation.

The book has an extensive bibliography that assembles for the first time a comprehensive international listing of the references important for interpreting and evaluating the structural developmental movement in the interpretation of faith and religion.

Stages of Faith and Religious Development was published in 1988 in German as *Glaubensentwicklung und Erziehung* (Gütersloh: Mohn). It joins the growing literature of interpretation, criticism, and application of research and theory in religious and faith development, and represents the most extensive international discussion on these issues to date. The American edition of this work owes a debt of gratitude to Karl Ernst Nipkow and Friedrich Schweitzer, who did most of the work of editing the German volume and kindly gave permission for its translation into the present volume. In the preparation of this book Emory University doctoral candidates Kurt Keljo and Norbert Hahn made significant contributions in editing and translating, respectively. The ordering of our translation of the extensive bibliography was largely the work of Karen DeNicola, administrative coordinator of the Center for Research in Faith and Moral Development at Emory University. Our editor at Crossroad, Frank Oveis, gave strong support and incisive suggestions at many points, which have significantly helped to improve the book.

James W. Fowler
Emory University

Introduction

KARL ERNST NIPKOW
FRIEDRICH SCHWEITZER
JAMES FOWLER

"FAITH DEVELOPMENT," as mentioned in the title of this book, is a new term in psychology of religion. It does not refer to any particular faith or religion; rather, it refers to the developmental process of finding and making meaning as a human activity. This concept of faith or meaning intends to be equally applicable to religious and nonreligious, Christian and non-Christian interpretations of self and world. It is a psychological concept of faith that abstracts from any particular content of faith or belief. At the same time, this concept of faith is designed in such a way that it can also be interpreted theologically and filled with substantive beliefs. At least this is the explicit intention with which James Fowler has chosen this concept, following mainly the philosophy of religion of Paul Tillich and Wilfred Cantwell Smith.

In this volume we are concerned with both the *development* of faith as defined above and the development of religious reasoning and knowing as introduced in Europe by Fritz Oser and his colleagues. We also focus, however, on the implications of theories of faith and religious development for religious education. We will investigate the implications for religious education that result from the phenomenon of faith development and the research related to it. Our approach will not be one of simply transferring or applying psychological theories to religious education. Rather, we will pose critical questions to the psychological theories concerning their empirical validity and range as well as their theological adequacy. In addition, we will have to search for theoretical alternatives and inquire into their relation to theories of faith development. We will also have to uncover the social and societal conditions that form the backdrop for contemporary religious education.

In the following pages we will clarify the larger context in which the contributions to this volume need to be seen and how they are related to one another.

1

Stage Theories of Faith Development
as a New Approach to Psychology of Religion
and to Religious Education

One of the psychological theories of the last decade that received world-wide attention is most certainly the theory of moral development by L. Kohlberg (1981, 1984). Following and extending the work of J. Piaget, this theory joins together a cognitive approach to moral psychology with a concept of development that focuses on the general structures of moral judgments. The combination of these three elements – the choice of a *cognitive approach,* the emphasis on the *developmental dimension,* and the focus on *structures* – proved equally stimulating for research and praxis, despite some recognizable disadvantages of a theoretical commitment of this kind.

The cognitive-structural theories of moral development found a counter-part in the domain of religion, when, in the mid-seventies, James Fowler and Fritz Oser began to conduct empirical research and proposed their theories of faith development and of stages of religious judgment, respectively. These theories, too, delineate structural stages through which persons pass, or at least can pass, in their development. It must be pointed out from the beginning that such structural stages are by no means stages of maturation, for the aging process does not provide an automatic advance to a high stage. Rather, it is a central feature of the cognitive-structural theories of development – and in this they are distinctly and entirely different from an older school of developmental psychology – that, on the one hand, they posit the existence of higher stages later in life, because they build on the earlier stages, while, on the other hand, development can be arrested at any of the earlier stages. Actually, it is precisely the distinction between *age* and *development* that facilitates more complex insights, for instance, into the heterogeneity of congregations or school classes.

Furthermore, one must pay attention to the *broad concept of "knowing* or *"meaning making"* which guides the cognitive approach. For we are not deal-ing with a psychological reductionism to intellectual or rational aspects to the exclusion of the emotional or the irrational. This contradicts a widely held though erroneous assumption in two ways: first, the process of "know-ing" as understood and investigated by Piaget, Kohlberg, Fowler, Oser, and others does include the emotional domain, although this is not done, for instance, as it would be in a drive theory of the instincts. Second, while the rational structuring of morality or religion forms the explicit goal of develop-ment, these theories propose the alteration of the concept of rationality in such a way that it provides a legitimate role for religion instead of pushing it aside or replacing it.

One ought to be particularly cautious of prematurely charging Fowler with intellectualism. In his recent book on faith development and pastoral care, he has extended his theory by integrating the personality psychology of R. Kegan, who attempts to describe the development of the "self" in a holistic fashion. As regards Oser, one has to take note that in his view the structures of religious judgment, which he has been investigating, are deep structures which feature a close proximity of cognition and emotion prior to the separation into feeling and intellect. This becomes clearly visible in more recent studies that Oser presents in his latest publication (1988). The answers given by respondents who were given dilemma stories reflect in many cases an internal struggle, especially in those instances where the case studies deal with the personally stressful and challenging problem of theodicy.

Although not replacing the psychoanalytical approach to psychology of religion, the cognitive-structural theories of religious development do provide a significant complementary perspective. To that extent they offer a new perspective and methodology. For this reason it is not surprising that particularly the theory of Fowler has found great resonance and stimulated a broad discussion in the United States. Initially, this discussion concerned typical issues in the psychology of religion, that is, issues of the adequacy of the approach, the empirical validity of the stages, the reliability of the methodology. Increasingly, however, the discussion centers on pedagogical and practical-theological issues, such as the implications of this theory for religious education, congregational ministry, and pastoral care. In the last few years, Fowler's own work has come to be focused on the practical theological implications of his theory. After an initial concentration on the development of a psychological theory of faith stages, which culminated in 1981 in the publication of the book *Stages of Faith*, Fowler has begun to address more strongly the issues of adult education (1984a) and pastoral care (1987a). Something similar holds true for Oser and his research team (1988), who now focus particularly on religious education in schools and begin to include religious education in the family.

On the Necessity of a Multidimensional Psychology and Pedagogy of Religion

The introductory overview of the development and current situation of research in the field of faith development suggests that both American and European scholars should take advantage of the international discussion for their work. This volume aims in that direction. At the same time, it attempts to raise the international debate to a new level. The 1986 publication of a collection of essays on Fowler (Dykstra and Parks) reflects only the North American discussion about this author. Moreover, that book dates back to a conference that took place in 1983. The present volume makes it possible to correlate the theories of Fowler and Oser and to examine them in their latest stage of development as they are presented in the opening essays. The theories of Fowler and Oser have achieved a degree of maturity in terms of inner differentiation, prudent self-correction, surprising extensions, and openness toward each other and toward other approaches (e.g., the psycho-analytic approach). Thus, it appears obsolete to base an evaluation of Fowler only on his 1981 publication and of Oser only on the work coauthored with Gmünder in 1984, although these publications have by no means lost their foundational status.

It may be helpful here to explore and clarify some of the differences between the central conceptions of Fowler and Oser (see Schweitzer 1987a). On the one hand, studies based on Fowler's broad concept of faith which take as their object (of investigation) human faith understood as a generic dimension of human meaning making will be challenged by Oser's twofold concentration on (1) the relation between persons and an ultimate (God), and on (2) the construct of an independently constituted logic of "religious judgment." The challenge will be to focus similarly on the specifically reli-gious search for meaning, including the God question. (This is already a bit more clear in Fowler's 1987 book.) On the other hand, anyone taking Oser as the starting point will recognize in light of Fowler's theory that the religious life includes important elements apart from just religious judg-ment: images and narratives that stimulate feelings and spur the imagination, a concept of symbolic functioning, the connections between worldviews and social responsibilities. Some of these components have already received intentional investigative attention by Oser's associates (on the concept of symbolic functioning in the interpretation of biblical parables, see Bucher 1987a, Bucher and Oser 1987b; on the role of religious worldviews, see Reich 1987).

However, the discussion in this volume does not limit itself to testing the compatibility of the two theories. In addition to making theoretical com-parisons, we must ask foundational questions. This entails, first, an examina-tion of the *theoretical stringency of the projects* and of their *construct validity* (cf. the contributions of Power, Parks, and Döbert). These chapters can be seen as a discussion among representatives of the same family of theories concerning possible improvements of their approaches.

Other articles reach much further beyond this frame of intraparadigmatic reference. In this regard a number of chapters explore *fundamental alter-natives* to the structural developmental paradigm. Moran's chapter provides a forceful alternative from the American scene. It extends his earlier critical and constructive book on religious education development (Moran 1983). With Heimbrock, we find an author who has already explicitly entered into the debate with the cognitive psychologies of Oser and Fowler in the

German-speaking realm (Fraas and Heimbrock 1986). Bittner's contribution constitutes an entirely alternative design from a psychoanalytical perspective.

A third set of interests is pursued in this volume. Several authors have taken on the task of relating theories of faith and religious development to their historically determined political, economic, and cultural contexts. The chapters by Durka and Hull have special relevance in this regard. Their chapters offer perspectives that are able to uncover the limitations of cognitive-structural theories of development. These critics are particularly attentive to the dangers that arise from the one-sided stress on individual development (individualistic reductionism) and the concentration on structures (structuralistic reductionism). Perhaps with some justification, theories of structural stages in developmental psychology often draw the criticism that they neglect the societal influences on the socialization of individuals as well as more concrete historical challenges. In light of this, the present volume intends to add to the discussion an *integrating and comprehensive approach*. It corresponds to approaches to religious education and to a practical theology which understand themselves as intentionally multidimensional. Such approaches are conscious of the need to join individual and society, individual processes and institutional conditions (family, school, church), development and socialization, life cycle and everyday life in order to do justice to the complex reality in which (religious) education must be done.

Is it possible to reflect on faith development without remembering that growth in faith is really a very old topic? One weakness of Oser's and Fowler's theories consists in the missing investigation of historical antecedents. Although this is understandable in the case of research guided by an empirical-analytical interest, it remains unsatisfactory for those who work in (religious) education and theology.

In cooperation with others, Fowler did attempt to illuminate historical biographies from the perspective of faith development theory (Fowler, Lovin, et al. 1980). Yet this constitutes a historic application of his theory, not a historical engagement and critical challenge. Such a step, however, is necessary, and it succeeds only when one searches for historical antecedents and contradictory conceptual models to the paradigm of developmental stages.

In anticipation of a more substantial study of his own, F. Schweitzer takes account of this fourth direction by pursuing the question concerning the emergence of the discovery of the religion of the child. As will be shown, precursors exist since the Reformation (J. A. Comenius, A. H. Francke, et al.), in a certain sense also in the eighteenth century. In different publications during the last few years, Karl Ernst Nipkow has investigated the similar, though more limited question of whether theological projects could be found which explicitly employ the term "stage," or the concept of sequential steps or phases, and which shed a different light onto the theme of faith development. This was true for M. Luther, J. A. Comenius, J. G. Haman (Nipkow 1983, 1987a,b), and S. Kierkegaard (Nipkow 1986, 1988).

Finally, this volume poses to the theories of Oser and Fowler *foundational theological questions* (Nipkow). They aim in particular in the direction of the domain of religious as well as general education. It does not require much imagination to envision that talk about stages of faith (Fowler) or about stages of religious judgment (Oser) not only elicit curiosity but also great irritation. The stage concept is the most disputed element in both theories. It is and will remain a controversial notion. It captures in particular crispness the problem of normativity, especially in regard to the "highest" stage. However, a prudent and cautious use of the stage concept is recommended not only by the pertinent essays in this volume but by the "architects" of the stage theories themselves.

A Critical Dialogue between Psychology of Religion, Theology, and Religious Education

Independent of the already controversial concept of stages, the term "faith development" joins two very different subject matters which, therefore, coexist in a tension-filled relation. They are "faith" as the central theme of Christian theology and "development" as the guiding category of a particular subdiscipline in psychology. Since in Fowler's work, unlike Oser, "faith" occupies a central position, the relation between psychology and theology deserves fresh treatment in contemporary discussion, though in fundamentally new ways.

Unnecessary confusion can be avoided, if one keeps in mind Fowler's very intentional definitions. With W. C. Smith, Fowler distinguishes between (1) "religion/s" — as the "cumulative traditions" of the various expressions of faith of people in the past dependent on ongoing remembering and reenactment; (2) "belief" — in the sense of the holding, and holding to be true, of certain ideas; and (3) "faith" — as the relation of trust and loyalty to the transcendent (Fowler 1981, 9ff.). These distinctions indicate immediately the intended thrust of the assertion that we are dealing here with a psychological concept of faith which, while abstracting from contents of faith, at the same time undertakes theological interpretations. Further, it is devised in such a way that its conceptual structure can be filled with particular content in correspondence with particular historical religions. Fowler's concept of "faith" refers to the act of faith, the act of fundamental, existential trust in life and loyalty.

Presumably in response to his North American critics, Fowler has been concerned for years with proving the same two things with which he is concerned in his contribution to this volume. It is a fundamental concern of his to show that his faith development theory has been grounded from the beginning—that is, its initial inspiration by H. R. Niebuhr—in theological presuppositions. These, however, have been intentionally formulated in such a way that the resulting psychological theory of development possesses the character of a general theory that is valid even outside the realm of theological presuppositions.

Fowler forcefully reemphasizes the fundamental theological concepts that were central already in *Stages of Faith* (1981): (1) the covenantal character and the fiduciary structure of faith; (2) the deep conviction that Christian faith is a process of ongoing conversion or *metanoia*; (3) the guiding concept of "radical monotheism"; and (4) the metaphor of "the kingdom of God." The last two of these both serve as images for the end point of faith development. Fowler regards the "transformational theology" of Niebuhr as key for his own thought. Viewed from that perspective, human transformation by the Holy Spirit can be correlated with psychologically describable faith "development" as human response to divine activity. Fowler's recent programmatic essays on practical theology and the applications of faith development theory to Christian adult education (Fowler 1984a) as well as to issues of congregational ministry and pastoral care reveal that Fowler, as a Christian theologian, now more than ever wants to make a contribution to the praxis of church and congregation.

At the same time, however, the psychological dimension of his stage theory is employed in the interest of making the search for meaning and faith under modern conditions and in a world of pluralistic worldviews plausible for as many people as possible, even outside the Christian church. For that reason, Fowler and his associates continue to elaborate the theory from the perspective of general personality psychology. Special mention is deserved for the combination of Fowler's own approach with that of Robert Kegan (Fowler 1987) and the now-completed coding manual for the execution and evaluation of interviews (Moseley, Jarvis, and Fowler 1986).

Can this intended balance and integration succeed and convince scientifically? Is it possible to move so easily from the domain of psychological to theological speech? Do not concepts like "faith" obtain different meaning when put in a psychological versus a theological frame of reference?

In his essay, Fowler attempts to respond to the question (Nipkow 1986) whether his psychological theory ought not be conceived more strictly as a general "*psychological* theory of faith *development*." For this would provide the freedom to develop more clearly a particular "*theological* theory of faith-*history*" as a Christian theological response to this subject matter. Then both the theological and the psychological approach would have to be related to each other. We are not just dealing with the problem of two different ways of representing the same subject matter; rather we are faced with the

question of compatibility, that is, the possibility or impossibility of cor-
relating elements that, at least in part, are of rather divergent nature.

Nipkow's contribution attempts to demonstrate that the degree of compatibility of theology and psychology depends also on the quality of the
theology that is employed. It appears that in the domain of theological
anthropology a theological model such as Fowler's, which leans toward the
Reformed tradition and stresses the Old Testament idea of covenant, the
concept of vocation, and human partnership with God in the cooperative
activity of the inbreaking reign of God, is much more receptive than other
theological positions to the psychological understanding of faith as human
activity. On the other hand, a theological point of view following, for
instance, Luther, which emphasizes the irreconcilable paradox of the faith
experience as well as the dialectic of sin and justification, is a much greater
obstacle precisely at those points where Fowler's theology speaks of the goal
of faith development.

With regard to the ongoing discussion, the conclusion suggests itself that
it is always necessary to examine what sort of specific, explicit, and implicit
anthropological-theological presuppositions underlie models in the psychology or pedagogy of religion. It is, indeed, problematic simply to join the *positions* of psychology and theology in general and of developmental psychology
and religious education in particular. Rather, it is necessary to examine
critically the "backside" of psychological and religious education theories. To
this end, Fowler and Oser are aware of the limits of their theories with
regard to other psychological models. This is not true, however, in regard
to theology. Oser undergirds his description of the highest stage (stage 5)
with a transcendental theological approach (based on H. Peukert and W.
Pannenberg). Things are similar for Fowler; he builds directly on a theological "position" most of which he shares with H. R. Niebuhr. These
approaches do possess certain strengths and justification, and the discussions
in this book reveal them nicely. However, analyzing the "backside" of these
two theories helps avoid a theoretical dogmatism. This concern is fully
shared by Fowler and Oser, who have expressly encouraged an ongoing
discussion of their theories' normative presuppositions.

Of course, this psychology–theology dialogue moves both ways. In light
of the new psychological theories of faith development, it is becoming evident how naïvely dogmatic certain theological religious education models
are regarding the human conditions that proclamation, pastoral care, education, and instruction must take into account. On the one hand, viewed
psychologically, we still discover behavioristic assumptions about the (Christian) impressionability of people, while, on the other hand, from a religious
point of view, children and adolescents are said to develop on their own.
Oser and Fowler reject both positions: over against the former they stress
that structural growth in faith occurs only as independent activity of the

individual. They warn proponents of the latter position against overlooking the regularities and laws of development.

As documented by S. Parks's superb summary of the critical discussion on Fowler in the United States, dialogical impasses can be overcome by pursuing the direction indicated above. Currently, neither the theological nor the psychological camp is fully satisfied with Fowler. For many Christian critics, the formalization of the fundamental theological assumptions lacks theological clarity. On the other side, it is precisely the strong Christian hue of the description of Universalizing faith that disgruntles his liberal, humanistic readers. They feel the influence from the Christian tradition, and they regard the description of the transition to the sixth faith stage as involving a breach from the ways the first through the fifth stages have been described.

In his own way, G. Moran currently contributes with his publications (1983, 1987) to a fundamental examination of the concept and the metaphors of stage development from the perspective of philosophy of religion. He, too, looks at the backside of the concept, and he begins his critique with the concept of development. He warns urgently against optimistic attitudes toward growth and against the achievement orientation with which the concept of development is loaded. According to Moran, it would be better to do away completely with any normative image for the end point of development (which is always implied when one speaks of development). How might that be possible?

In Moran's own vision neither development toward "autonomy" nor "the way up" can be the final word, but "the way inward" and the "communion" of all living creatures and life forms. This, however, turns out to be another normative image of a developmental goal. Therefore, it appears most appropriate to the current state of this discussion to remain open to various images of mature faith. Then the existing psychological images of a highest stage represent only one possible descriptive attempt. At the same time, they function as an invitation to theologians to continue this thought process together.

A Social-Scientific Examination of Stage Theories of Faith Development

The question inevitably arises of the status of a stage theory of religious development, when the final stage of its "developmental logic" suddenly becomes arbitrary or, at least, is confronted with an unexpected array of alternative descriptions. Developmental theories in the Piagetian school are necessarily "upside down," that is, their stage sequentiality must be logically reconstructed from the highest stage backward.

Oser's contribution to this volume is much more intentional than Fowler's in self-critically examining the scientific claims of his own theory, especially the construct validity. Furthermore, in a special segment, he addresses the criticisms made in various publications by his associates (Fetz and Bucher) and others (Ebert, Englert, Fraas, Grom, Mette, Schmidt, Schweitzer). As long as cross-cultural research is lacking—which, by the way, is the case also for Fowler's work—Oser shies away from claiming the final validity of his hypothesis of a *universal* stagelike logic of development in the domain of religious judgment independent of cultural influences. However, according to Oser, an age trend is clearly recognizable in all research conducted by him. Another piece of strong evidence is provided by the convergence of the results from the various dilemma stories. Furthermore, some clues to the universality of the developmental sequence can be gained from initial comparative, intercultural studies (Dick). Thus, Oser seems relatively certain in regard to the universality of the first four stages. Nevertheless, it is appropriate to raise the critical question whether the theory actually measures what it pretends to measure. It might be assumed that different forms of religious judgment are perhaps *parallel* types of judgment or reasoning rather than *sequential* stages. Perhaps they are predominantly a result of different socialization influences and not expressions of a universal paradigm of development.

These issues can be examined from various angles, depending on one's own theoretical standpoint. C. Power, a close associate of L. Kohlberg, examines in his essay both theories according to their shared starting point, the theoretical paradigm of Piaget. According to this model, stage theories must satisfy, among other things, the following: the proof of sequentiality, a *structuralism* that is independent of any content, the assumption that the developmental aspects of any stage form a structural whole.

Concerning the first point, Power believes that Oser's theory is closer to Piaget than Fowler's: Oser's theory pays stricter attention to proving the developmental logic (sequentiality). Furthermore, Power asks whether Fowler's theory may not actually measure to a large degree content-related competencies of reasoning and speech and not just the "operations" of a basic underlying "structure." Further, he raises the question whether the seven aspects of "faith" in Fowler's theory really constitute a structural whole. All these are criteria of a theory of "hard" universal stages. But is it really necessary for developmental theories oriented toward the psychology of religion to be "hard" theories? Can they even be "hard" theories? Power's essay reveals in undogmatic fashion that when dealing with issues of religion and faith, certain things do look different from research into operations in the domain of mathematics and the natural sciences. The criteria of "hard" stage theories are important for adding precision, but they must not become coercive.

From the perspective of the sociology of religion, R. Döbert focuses his inquiry on the relation between structure and content. He doubts whether it is possible at all to discover in the domain of religion (and morality, contra Kohlberg and Power) an "operational basis" compatible with Piaget's "cognitive structures." As a sociologist, Döbert justly reminds us of the force of social and historically determined influences. He wonders whether the remarkable distancing from traditional religious concepts that occurs in both theories (Oser's stage 3, Fowler's stage 4) may be attributed to the decline of religious traditions and the emergence of secularistic and individualistic orientations.

One will have to concede that, in comparison to Piaget's and Kohlberg's subject matters, it is more difficult to conceive of and investigate independent forms of religious judgment. However, the data collected by Fowler and Oser do indicate clearly the existence of religious development.

Overall, the central hypotheses of the stage theories under discussion are not regarded as falsified by the contributions of this volume; however, there are theoretical alternatives. With the psychoanalytically oriented contribution of G. Bittner, this volume is introducing a clearly outlined counterproposal. According to Bittner, religion shall be conceived of as fundamentally different: as spontaneous emotional experience, as "knowing through emotions," with deep roots in early-childhood developments the illumination of which constitutes the domain of psychoanalysis. But does it make sense to assume a mutual exclusivity of structural stage theories and psychoanalytical perspectives? Theories cannot be falsified by other theories. Again, we must emphasize the necessity of complementary approaches. Only in this way it is possible to profit from the unique explanatory power of each approach.

H. G. Heimbrock's essay, grounded in the psychology of religion, documents that both of the currently predominant models in developmental psychology, that is, the structural and the psychoanalytical, undervalue the dimension of religious *rituals*. This paper attempts more than merely to advance a sketch of an independent "theory of human ritualization potential" with implications for the praxis of worship and religious education. It proves how constructively the entire discussion can be enriched by a school of thought contrary to the Piagetian tradition.

The Historical and Social Context and the Pedagogical Significance (of Developmental Theories)

How can we estimate the pedagogical significance of the cognitive-structural theories of religious development? We can do justice to such an evaluation only if we consider them in their historical and societal matrix.

Religious education is subject to historical change. In many respects, it is confronted today with new questions that result mainly from changes in family and society and from a changing role of religion in society. Simultaneously, there occurs an increasing differentiation between individual religiosity and institutional religion. It appears that less and less religious education occurs in the family. In a decreasing number of cases, parents are the first mediators of religious content, and children and youth only rarely articulate religious questions in the traditional terminology offered to them by the church.

These changes explain why the sociological opinion research and polling sponsored by churches frequently gather only superficial results: the questions presume traditional religious content. As far as religious education is concerned, the theories of religious socialization are, in this situation, of diminishing helpfulness, for they focus entirely on the family (e.g., in the emphasis on the so-called primary socialization in early childhood). Compared to this, the cognitive-structural theories, with their open approach to the life cycle as a whole and to religion in the wider sense, offer promising possibilities for illuminating the central points of reference for religious education in family, school, church, everyday life, group life.

The value aims of the cognitive-structural theories of religious development display a preference for autonomy, rationality, and subjectivity. This reveals how deeply they are indebted to modern, and largely secular, ways of thinking. Therefore, it is appropriate to view these theories as an expression and continuation of such thinking—with the result that the philosophical and theological critique of a one-sided orientation to autonomy, rationality, and subjectivity must also be applied to the structural theories of religious development.

One must not overlook, however, that these theories have been conceived and are being extended with the intention to *overcome* such a one-sidedness. Both Oser and Fowler firmly insist that rationality and autonomy are misunderstood when and as long as they exclude religion. Viewed from this angle, the cognitive-structural theories of religious development grow out of the concern to counter the amputating or narrowing of the modern image of the person and the modern image of development. Thus, it will be necessary to examine in each individual case whether a theory of faith development based on the paradigm of developmental psychology or a particular concept in religious education leans more to one side or to the other, that is, whether religious development and education refer to an accommodation to secular culture or whether they mean resistance in the name of a postmodern form of religion (Schweitzer).

Phases in Research and Perspectives for the Future

This book marks the beginning of a new phase in the discussion of cognitive-structural theories of religious development and their significance for religious education. Although the identification of phases in contemporary scientific discussions can proceed only with great caution—a lack of distance renders any judgment relative—such a step, nevertheless, serves an orientation function in regard to the development, history, and reception of a theory. In this limited sense, we can speak of three phases or stages through which the cognitive-structural psychology of religion has passed up to this point.

A first phase was determined by the increasing attention which the cognitive-structural developmental psychology, initially represented generally by Kohlberg's work on moral development, received in the United States and later on also internationally. Kohlberg's psychology rests on the assumption that moral development occurs independently of religious influences. Therefore he paid only marginal attention to religious development; or, to be more precise, only after the end of the moral development sequence, at stage 7, does religion begin to play a role again in Kohlberg's scheme (Kohlberg 1981b, 311ff.). This neglect of religion in cognitive-structural psychology functioned as the backdrop for the research of Oser and Fowler, who began to employ the methodological and theoretical means of cognitive-structural psychology for proving the existence of the phenomenon "religious development" as well as for documenting the religious aspects of moral development.

The studies of this first phase, which corresponds roughly to the second half of the seventies, was overshadowed by Kohlberg and his psychology. In a few brief years, however, Fowler and Oser became recognized as theorists in their own right with the publications of their major theoretical works in 1981 (Fowler) and 1984 (Oser-Gmünder). These literary successes clearly mark the public establishment of a second phase. The tenor of this phase was set by the fundamental objections that were fielded against these theories (see, e.g., the collections of essays edited by Dykstra and Parks [1986] and Fraas and Heimbrock [1986]; and the review by Schweitzer [1986a]). Many of these objections sound like a debate among competing schools of thought: one theory is marshaled against another; one fundamental conviction opposes another. Psychoanalytically and sociologically oriented authors complain, from their respective perspectives, about the lack of attention to those central elements that they view as important: ego development or religious socialization. A complete rejection or, at the very least, a fundamental criticism of the cognitive-structural theories seemed to suggest itself.

The harshness of the criticisms becomes a bit more understandable when one recognizes the basic claims implicit in the titles of Oser's and Fowler's writings on these matters: Oser's next book is titled in German *Der Mensch— Stufen seiner religiösen Entwicklung* (The Person—Stages of His or Her Religious Development; in English it will be *Religious Judgment: A Developmental Perspective*). Fowler's main theoretical book carries the title *Stages of Faith: The Psychology of Human Development and the Quest for Meaning*.

With such titles for the two major works (chosen apparently with some regard for the marketing interests of the publishing houses) it seemed a bit difficult not to raise the impression of some sort of monopolistic claim in the psychology of religion, although Fowler attempted early on to include psychoanalytical perspectives.

A new phase in the discussion is clearly suggested by a very intentional openness of the cognitive-structural theories of religious development in two areas: (1) Oser and Fowler seem to be more receptive to the parallels in each other's work as well as to other psychological and sociological approaches; and (2) the cognitive structural psychology of religion is beginning to be integrated into a multiperspectival model of religious education. This third phase surfaces repeatedly and in various ways in the contributions to this volume and is addressed by both Oser and Fowler. Thus, the cognitive-structural theories of religious development represent nothing more—but also nothing less—than *one* interpretation of religious development. This interpretation must be complemented by others; other interpretations must be supplemented by it.

The relation between the religiophilosophical/psychological sides of the developmental theories and their theological groundings is still very open. Shall we follow Fowler and aim at a confessional theological elaboration of the theory of faith development—not the least because of the self-critical insight that one's own standpoint permeates, openly or hiddenly, one's scientific work? Or shall we follow Oser and strive for a strict religiophilosophical/ universal version of developmental theory, which would require a repeated self-critical liberating of the theory from any confessional and positional limitations? Or is it possible to do both in such a way that religiophilosophical and theological perspectives can be joined dialogically?

Finally, the pedagogical, religious education, and practical theological significance of the cognitive-structural theories clearly demands attention. Theoretical attempts to make these theories fruitful for the school and for instruction (see, e.g., Nipkow 1982; Schmidt 1984; Schweitzer 1986b) raise deep questions: How can a stronger integration be achieved between the developmental theories and the theories of religious education? How must one prepare and lead a classroom session so that it does justice to the developmental level of the students?

The application for church and school instruction by no means exhausts the pedagogical significance of the cognitive-structural theories (see Schweitzer 1986c). Congregational and social-pedagogical tasks as well as adult church education appear in a new light when viewed from the perspective of religious development (Nipkow 1988). Fowler's latest book on faith development and pastoral care (1987a), which deals also with questions of congregational formation, indicates the direction for future studies: How do the different developmental stages present among adult members in a congregation affect congregational ministry and mission, pastoral care, and Christian education? What tasks and possibilities does this yield for the adult education programs of the church? And what developmental assumptions are contained in programs such as "ecumenical learning" when they aim at a universal orientation toward church and humanity on this one planet?

In contrast to traditional studies in developmental psychology, these pedagogical and practical theological questions demand a stricter interactive orientation when investigating how teachers discern which stage characterizes the children, youth, and adults with whom they work. One needs to be concerned with the way teachers, educators, and adult education workers perceive these stages and how they react. It is not the particular developmental stage that is pedagogically decisive here but the interaction among persons of different developmental stages. Little is known at this point regarding such important questions for the pedagogical employment of developmental theories. Perhaps a closer cooperation between educators and psychologists, a possibility exemplified in this volume, may give impetus in these directions.

Part 1

Two Developmental Approaches to Faith and Religious Knowing

1

The Vocation of
Faith Developmental Theory

JAMES W. FOWLER

KARL ERNST NIPKOW has pressed a set of questions that helped to shape the approach to this chapter. Nipkow read this author's books and articles written since the publication of *Stages of Faith* in 1981. He noted in them a turn toward engagement with issues in practical theology. He referred to a 1983 essay entitled "Practical Theology and the Shaping of Christian Lives," which he, rightly, interpreted as having been a programmatic essay for future work. There faith development theory and the stages of faith were identified as one constituent component of a more comprehensive practical theology of Christian formation and transformation. Noting this practical theological direction and interest, Nipkow posed the question of the future of faith development theory taken as a general, comprehensive, and potentially universal accounting for faith. While not denying its value as a component of practical theological work, he expressed concern that faith development research and theory should not relinquish its promise as a social-scientific, general theory of human development.

Nipkow's concern led to a course of reflection on certain patterns and tensions in this work, which I recount in this chapter. These comments are intended to examine the relations between normative theological interests in faith development work and interests in social-scientific research and theory building. Let us begin with a consideration of the relation of theological themes and social-scientific intent in the 1981 volume, *Stages of Faith*.

Theology and Psychology in Faith Development Theory

With the publication of *Stages of Faith* in 1981 ten years of research and analysis, and of theoretical and theological reflection, found comprehensive

formulation. How should we characterize the book *Stages of Faith?* What genre describes what it tried to achieve? What discipline or focus captures its contribution? Let us consider the elements that constitute the book:

Part I is entitled "Human Faith." It represents an effort to describe the phenomenon of faith from a variety of angles of vision. Theologically it draws on the work of Paul Tillich and H. Richard Niebuhr, both of whom stand in the tradition of Ernst Troeltsch and the nineteenth-century German liberalism that goes back to Friedrich Schleiermacher. Of the two, Niebuhr's theological influence is the more fundamental for the faith development project, with its distinctive style of affirming the sovereignty of God while correlatively taking seriously the patterns and dynamics of human responsiveness to and interpretations of the divine–human interaction (Fowler 1974b, 1985). Both Niebuhr and Tillich wrote incisive treatises on faith in which they treated it as a dynamic pattern of human action involving "the state of being ultimately concerned" (Tillich 1957) or the "attitude and action of confidence in, and fidelity to, certain realities as the sources of value and the objects of loyalty" (Niebuhr 1960, 1989). The biblical and Reformed sides of Niebuhr's background and his indebtedness to the American idealist philosopher Josiah Royce (Royce 1908, 1912) led him to stress the covenantal or "triadic" character of faith. This understanding affirms both the social nature of selfhood (which Niebuhr also derived from George Herbert Mead) and the claim that any lasting human relation or community involves mutual or shared trust in and loyalty to a "third" or "thirds" which constitute superordinate centers of value and power. These centers of value—these "thirds"—confirm the mutual trusts and loyalties of their members and link them in community. In *Radical Monotheism and Western Culture* (Niebuhr 1960) Niebuhr identified three types of relation between self and others and their common relatedness to transcending centers of value and power: *polytheism*, where there are multiple but minor centers of trust and loyalty, no one of which exerts ordering power on the others; *henotheism*, where one center of value and power (idolatrous, from a theological standpoint) exerts ordering power on the others, binding one to a closed community of loyalty; and *radical monotheism* in which allegiance to the "God beyond the gods" relativizes and orders the self's attachments to other value centers and binds one with loyalty to a potentially universal community of faith.

Niebuhr, as did Tillich in a different way, developed the importance of both non-Christian and nonreligious patterns of trust and loyalty as manifestations of human faith. At the same time, he set forth in a variety of places (Niebuhr 1941, 1957, 1989) his conception of the life of Christian faith as a process of ongoing conversion (*metanoia*)—a continuing process of relinquishing centering commitments to finite centers of value and power, and movement toward commitment in radical trust in God as the source and center of all value and power. Niebuhr's transformational theology holds an important clue for understanding the relation between faith development theory, as a general theory of human faith, and the accounts in more recent books (Fowler 1984a, 1987a, 1991) and articles (Fowler 1983, 1985) of conversion and development in Christian faith. We will consider these recent writings more fully in a later section.

Also included in Part I of *Stages of Faith* is a section that draws on the important work of the historian of religion Wilfred Cantwell Smith. This discussion of Smith's work pursues two particular objectives: The first objective is to clarify distinctions, implicit in Tillich and Niebuhr, between religion, belief, and faith. The second is to corroborate, on the basis of Smith's extensive and original studies in the Buddhist, Hindu, Muslim, Jewish, and Christian traditions (Smith 1962, 1977, 1979), that faith is *the* generic and universal religious (and human) category.

After the brief exposition of Smith's contribution, there follows a discussion of faith as an expression of imagination. This explanation is based on Samuel Taylor Coleridge, Richard R. Niebuhr, the Rev. William F. Lynch, and others (Parks 1986a). It draws the implications of understanding faith as involving a particular use of imagination understood as *Einbildungskraft*. This compound term means "the power of forming into one." Faith is a composing, a dynamic and holistic construction of relations that include self to others, self to world, and self to self, construed as all related to an ultimate environment. This view has been scorned by some critics for not providing a more unitary and precise definition of faith (Fernhout 1986). It tries to evoke an awareness of faith as a multidimensional, central form of human action and construction. Faith involves both conscious and unconscious processes and holds together both rational and passional dynamics. Faith holds together both religious and nonreligious directions and forms.

Faith, Religion, Belief: An Interlude

Before continuing on to discuss the subsequent parts of *Stages of Faith* it may be useful to provide the reader with a brief summary of the major points required for understanding the perspective on faith offered in that book. Faith understood generically as a human universal includes but is not limited to or identical with religion. You can have faith that is not religious faith. Common examples include communism, materialism, or what some fundamentalists call "secular humanism." A religion, as a cumulative tradition, is made up of the expressions of the faith of people in the past. It can include scriptures and theology, symbol and myth, ethical teachings and prayers, architecture and music, art and patterns of teaching and preaching. Religion, in this sense, gives forms and patterns for the shaping of the faith of present and future persons. Religions are the cumulative traditions that we inherit in all of their varieties of forms. Religious faith, on the other hand, is the personal appropriation of relationship to God through and by means of a religious tradition (see W. C. Smith 1962; chs. 6, 7; Fowler 1981, x–36).

Just as we can distinguish faith from religion, it is important also to clarify the relation between faith and belief. Belief is one of the important ways of expressing and communicating faith. But belief and faith are not the same thing, particularly in the period in which we live. Since the Enlightenment of the eighteenth century, many people have come to understand belief as intellectual assent to propositions of dubious verifiability. Faith is deeper than belief. We hope that our beliefs are congruent with and expressive of our faith, but faith is deeper and involves unconscious motivations as well as those that we can make conscious in our belief and in our actions.

In speaking of faith as a generic feature of human lives—as a universal quality of human meaning making—I make the claim that God has prepotentiated us for faith. That is, as human beings we have evolved with capacities and the need for faith from the beginning. Whether or not we are explicitly nurtured in faith in religious or Christian ways, we are engaged in forming relations of trust and loyalty to others. We shape commitments to causes and centers of value. We form allegiances and alliances with images and realities of power. And we form and shape our lives in relation to master stories. In these ways we join with others in the finding and making of meaning. Let us look at these three dimensions of living faith in more detail.

First, faith is a dynamic pattern of personal trust in and loyalty to a *center* or *centers of value*. What do I mean by the term "center of value"? We rest our hearts, we focus our life in persons, in causes, in ideals, or institutions that have great worth to us. We attach our affections to those persons, institutions, causes, or things that promise to give worth and meaning to our lives. A center of value in your life or mine is something that calls forth love and devotion and therefore exerts ordering power on the rest of our lives and our attachments. Family can be one such profound center of value in our lives. Success and one's career can be important centers of value. One's nation or an ideological creed can be of life-centering importance. Money, power, influence, and sexuality can all be idolatrous centers of value in our lives. For some persons and groups religious institutions constitute dominant centers of value. All of these and much more can be centers of value in our lives. And, of course, from a religious standpoint, God is meant to be the supreme center of value in our lives.

Second, faith is trust in and loyalty to *images and realities of power*. You and I are finite creatures who live in a dangerous world. We and those we love are vulnerable to arbitrary power and destruction in this world. How in such a world do we align ourselves so as to feel sustained in life and in death? "The Lord is my Shepherd, I shall not want." That is a statement about alignment with power and the placing of our reliance on security. You could also say, "My stock portfolio is my shepherd, I shall not want." Or we could say, nationally speaking, "The Star Wars missile defense system is our shepherd, we shall not want." Ernest Becker said that, in the face of death, we all try to build *causa sui* projects, projects of self-vindication, projects that help us have the sense that we will continue on even after we die (Becker 1973). When I held my first book in my hand, which had an ugly cover but a beautiful title — *To See the Kingdom* — I looked at it and said to my wife, "Dear, it's slender immortality, but it is immortality." It will live after I'm gone. With what centers or images of power do we align ourselves in order to feel secure in life? The question of how we align ourselves with power to sustain us in life and death is an important faith question.

Third, faith is trust in and loyalty to a *shared master story* or *core story*. In the 1960s Eric Berne offered his neo-Freudian theory of personality growth and change called transactional analysis. One of the key ideas in transactional analysis is the notion that each of us in early childhood forms a *script* — a kind of unconscious story that takes form in us before we are five years of age. This script, like a fate, in a sense, shapes and guides unconsciously the choices and decisions that we make as we move along in our lives. A master story is a little like that. It often begins unconsciously, and gradually we make it more conscious and explicit as something we are committed to. An acquaintance of mine studied prisoners in a federal prison some years ago and he found that of those who had tattoos, 60 percent of them had tattooed into their skin some variant of the phrase "born to lose" as a kind of master story engraved into their skin.

Unlike the unconscious scripts of Berne and the fated label on the felons, however, a faith master story gives direction, courage, and hope to our lives. It provides life-guiding images of the goodness — and the Godness — for which we are made. A master story shapes our consciousness regarding the character of the ultimate power and reality with which we have to do, and how we should shape our lives with our neighbors in light of that relation.

Faith is covenantal in structure. We are not alone or solitary in our faith. Faith involves trust in and loyalty to other persons. But that trust and loyalty with others are confirmed and deepened by our shared trust and loyalties to centers of value, images of power, and stories that transcend us as individuals and bind us together with others. This is what we mean by *covenant*. Covenant is trust and loyalty, commitment between persons and within groups, that is ratified and deepened by our shared trust in and loyalty to something, someone, Reality, God, or some set of values that transcends us. Faith always has this triadic, covenantal structure.

Stages of Faith: Continuing the Account

Part II of *Stages of Faith* attempts to expound in interrelated and readable fashion, the main assumptions and groundlines of the theories of human development of Erik Erikson, Jean Piaget, and Lawrence Kohlberg. Here these theorists are treated as philosophical psychologists, with attention drawn to the normative as well as the descriptive interests of their theories. The different foci of their research efforts are distinguished, as are the differences in the meaning they give to terms like "stage," "transition," "genetic," and indices of maturation.

Part III constitutes a brief theoretical coda that indicates how each of these three perspectives contributes to faith development theory. It clarifies the theoretical relations between psychosocial and maturationist theories such as those of Erikson and Daniel Levinson and constructive developmental theories like those of Piaget and Kohlberg. It indicates that faith development theory, while indebted to the psychosocial theory of Erikson, finds its principal theoretical grounding in the constructivist tradition.

Part IV gives the longest and fullest exposition to that date of the research findings regarding stages of faith. In about one hundred pages the stages are characterized through a combination of formal descriptions and the liberal use of illustrative quotes from some of the 359 interviews which had been conducted up to that time. This section does not describe the stages by structural "aspects" but rather tries to give the reader vivid and personalized images of the stages as "structured wholes" and as distinctive ways of being in faith. By citing several persons with different faith orientations in each of the stages the effort was made to clarify the distinction between the "structuring" and the "contents" of faith, following in the Piaget-Kohlberg tradition. Readers unfamiliar with this work may find it helpful to examine a recent, very brief and telegraphic accounting of the structural developmental stages of faith.

Stages of Faith: A Brief Summary

Primal Faith (Infancy): A prelanguage disposition of trust forms in the mutuality of one's relationships with parents and others to offset the anxiety that results from separations which occur during infant development.

Intuitive-Projective Faith (Early Childhood): Imagination, stimulated by stories, gestures, and symbols, and not yet controlled by logical thinking, combines with perception and feelings to create long-lasting images that represent both the protective and threatening powers surrounding one's life.

Mythic-Literal Faith (Childhood and beyond): The developing ability to think logically helps one order the world with categories of causality, space, and time; to enter into the perspectives of others; and to capture life meaning in stories.

Synthetic-Conventional Faith (Adolescence and beyond): New cognitive abilities make mutual perspective taking possible and require one to integrate diverse self-images into a coherent identity. A personal and largely unreflective synthesis of beliefs and values evolves to support identity and to unite one in emotional solidarity with others.

Individuative-Reflective Faith (Young Adulthood and beyond): Critical reflection upon one's beliefs and values, utilizing third-person perspective taking; understanding of the self and others as part of a social system; the internalization of authority and the assumption of responsibility for making explicit choices of ideology and life-style; all open the way for critically self-aware commitments in relationships and vocation.

Conjunctive Faith (Mid-life and beyond): The embrace of polarities in one's life, an alertness to paradox, and the need for multiple interpretations of reality mark this stage. Symbol and story, metaphor and myth (from one's own traditions and others') are newly appreciated (second, or willed naïveté) as vehicles for expressing truth.

Universalizing Faith (Mid-life and beyond): Beyond paradox and polarities, persons in this stage are grounded in a oneness with the power of being. Their visions and commitments free them for a passionate yet detached spending of the self in love, devoted to overcoming division, oppression, and violence, and in effective anticipatory response to an inbreaking commonwealth of love and justice.

The Normative End Point as Contested Concept

In the course of completing the account of stages in *Stages of Faith* it was necessary to engage head on the question of the normativity of the theory's end point, and the precommitments informing the theory. The chapter on Universalizing faith acknowledged that the normative image of most developed faith derives principally from H. Richard Niebuhr's complex representation of the Christian and biblical traditions' vision of mature faith. There we see persons whose wills, visions, and patterns of living are grounded in and congruent with the divine intention and modes of action disclosed in the elaborated eschatological metaphor "kingdom of God." Citing the proclamation of the kingdom of God as the central image and impulse of Jesus' preaching and mission, the chapter tackled the question of the particular and the universal as they are raised by this entire discussion. Its fundamental claim, misunderstood by many critics and interpreters (Moran 1983; Schmidt 1984), derives in part from the spirit of Wolfhart Pannenberg's theology (Pannenberg 1976) as well as from that of Niebuhr: It is that claims to *revelation* in the biblical tradition, if justified or justifiable at all, must be taken seriously as the disclosure of the nature and *Tendenz* of Ultimate Reality and of the appropriate human response of obedient partnership. Revelation is not just for and within a particular "salvation history," but must be apprehended as generally and universally significant. Extreme care must be taken, of course, to avoid an uncritical identification of God's self-disclosure and its reality content with the *formulations* and *interpretations* made about it by those who are drawn to it as truth. In this regard a distinction is made between absoluteness as meaning "bearing the quality of ultimacy," and absolutes, which are the reified formulations and symbols through which absoluteness is grasped, communicated, and — inevitably — reduced and distorted. Claims of ultimacy can be made for aspects of a revelatory tradition, the book argued, without having to make the correlative claim of its exclusivity or singularity. Universalizing faith, from this standpoint, is faith that is shaped by centering responsiveness to and decision for the Reality and Possibility that are disclosed and symbolized in the metaphor "kingdom of God." More on these knotty issues will be found later in this chapter.

Part V of *Stages of Faith* is called "Formation and Transformation in Faith." The first section of this part, "Mary's Pilgrimage," presents the edited transcript of a compelling faith development interview with a young adult whose faith journey involved alienation from her family of origin, a phase of immersion and drifting in hippie and drug culture, an event of self-confrontation and "conversion" at a rock-bottom time, and then a succession of involvements with charismatic and authoritarian Christian cults and groups. Mary's story was chosen, although it had some irregular features as a faith development interview, with the hope that an analysis and discussion of it would make possible the achievement of the following: (1) the introduction and demonstration of the analytic use of the structural "aspects" of faith development theory; (2) the correlation of insights derived from structural-developmental analysis with those derived from the psychoanalytic and ego-psychology perspectives of Erikson; (3) an illustration of the need for a more complex understanding of conversion as a process, through combining and contrasting faith development stage change with the phenomenon of a redirection of mind, heart, and will as regards the "contents" of faith; and (4) the contention that "conversion" is not complete — and can even be destructive — if care is not given in helping persons heal, rework, and reintegrate damaging and distorting experiences from their pasts in light of their new affections and directions of the heart.

The next-to-last section of the book takes up the question of changes in the "affections and directions of the heart." Conversion is characterized there as "a significant recentering of one's previous conscious or unconscious images of value and power, and the conscious adoption of a new set of master stories in the commitment to reshape one's life in a new community of interpretation and action" (Fowler 1981, 281–82). Conversion, the text argues, involves principally an alteration in the "contents" of one's faith. On the interrelation of form (structuring in faith) and content it says,

> Reflection on a life story like Mary's . . . helps us see how the structuring activity that is faith involves *both* the formally describable operations of her knowing and valuing and the structuring power of the symbols, beliefs and practices of the faith community of which she is a part. In faith both the "forms" and the "contents" exert power in shaping a person's life-sustaining, life-guiding meanings. . . . To try to account for the interplay of structure and content in faith means to look more radically and inclusively at faith as a *particular* person's way of constituting self, others and world in relation to the particular values, powers and stories of reality he or she takes as ultimate. (Fowler 1981, 273)

This closing part of *Stages of Faith* manifested not only a theoretical interest in acknowledging the importance of the "contents" of faith but also a passion for returning to constructive engagement with substantive theological issues:

> There is a limit to how much one can talk about faith and development in faith without acknowledging that the question of whether there will be faith on earth is finally God's business. Faith development theory, focusing resolutely on the human side of the faith relationship, comes up against the fact that the transcendent other with whom we have to do in faith is not confined by the models we build or to the patterns we discern. In the biblical tradition, at its best, the radical freedom of God is a central and indispensable testimony. God is recognized as sovereign reality—as creator, ruler, and redeemer of *all* being. (Fowler 1981, 302)

The intent of the foregoing review of *Stages of Faith* has been to lift up the theological foundations, themes, and precommitments of a book that has received rather broad acceptance as a contribution to the social-scientific literature on human development. This review aimed to highlight the elements of a tension in the faith development project resulting from what appears to be a duality between normative theological interests, on the one hand, and interests in social-scientific research and theory building, on the other. Both of these interests seem to lie close to the heart of the work. Let us look now at more recent writings which to some readers may seem to have resolved the duality in the direction of theological interests and intent.

Faith Development Theory and Practical Theology, 1983–1987

The 1984 book *Becoming Adult, Becoming Christian* was intended for general audiences. It used developmental theories (Erikson, Levinson, Gilligan, and Fowler) both as points of contact with an interested public and as serious efforts by philosophical or theological theorists to offer descriptive and normative conceptions of the human vocation. It treated these theories, including faith development theory, as contemporary "myths of becoming," addressed to the fermentive cultural confusion regarding the nature and destiny of humankind. I do not believe that the use of faith development theory in this book compromised its status as a general theory of human development with a special focus on faith. The only concession the author made in that regard to the overall constructive theological intent of the book was to illustrate the account of the faith stages dominantly with Christian examples. (The exception to this is in the Universalizing stage, where Gandhi was used as the example.)

In an approach described by David Tracy as a "mutually critical correlation" (Tracy 1983) *Becoming Adult, Becoming Christian* sought to develop central themes from the Christian story and vision regarding the human vocation and to bring them into mutually critical dialogue with cultural images of destiny and "self-actualization." In its handling of the Christian story and vision the book relies on Tracy's Gadamerian concept of the "religious classic" (Tracy 1981). In a spirit that intends to honor the faith traditions of others in a pluralistic world, while not compromising the integrity and power of its own witness, the book endeavors to offer central Christian themes as elements of the "Christian classic." Among these it paints, in broad strokes, the "narrative structure" of the Christian classic. It also develops the themes of covenant and vocation and offers a preliminary account of the human vocation, as depicted in the Christian story and vision, as the calling to be partners in God's work of creation, governance, and liberation/redemption.

The book then attempts to delineate the elements of a theory of Christian character. In the context of discussing the purposes of Christian community and its praxis, the book gives an account of specific Christian virtues, passions, and affections (the latter understood as deep-going, pervasive emotions that give direction and power to our lives). In its final movement the book points to the transformation that begins when the stories we are authoring with our lives come into regrounding and redirecting interplay with God's story. In a preliminary way, *Becoming Adult, Becoming Christian* moved toward an integration of development in faith, as illumined in stage theory, with conversion, understood as the disjunctive and redirecting encounter with God's grace as a liberating expression of God as the power of the future. In that connection there comes what may be the most passionate statement of that book:

> The transformation toward vocation of which we speak requires not only development but also *conversion*. By conversion, here, I . . . mean *an ongoing process . . . in which people (or a group) gradually bring the lived story of their lives into congruence with the core story of the Christian faith*.
>
> Conversion means a release from the burden of self-groundedness. It means accepting, at a depth of the heart that is truly liberating, that our worth, our value, our grounding as children of God is *given* as our birthright. It means embracing the conviction that we are known, loved,

supported, and invited to partnership in being with One, who from all eternity intended us and who desires our love and friendship. Conversion means a recentering of our passion. It is a falling in love with the God who became like us and who invites and empowers us to a relation like that of parent to adult son or daughter. It means making an attachment to the passion of Jesus the Christ—a loving, committed, and ready-to-suffer passion for the inbreaking commonwealth of love (and justice). Conversion means a realignment of our affections, the restructuring of our virtues, and the growth in lucidity and power of our partnership with God's work in the world. (Fowler 1984, 140)

Becoming Adult, Becoming Christian tried to do many things. Underneath it all, the book was both an effort in apologetics and the offering of a nascent theory of the praxis of Christian formation and transformation in community. In its direct use of faith development theory it intended not to compromise its character as a social-scientific, general theory. However, in addressing the question of Christian character—the virtues, passions, and affections of Christian selfhood—it did signal concern for an enriched model of selfhood, one that would necessarily have to extend the implicit and formal account given in structural stage theories. In its discussion of conversion, it focused, without solving, the problem of accounting for how developmental stages can constitute plateaus of augmented defensiveness or self-groundedness, and *can* represent only a sequence of more sophisticated patterns of self-deceiving world construal. We shall return to these issues at a later point in this chapter.

Karl Ernst Nipkow's concern regarding the social-scientific, general theory side of faith development work undoubtedly received little reassurance from the 1985 article entitled "Practical Theology and Theological Education." There again the stages of faith are portrayed as an essential but limited dimension of a more comprehensive practical theology. In the research for that article Johannes Metz's phrase "becoming a subject before God" (Metz 1980) offered itself as a way of capturing and holding together two of the important dimensions of the vocation of human beings which this practical theological use of faith stage theory intended. Metz's phrase promised to hold together (1) the developmental and emancipatory thrust of the stage theory, as an accounting for a subject's stadial process of disembedding from assumptive constructions of reality toward self-aware and critically responsible selfhood, with (2) the covenantal and vocational dimensions constitutive of the effort to conceptualize the human calling to partnership with a sovereign God. With this unifying conception, "becoming a subject before God," the question of the relation between faith stage theory as an independent, general theory and its role in practical theology becomes more complex.

The foregoing themes receive more elaborated treatment in *Faith Development and Pastoral Care*. This book, written as part of a series on theology and pastoral care edited by Don S. Browning, had to be limited to 120 pages of text and was intended for address to a pastoral audience. This book may be seen as a prolegomenon to an eventual longer and more comprehensively argued practical theology. Let us put to it Nipkow's question: What advance or contribution to faith development theory, as a general social-scientific enterprise, occurs in *Faith Development and Pastoral Care?* In this regard there are some interesting considerations: First, as regards the Metz formulation mentioned above, the theological program outlined in chapter 3 of the book anticipates integrating the stage theory into a comprehensive accounting for the processes and stages through which human beings can fulfill our calling to be the conscious, reflective, critically self-aware, and responsible members (*imago dei*) of nature. Such growth and development are intrinsic to God's call to humankind to partnership on behalf of God's intentions for creation. Here, the theological grounding and framework that have been *implicit* in faith development theory and research have been made *explicit*. Moreover, the theological grounding makes it possible to introduce concepts of personal and corporate sin, distortion, defensiveness, and self-deception into the theory, a matter of some difficulty when the faith stages are too quickly assimilated to the enlightenment, rationalist framework of the Piaget-Kohlberg tradition.

We should not conclude that faith development theory relinquishes its "scientific" status if it acknowledges and rationally explicates its theological grounding. Cognitive and moral development theories require extensive philosophical explication and justification of their ground commitments and assumptions. Even a general scientific theory of faith stages cannot and should not stand alone, without theological or philosophical foundations or frame. Rigorous empirical testing and validation studies are by no means disqualified on account of such acknowledgments.

The second advance made in *Faith Development and Pastoral Care* enriches the account of the stages by the inclusion of correlations with Robert Kegan's theory of the stages of evolving selfhood (Kegan 1982). This move also makes explicit much that was already implicit in faith development theory (Kegan was a member of the faith development research team at Harvard from 1974 to 1976). The dialogue with Kegan's mature work in the last two years, however, has led to new theoretical insights and connections. The formulation of stages of faith and selfhood in the 1987 book reached toward a substantially new level of theoretical coherence and comprehensiveness. I believe it lays the basis for enriched empirical studies through which to assess and refine the now more comprehensive vision of "persons in motion" captured by the stage theory. Moreover, Kegan's way of addressing both the troublesome division of the "cognitive" and the "affective" in the Piagetian tradition and the difficulty in accounting for the dynamic unconscious in structural developmental theories holds real promise.

With this new set of formulations we have a way to capture Metz's phrase about "becoming subjects before God" in a more richly textured and multidimensional, if still formal, developmental model.

Third, chapter 5 of *Faith Development and Pastoral Care* extends faith development theory in the direction of systems theory. There are always questions—some thoughtful, others mindless—about the purported "individualism" of psychological theories of development. Despite declarations and demonstrations of the social-interactionist dynamics of the theory, many persist in reading it in individualistic terms. In attempting to characterize congregations of the church as ecologies of diverse, interliving styles of faith consciousness, we begin to illustrate the possibility of a more adequate account of the influences of group roles and membership, and of the faith development "atmosphere" of corporate bodies, upon the faith constructions of individual members. Preliminary work in dialogue with family systems theory (Friedman 1985; Fowler 1990) and with studies of the moral atmosphere of schools and prisons (Power, Higgins, and Kohlberg 1988) suggests that faith development theory can provide rich models for capturing the structural styles and dynamic patterns of face-to-face groups. This begins to operationalize and elaborate the notion of "modal developmental levels" of faith and moral development mentioned at points in our earlier work (Fowler 1982, 1987a). As we pursue such studies we will need to conceive richer and more complex, and necessarily new, empirical and theoretical approaches to understanding the interaction of persons with the groups, institutions, and larger cultures of which they are members.

Empirical and Theoretical Advances since 1981

During the time covered by this paper significant progress in other areas has been made in the strengthening and extending of the stage theory of faith development. From 1982 to 1986, through several drafts, work has proceeded on the elaboration, testing, and refining of the *Manual for Faith Development Research* (Moseley, Jarvis, and Fowler 1986). This 195–page volume has come to provide the basis for training interviewers and analysts for faith development research. Innovations in research procedure since the publication of our earlier questionnaire and coding methods in the appendix of *Stages of Faith* include the following:

1. The use and incorporation of the "Unfolding Tapestry of My Life" self-enquiry instrument (see Fowler 1987a, 122–25). Respondents are asked to complete this autobiographical study prior to coming for the interview session. It has proved to enrich the data considerably and systematically in the direction of strengthening our ability to see transitional times in respondents' lives, and to correlate probable life-cycle transition times with times

of stage change as interpreted in structural developmental faith and self-hood terms.

2. The provision of a standard scoring worksheet. This simple but important innovation leads in the eventual direction of facilitating computer analysis of data, making it possible easily to calculate frequency of responses assigned to each of the aspects and testing for cross-aspect congruence or deviance.

3. The elaboration of the interview questionnaire, identifying the particular faith development aspects particularly targeted by each question. This augments standardization of interview depth and thoroughness while strengthening the new interviewer's grasp on the purpose of each question.

4. Clearly stated and precise criteria, given aspect by aspect, for making structural stage assignments for the structure-indicating passages of the interview. While effective scorers must still learn to think structurally and to analyze structure-indicating passages on the basis of their underlying organizational patterns, these criteria, which include indications for exclusion as well as inclusion, make that task far less susceptible to subjective distortion. The manual makes it possible to learn the interviewing and analysis procedures at a distance from the Center for Research in Faith and Moral Development. There are standardized interviews that can be analyzed in order to demonstrate proficiency in the use of the manual. Trained scorers, using the manual, are achieving blind interrator agreement at better than a 90 percent rate. The completion of the manual in this form opens the way for a variety of correlational studies with other theoretical systems. It provides the explicit basis for ethnographic and cross-cultural research on faith development, and it makes possible the pursuit of rigorous construct validation studies, which we have in view for the coming years.

During 1986–87 Dr. Romney Moseley and Dr. Cand. Ken Brockenbrough conducted a pilot round of new research with very young children. They worked with children under six (and as young as three) and with their families, using the *Manual*'s interview with adults, but employing experimental projective approaches with the children. The aim of these videotaped interviews has been to focus especially on the affective and symbolic-aesthetic structuring exhibited by these young children. Preliminary results are confirming of descriptions of our early stages, but are adding nuances and richness not previously attended to. Further, the continuities and compensatory differences we are finding between parents' and childrens' faith open unprecedented areas of richness. In this regard, theoretical engagement with the relations between descriptions of early faith stages (Primal and Intuitive-Projective stages) and the object relations theories of Margaret Mahler and D. W. Winnicott seem particularly promising. Mahler's notion of "constancy" intrigues us as a way of focusing and accounting for the early development (or failure of development) of a foundational element in infantile faith (see Moseley and Brockenbrough 1988).

Building on the Moseley-Brockenbrough research and the theoretical perspectives of Daniel N. Stern, this author has written an exploratory study of the dynamics of selfhood and faith in the first two years of life (Fowler 1989).

In 1990 John Snarey, based on the analysis of sixty respondents from his study of moral and faith development among Israeli kibbutzim, has marshaled compelling evidence for the construct validity of faith development theory (Snarey 1990).

Conclusions

The stage theory of faith development has achieved a fair amount of empirical establishment. We are aware of more than two hundred research projects engaging in faith development research through the Center for Research in Faith and Moral Development (DeNicola 1990a). The bibliography delineating publications on or related to faith development research numbers more than twenty-seven closely packed pages (DeNicola 1990b). Despite the growing empirical verification, however, its theoretical framework and grounding indisputably rest on theological foundations and reasoning. These foundations have convictional status and finally rest on the faith commitments of the theorist and of the faith tradition of which he or she is a part. They can be rationally explicated, however, and are subject to statement in largely formal and functional terms. To a degree not yet fully tested, they seem capable of being stated in terms derived from other traditions and cultures not Christian or Western. It is a principal thesis of this chapter that the acknowledgment and rational explication of these broadly theological foundations do not jeopardize the theory's claim to scientific integrity. In this regard there are parallels with the conviction-laden philosophical rationales for normative and descriptive theories of cognitive development and for developmental theories of moral and religious reasoning.

This chapter has sought to illustrate that the stage theory of faith development has found formulation in two different genres. The first, best characterized by the book *Stages of Faith* and by such articles as "Faith and the Structuring of Meaning" (Fowler 1980a, 1986) and "Strength for the Journey: Early Childhood Development in Selfhood and Faith" (Fowler 1989), presents the work as a general social-scientific theory, dependent on the operationalization of its key concepts for testing and refinement through empirical research. The second, best characterized in the articles on practical theology and in the books *Becoming Adult, Becoming Christian, Faith Development and Pastoral Care,* and the forthcoming *Weaving the New Creation* (Fowler 1991), treats the theory as a contribution to theological anthropology and integrates it into a more comprehensive, confessional theological account of the Christian understanding of the human vocation. Pains have been taken to present this Christian theological perspective in public language and to offer it, in its integrity, as an expression of the "Christian classic." It intends to be confessional in a way, therefore, which avoids Christian imperialism and sectarian exclusivism and invites dialogue with persons of secular orientations as well as of other traditions. The social-scientific foundations of faith development theory and the formal, functional statement of its central concepts seem to have facilitated dialogue with persons from other traditions and with secularists. Critics of the theory, however, have not been slow to charge it with "religious imperialism" in its use of biblical themes, symbols, and metaphors to characterize faith. Others have questioned how theory and research, which intend to claim scientific status, can begin with a *prescriptive* conception of the most developed stage. Though this response must necessarily be brief, it seems important to indicate the directions of answers to these objections.

First, the charge of Christian or biblical imperialism. Recently in conducting a fresh and in-depth review of Wilfred Cantwell Smith's work on faith in several major religious traditions (Fowler 1987b), it was intriguing to see the structural resonances between radical monotheistic faith, oriented toward the kingdom of God, and several of the central images and ideas Smith explicated as characterizing the goal of faith in human transformation and completion in other traditions. In dealing with early Theravadin Buddhist scriptures, for example, Smith speaks of *nirvana* in ways that formally parallel and functionally resemble Niebuhr's discussion of the kingdom of God. He discusses *dharma*, the moral law, as the absolute basis of enlightenment, but makes it clear to his readers that *dharma*, as the absolute form of life leading to enlightenment and *nirvana*, is not to be taken as identical with *any* of the time-bound, historical formulations of the moral law. Through response to the Buddha and the moral law, Smith says, "men and women were enabled to recognize, yes, but more important, to discover, that transcendence is not another world, afar off; it is this world lived in truly, compassionately. . . . They tasted transcendence; and accordingly their lives were touched by compassion and courage and serenity and ultimate significance" (Smith 1979, 32). A similar discussion can be found, though with more attention to the disjunctures between Buddhist and Christian thought patterns than Smith acknowledges, in the important work by John Cobb, *Beyond Dialogue: Toward a Mutual Transformation of Christianity and Buddhism* (Cobb 1982).

In another instance we have Smith's discussion of faith as understood in Hindu traditions. There faith (*Sraddha*, to "rest one's heart" in Sanskrit) seems inseparably connected to notions of knowing, of insight into, and of participation in transcendence. The following passage attempts to capture the heart of a considerable number of complex pages that Smith devoted to

explicating *Sraddha: Sraddha,* with its resting of the heart, connotes the
attitude of engagement or involvement with something. It conveys the sense
of an alert and insightful penetration of the deep meaning of things. It
implies an attentive receptivity and a deep eagerness to receive and embrace
truth. It involves a risking and effortful investment of the total self to "get
the point." *Sraddha* seems to carry the powerful sense of a commitment with
sufficient emotional depth and intelligence that it guides wisely and orders
justly the other longings and desires of the heart (Fowler 1987a, 18–19).

These brief excursions into comparative examinations of the human vocation religiously understood—and of the changes or transformations
necessary to fulfill it—illustrate the possibility of testing the claim that
Universalizing faith has structural features that are truly universal. However,
as we have observed at other points in this chapter we should not expect to
find these structural features apart from their integration with the "structuring power" of the normative "contents" —the symbols, beliefs, rituals, stories,
and ethics—of particular religious or philosophical traditions.

This brings us to the second of the two issues identified above—the question of how a theory and supporting research, which intend to be scientific,
can begin with a normative end point determined by one interpretation of
the vision of a particular religious tradition. To answer this question fully
would involve an excursion into the philosophy of science, which cannot be
pursued now. The following observations, however, will perhaps indicate
the directions that a more substantive and comprehensive account might
take. The normative end points, or the descriptions of most adequate development which inform theories of this sort, are essentially contested conceptions. They are also conceptions expressive of faith. Whether we speak of
Habermas's ideal of an undistorted communications situation, Marx's vision
of the classless society, Piaget's utopia of formal operational thinking,
Erikson's conception of "integrity" or Kohlberg's "universalizing principles
of justice," we are dealing with normative visions deriving from particular
philosophical commitments and traditions. These can, of course, be philo-
sophically argued for and explicated. But they have not been—and cannot
be—empirically established as most developed, most true, or most adequate
by strictly value-free procedures of inquiry. Nonetheless, they provide the
grounding values and visions from which the systems to which they give rise
derive their direction and integrity.

Similarly, to speak of "Enlightenment" in early Buddhism, "Satori" in Zen,
"Theosis" in Orthodoxy, "Sanctification" in Protestantism, or the "Unitive
Way" in Catholic spirituality, is to refer to elaborated conceptions, informed
by centuries of revealed and evolved wisdom, which order and direct our
understandings to the most richly developed possibilities of human realization. My point is not to say, in some simple sense, that all these normative
statuses represent just so many ways of referring to the same ultimate human
destiny. Rather, my point is that any developmental theory involving an

accounting of qualitative transformations in human knowing, valuing, committing and acting, must derive its *Tendenz* and normative direction from some faith vision of the excellence to which humans are called and for which we are potentiated. We could not investigate "faith development" in the absence of any conception of the most developed forms of faith in relation to which relative realizations could be located and assessed. By the same token, we could not establish the normative qualities of the most developed stage by mere open-ended, "value-free" empirical research.

In view of the foregoing observations it is arguable that "science," in this regard, involves being as clear as possible about the sources informing the normative visions that shape developmental research. Then, having clarified the relation of structure and content in one's initial formulations of the most developed stage, research of two kinds must be pursued in order to test and refine the possibility of a Universalizing stage of faith: (1) There must be extensive examination of implicit and explicit images of most developed faith in the texts and practice of various of the religious and philosophical "classics" that make up the world's great religious traditions. In our discussion of Smith's work above we got just a hint of how that work could proceed. (2) There must be extensive interview research with persons from a variety of religious, ethnic, ideological, cultural, and national backgrounds, nominated by thoughtful and knowlegeable others as being of mature and extensively developed faith. (Such interviews must be coupled with corroborative questioning of those who make up the surrounding social realities of the persons.) Through the analytic interplay of perspectives from traditions, from the study of the knowing, valuing, committing, and acting of particular persons, and from the testing and refinement (or replacement) of present structural descriptions of the aspects of Universalizing faith, there should come, in time, an adequate theory of this stage.

In conclusion, this chapter has highlighted the tensions between the contributions of faith development theory as a social scientific enterprise and as a contribution to practical theology. It has been the author's experience that working with the theory in both these modes provides mutual enrichment for both sides. There is, however, a central and unifying task of faith development theory and research that holds together, with some overlapping and tension, these two genres. This is the vocation of faith development theory and research to account for the process and stages by which persons and groups successively disembed themselves from and take conscious and critical responsibility for their memberships, beliefs, values, and actions. Correlated with this disembedding, the theory also accounts for the rebindings, at new levels, of persons into community and into shared systems of meaning. In this sense it is appropriate to describe this work, in both its status as a general theory, and in its contribution to practical theology, with the earlier quoted language of Johannes Metz: It *is* a theory of our "becoming subjects before God."

2

Toward a Logic of Religious Development: A Reply to My Critics

FRITZ K. OSER

THIS ARTICLE CONTAINS three parts. In section I the stages of religious judgment development are outlined and an overview of a large-scale research program is presented. The second part is a brief report on a study regarding the relations between life-cycle phases and stages of religious judgment as well as the various ways in which subjects retrospectively reconstruct their own religious development. Some cases are presented. The last part consists of replies to six clusters of criticisms that have been raised against this theory of religious development.

Religious Development: Foundations, Stages, and Construct Validation

The Focus of the Theory: Qualitative Changes in Construing the Relationship between Humans and Ultimate Being

We begin by defining religious consciousness in terms of persons' constructions of their relationship with an Ultimate Being. In this approach we do not rely on an *a priori* definition of the Ultimate Being but rather focus on capturing the human–divine relationship itself. This relationship is constructed by a dynamic, interactional cognitive activity by which a person copes with contingencies, gives religious meaning to situations, interprets religious messages, and engages in prayer. Our effort is to understand our

---

* The present English version of this article is edited for length and North American comprehension. For the full statement of Oser's position, see the original in the German version in Nipkow, Schweitzer, and Fowler 1988, pp. 48–88.

subject's structuring of the relation to an Ultimate Being by utilizing psychological categories.

When we focus on the structuring of the relation between humans and God that constitutes religious consciousness, we start with the following two observations: First, we hold that this structure is holistic, that it has its own self-regulatory power that is used to solve problems encountered in life through religious categories. Second, the structure develops; that is, it changes. That means we have to question the generative status of such forms of thought: How did this structure develop? What has been there prior to it? What will follow after the loss of plausibility of this line of thought? This leads to a fundamental question: Is development in religious knowing governed by an innate or natural lawfulness? Does it follow a regular order? Is it possible to argue for a natural necessity for growth through a sequence of stages?

In order to test these assumptions and to answer these basic questions, we must empirically identify the ways in which subjects conceive the relationship between humans and an Ultimate Being. For purposes of analysis the following foci are important in allowing us to compare responses across the range of our subjects:

Transcendence versus Immanence

The subject who finds himself or herself in a life situation that stimulates religious interpretation, asks how the Ultimate Being might intervene in the world, in a human person, in society.

Freedom versus Dependency

The individual's feeling being cast into this world and to experience his or her natural limits day by day is often rationalized by the notion of "depending" on an Ultimate Being's decision making. How a person balances freedom from the Ultimate Being with dependency on the divine is the focus here.

Trust versus Fear

A fundamental religious belief promises that if you have trust in the Ultimate Being, your life will be saved and meaningful. Nonetheless, we experience fear of death; we suffer from illness, from ruptures in life, and from loneliness. This criterion focuses on how such experiences are coordinated with underlying trust. It is precisely the experience of fear which provides a basis for trust, and that trust in an Ultimate Being grows in the course of coping with anxiety.

There are four additional polar dimensions that I cannot address in detail: the Holy versus the Profane; Hope versus Absurdity; Eternity versus Ephemerality; and Functional Transparency versus Opaqueness.

When we interview our subjects we do not ask them, Do you trust, or do you fear; do you believe (and in what), or what do you think about dependency on God? This way of inquiry would not have taken us beyond the surface of knowledge or belief. To gain access to persons' ways of constructing their relations with the Ultimate Being, we attempted to analyze how individuals deal with concrete situations that have in themselves a kind of archetypical character. These situations, set forth in religious judgment dilemmas, refer to questions of theodicy, predetermined destiny versus freedom of choice, death and eternal life, mystery and hidden forces, good and bad luck, and the like. In questioning subjects about such situations we seek access to how they resolve the seven polar dimensions mentioned above.

Through these means we have discovered five structural stages that describe persons' ways of constructing their understandings of the human–divine relationship. In the following section we give a brief description of these stages.

The Logic of Religious Development

A comprehensive description of the developmental hierarchy of the religious judgment stages would require spelling out each of seven polar dimensions for each of the five stages separately, demonstrating that they form a structured pattern — the distinct quality we can call "stage." Space limits do not allow for such a detailed presentation. For this reason we confine our description to the most characteristic features of each stage. Note that this is only a very rough outline, aiming to provide a basis for the subsequent discussion of the developmental logic.

Stage 1. There is an Ultimate Being who protects you or sends you something hurtful, dispenses health or illness, joy or despair. The Ultimate Being influences you (and all other living beings) directly. The Ultimate Being's will must always be fulfilled. Otherwise, the relationship is broken.

At Stage 1 the interactional quality is one-sided; as a child in many daily situations depends on her parents, so is the relationship to the Ultimate Being one of dependence. At a particular moment there is total hope; at another there is downright despair. The integration variables are completely separated from the differentiation variables. Dependence is at the same time protection; absurdities are avoided through direct intervention of the Ultimate Being (God); when viewed from God's perspective, all is transparent, etc.

Stage 2. The Ultimate Being can be influenced by prayers, offerings, the following of religious rules, etc. If one cares about the Ultimate Being and passes the tests He sends, He will act like a trusting and loving father, and you will be happy, healthy, successful, etc. An individual can influence the Ultimate Being, or he or she can fail to do so, depending on his or her needs and free will.

At Stage 2 there is a shift: the subject now sees the possibility of and the means for influencing the Ultimate and thereby introducing security measures for his or her own well-being. There is a concern for God and a more secure knowledge of what He does and, on the other hand, a greater effort to do all we can for Him. Life becomes more calculable, because the actions of the Ultimate Being seems to depend on us, on our deeds, and not on His arbitrary decisions. God's action and our action are seen as connected: dependence is mutual.

Stage 3. The individual assumes responsibility for his or her own life, and for matters of the world. Freedom, meaning, and hope are linked to one's own decisions. The Ultimate Being is apart. He has His own field of action; we have ours. The Ultimate Being's wholeness encompasses a freedom, hope, and meaning that are different from the human ones. Transcendence is outside the individual but represents a basic order of world and life.

At Stage 3 the two realms (humans–Ultimate Being) are conceived as independent, mostly seen as being in a state of "peaceful coexistence." This more differentiated view posits that ultimately every human being's action is independent of a religious or metaphysical power but that there exists dependency concerning other things, such as the spiritual growth of humanity and individuals, such as love, secrets of nature, and hidden forces. Stage 3 is the typical stage of members of so-called youth religions, but certain forms of atheist thought can also spring up at this Stage 3: in regard to the new option "humanity or God?" the youth religions opt decisively for God, the atheists for humanity. Because the subject's thought must go from a conception of a direct influence administered by the Ultimate Being to a conception of a mediated relationship, he or she needs this intermediate stance of separating things from one another (like daughters and sons have to go through a period of detaching from the parents, hopefully without breaking the relationship to their parents) (Fasick 1984).

Stage 4. Now an indirect, mediated relationship with an Ultimate Being has come into existence. The individual continues to assume responsibility, but he or she wonders about the conditions for the mere possibility to carry responsibility. He or she sees his or her commitment as a way to overcome lack of meaning and hope, as well as absurdity. The transcendence is now partly inside (immanence): the Ultimate Being becomes the condition for the possibility of human freedom, independence, etc., via the divine plan.

At Stage 4 a mediated and correlational relationship to the Ultimate Being emerges anew, more equilibrated than ever. After a person has begun to realize the secularity of the many domains of life (differentiation), he or she integrates the Ultimate Being in his or her life in a new fashion: Whatever a person does or experiences, there is an unexplained part in it, which does not make sense unless referred to the existence of the Ultimate Being. This Being becomes the metaphysical *a priori* of human freedom (in a life of dependency) and of encounter. There is the governing notion of an invisible plan for everything, a kind of universal "It is all right as it is"; at rock bottom we live in a God-given security. Dependence is the reconstructed human limitation and, at the same time, a possibility that invites exploration.

Stage 5. The Ultimate Being (God) appears in every human commitment, yet transcends it at the same time. The Ultimate Being becomes apparent in history and in revelation. Transcendence and immanence interact completely. This total integration renders possible universal solidarity with all human beings. The "realm of God" becomes a cipher for a peaceful and fully committed human potential, which creates meaning not in options detached from the world but rather in a truly social perspective.

At Stage 5 there is a complete complementarity with regard to all dimensions. There is no profane without the holy; there is no holiness without profane, trivial aspects to it. There is no hope without absurdity; there is no absurdity without hope. The divine is completely transcended by the human, and it is not conceived as divine security (holy plan) anymore. Every person becomes a unique contributor to and participant in divinity, and it is understood that the divine is universal through human universal connectedness. ("God became human" is the absolute and universal cipher of a lived Stage 5 relationship.) Suffering and death are part of this integrative human solidarity. This solidarity needs a new elaboration in every situation. At Stage 5 revelation is continued by humans; there is no other ordering of life, no security other than belief. This is clearly expressed in a statement of Paul Tillich to which I would like to subscribe: "To be religious means to question passionately the meaning of our life and to be open for answers even if they trouble us profoundly. Such a position makes religion something universally human, even if this is not the usual meaning of the word religion" (Tillich 1958, 8). (I quote Tillich without agreeing with the entirety of his theology. Although his definitions are immediately appealing, Tillich runs the danger of disconnecting an individual's religion from what it is referring to. Critical remarks by K. E. Nipkow to that effect have stimulated my thinking.)

A careful analysis of these stages reveals that the succession rests on related changes in autonomy and connectedness, differentiation and integration, universality and uniqueness of thought.

Some Remarks on Research Methodology

For our research purposes we primarily utilize the semistructured ("clinical") interview method as designed by Piaget. We believe that confronting individuals with standardized situations, while still giving them extensive opportunity to unfold their thinking, yields the following advantages: (1) The probe questions can be structured according to an underlying theory. (2) The subjects' answers can be compared in a clear and reliable way. (3) It is possible to construct a scoring manual for classifying responses in an intersubjectively valid approach. (4) In order to understand the developmental core, we can use prototypical answers as criterion judgments for assigning specific stages (Oser and Gmünder 1984, 143–73; 1988, 130–58). (5) Dilemma stories stimulate in-depth reasoning rather than the expression of simple beliefs. They help to uncover real religious thinking, including explanation and justification of subjects' assumptions. The interviewing permits us to infer judgmental competences: the subject can be "pushed" toward the limit of his or her optimal reflective abilities. (6) On the basis of the scoring manual a method for stage calculation can be devised (RMS = Religious Maturity Score), the result of which can easily be compared with other psychological measures.

Three dilemma stories are used in our recent research: (a) the "Paul-Dilemma," which revolves around a promise to God given in a peril to Paul's life and the question whether the promise has to be kept after rescue; (b) the "Theodicy-Dilemma," which tells of bad things happening to a good person and leads to the question of whether after all the person should still try to believe in God; (c) the "Chance-Dilemma," in which probability calculation stands against the assertion that luck is a gift of God, a sign of his grace in life.

Validation of the Stage Concept: Outline of a Research Program

Our research focused on three different, though connected, objectives: to validate our conception of religious judgment development across various samples; to develop and evaluate educational intervention strategies designed to stimulate religious consciousness; and to explore effects of changes in religious judgment on other constructs (criterion validity).

Religious Judgment Development across Various Samples

1. The construct "religious judgment" was explored and validated by a study in a medium-sized Swiss town, the assessed independent variables being age, religious orientation, and social status; the sample size was N = 112 (Oser and Gmünder 1984, 179–222; 1988, 164–203). Several hypotheses could be confirmed: there is a clear age-related trend in religious judgment development (see fig. 1); variables related to religious orientation and sex do not influence this development significantly.

The hypothesized consistency of structures is supported by congruent findings on the basis of different dilemma stories (see Oser and Gmünder 1984, 184ff.; 1988, 165ff.). Numbers and percentages of correspondences are presented in table 1. One hypothesis had to be dismissed: that religious judgment does not depend on social class and educational training. It does, in terms of the stages achieved (see fig. 2).

All in all, this study indicated that religious judgment stages actually can be conceived as "structured wholes," and the results are not contrary to the notion that the stages actually follow an invariant sequence.

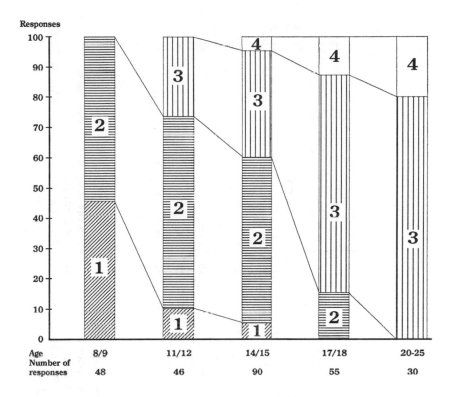

Fig. 1: Percentage of stage 1-, stage 2-, stage 3-, and stage 4-rated dilemma responses for various age groups (all dilemmas).

2. A study conducted by Dick (1982) addressed the question of universality: Can our religious judgment stages also be found in a non–Judeo-Christian context? Dick interviewed Hindus and Jains in Rajasthan (India), Mahayana Buddhists near the Tibetan border, as well as two samples in Rwanda (Africa) who practiced ancestor worship or were members of a Christian missionary group, respectively. Dick used the "Paul-Dilemma" adapted to the respective sociocultural contexts. All samples show a significant age trend. Unfortunately, the samples were too small and too specific to allow for truly cross-cultural comparisons. Thus the definite empirical support for the hypothesized universality of our stages has still to be put forward.

3. Given the conviction that having to cope with the contingencies of life is implied in being human, regardless of religious beliefs, Achermann

	PAUL 1		HIOB 2		UNGL 3		EWHL 4		SCHULD 5		LIEBE 6		SEMO 7		HEIRAT 8	
	+	-	+	-	+	-	+	-	+	-	+	-	+	-	+	-
PAUL 1			84.85	15.15	78.26	21.74	50.00	50.00	-	-	75.00	25.00	81.82	18.18	70.59	29.41
HIOB 2	28	5			79.41	20.59	60.87	39.13	72.73	27.27	-	-	55.56	44.44	57.14	42.86
UNGL 3	18	5	27	7			65.71	34.29	60.87	39.13	50.00	50.00	-	-	63.64	36.36
EWHL 4	6	6	14	9	23	12			71.88	28.12	70.00	30.00	80.00	20.00	-	-
SCHULD 5	-	3	8	3	14	9	23	9			60.61	39.39	80.95	19.05	100.00	0.0
LIEBE 6	9	3	-	-	6	6	14	6	20	13			79.41	20.59	80.95	19.05
SEMO 7	18	4	5	4	7	-	8	2	17	4	27	7			75.76	24.24
HEIRAT 8	24	10	12	9	7	4	-	-	9	0	17	4	25	8		

Table 1: Consistency of the stage scores in the 8 dilemmas:

(+) Consistency, i.e. the subject's responses were rated at the same stage in both dilemmas

(-) Inconsistency, i.e. the subject's responses were rated at different stages

Stage 1 = RMS 100-133, stage 2 = RMS 166-233, stage 3 = RMS 266-333, stage 4 = RMS 366-433.

Absolute frequencies are shown below the diagonal, percentages above.

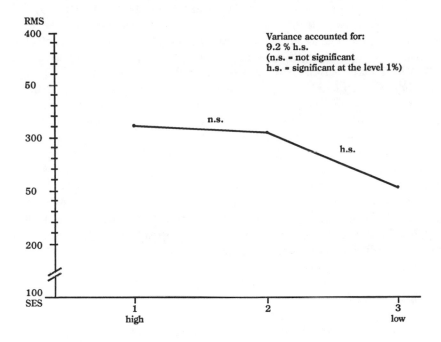

Fig. 2: Influence of the socio-economic status (SES) on the religious judgment

investigated the thinking of fifty declared atheists (Achermann 1981). Data are consistent with a description of types that display some remarkable similarities to the religious development stages: determination from outside (in this case, society, etc.) and fatalism at the one pole; self-determination via social commitment at the other. We do not take this as a proof that our stages account for nonreligious thinking as well (this was not even a full-fledged cross-sectional study and thus not suited to identify any kind of development, for that matter), but the structural congruences remain noteworthy.

4. In an additional study, von Brachel and Oser (1984) interviewed fifty subjects, equally distributed as to age, sex, and religious orientation, about their views on their own religious development. Contrary to an initial hypothesis, it is not the brief, critical life event that gives rise to a transition of consciousness; individuals rather report phases of change in life (e.g., leaving home, beginning of working life, marriage) as factors in abandoning former lines of thought and constructing new visions of world and God. Another major finding of this study gave some support to the developmental theory: most of the subjects were well aware that in former times they had thought

about religious issues and had related to God differently than they did by the time of the interview. Insofar as they reconstructed their own former ways of religious thinking, no elements emerged that did not fit into our stage descriptions—the descriptions of stages prior to subjects' current stages.

5. Additionally, various psychohistorical explorations attempted to utilize the religious judgment stages as a frame of reference in analyzing the genesis of thought in personalities who were well known not only for their work but also for a highly mature religious development, utilizing Erikson's model of ego development as well as our stage model. These studies show the feasibility of reconstructing the stages of religious consciousness (in the sequence described by the theory) from written material. Further analyses of this kind seem necessary to permit empirical statements regarding the question of a terminal point in structural development. This latter question is the focus of another study, still in its beginnings (see Oser, Althof, and Bucher 1986), which will attempt to explore the common features of thought in subjects intuitively considered as wise and experienced.

Educational Studies

6. Oser and Gmünder hypothesize that religious content, especially when presented in textual form, is assimilated in a manner isomorphic to the structure of religious judgment, that is, by a given person at his or her actual stage (1984, 261; 1988, 218). Empirical support for this hypothesis was adduced by a study of the understanding of parables of the New Testament exhibited by children at different levels of religious judgment development (Bucher 1987a; Bucher and Oser 1987b). Bucher postulated a four-stage model claiming to describe and explain the development of understanding with regard to parables not only in the Bible but in literature in general (1987a, 1987b).

These results seem to be of special significance for any kind of religious teaching working with text material. They provide strong indicators that students assimilate religious texts to structures of understanding that are qualitatively different from those of adults. Unidirectional transmission of theological texts is not sufficient, because either students do not understand them (and consequently reject them) or they reinterpret them according to their religious reasoning level. This can be clearly exemplified by the reactions to the parable of the workers in the vineyard, who are paid the same wages regardless of how long they had worked during the day. When children of lower stages of religious maturity were asked if the master's acting in the story could be understood as an example of God's acting, subjects answered no, full of indignation: How could this man be like God? Does not God reward people according to their performance and punish them according to their failures and misdeeds (bipolar reciprocity)?

7. A large-scale interventional study with seventh-grade students confirmed that religious judgment development could be effectively stimulated (Oser 1988). The average increase after two and one-half months of intervention amounted to more than half a stage. The treatment included (a) the discussion of religious dilemmas (real-life conflicts as well as dilemmas taken from religious texts) combined with a systematic stimulation of higher-stage patterns of argumentation, and (b) a metareflection on the discussion process. There is clear evidence that this kind of educational method (both treatments) is likely to provoke not only exchanges of opinion but also inner confrontations which, in the long run, break up the given stage of religious judgment and give way to structural transformations.

8. Another study, conducted by Schildknecht (1984), is situated in a similar context. This study investigated the development of competences in moral and religious argument. Following the prior work of Berkowitz and collaborators, competence was measured using the concept of "transactive discussion," which refers to the degree of cross-reference to the partner's arguments. Results show a clear age trend in the degree of transactive modes of dialogue. Figure 3 shows that in middle childhood no transacts are displayed, whereas in adolescence (14 through 17 years) 25 percent of the statements can be categorized as transactive. On the basis of these data Oser, Althof, and Berkowitz (1986; Berkowitz, Oser, and Althof 1987) developed a preliminary model of levels of argumentative logic.

9. Finally Klaghofer and Oser (1987) carried out a study of the "religious climate" in families. In this study, a questionnaire for assessing the religious atmosphere in families was constructed and factor analyzed. The authors uncovered two dimensions: (a) religious handling of contingency (i.e., unpredictable possibilities and dangers) and religious activities in the family; (b) religious discourse in the family. Further analyses of the general family atmosphere and of patterns of educational behavior fit well to both of the scales and demonstrate their usefulness. In the same context, Niggli (1987/ 1988) could show that higher stages of religious judgment are significantly related to support by the mother and the father, but not with pressure from either parent.

Religious Judgment and Other Domains of Development

10. The relationship between religious and moral judgment as conceived by Kohlberg (1981b, 1984) has been of particular interest. The study of Gut (Oser and Gmünder 1984) yielded discrepant results with respect to a widely accepted thesis, namely, that moral judgment development emerges prior to religious judgment development: twenty-four subjects proved to be

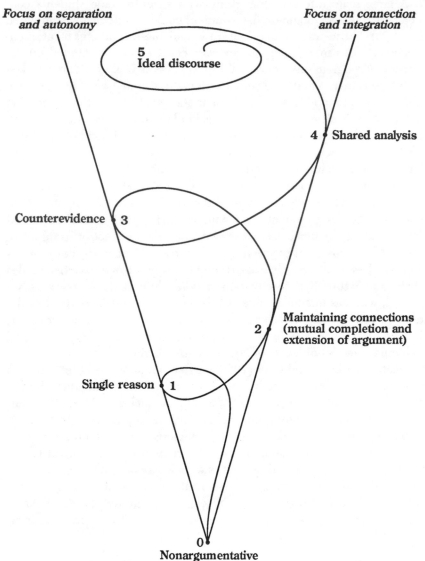

Focus on separation and autonomy

Focus on connection and integration

5
Ideal discourse

4 ● **Shared analysis**

Counterevidence ● **3**

Maintaining connections
(mutual completion and
extension of argument)

2 ●

Single reason ● **1**

0 ●
Nonargumentative
Use of argumentative elements is
arbitrary, experimenting, associative, and fragile.

Fig. 3: Oscillating styles
(From: Berkowitz, Oser, and Althof, 1987, p. 347.)

higher in level of moral judgment; sixteen subjects displayed parallel reasoning levels in both domains. Contrary to the stronger hypothesis, however, that moral judgment development is a necessary (but insufficient) condition for the development of an "isomorphic" religious judgment stage, ten subjects were more mature in religious than in moral reasoning. Oser's result (Oser 1988) supported Gut's findings. On the other hand, a study conducted by Caldwell and Berkowitz (1987) did support even the stronger hypothesis. More refined research is needed, as discussed by Oser and Reich (1987b).

11. Another research project compared religious judgment stage and the "world view" of sixty subjects, aged 5 to 19—that is, ontological and "cosmological" aspects of thought (Fetz and Oser, 1985/1986). As regards cosmology, most of these children gave superficial explanations: they assumed that in the beginning of the world God produced, in a craftsman's style, things of nature, such as mountains and trees, and even artifacts such as big buildings, etc (see Piaget 1926, 1929 for a discussion of artificialism). These children had a literal understanding of the biblical Genesis; at the same time they displayed low stages of religious judgment. After going through a hybrid stage (and apparently not before the age of 11), a differentiation of biblical and scientific belief systems takes place: from now on, "sky" and "heaven" can be understood in both the scientific and the symbolic and religious sense, respectively. A follow-up study four years later (Fetz, Reich, and Valentin [in preparation]) permitted the refinement of understanding of this development while confirming the main features described.

12. These data address a more general question: What can be said about the development of the ability to think in terms of *complementarity*, that is, to coordinate two different explanations (in the Fetz study, evolution theory and Genesis) of the same entity (beginning of the world). Oser and Reich (1987a, 1987b) carried out a pilot study, which is currently followed by a more extensive investigation. These authors confronted twenty-eight subjects with nine different problems, providing subjects with two distinct explanations for each problem and asking them which one was the right one, if both of them are necessary, and so on. On the basis of these data the authors constructed a preliminary model of five levels of thinking in "terms of complementarity."

Life Span Development and Religiosity: Continuity—Discontinuity

Two Possibilities of Investigation

Development is a lifelong enterprise. With respect to the logic of Piaget-type general cognitive development, extensive analyses of progress in

adulthood have been made (see the discussion of knowing levels in Campbell and Bickhard 1986). However, we do not yet possess such analyses in
the domain of religious development. Moreover, we do not yet know what
the environmental influences are on developmental changes; we do not
know enough about how persons experience the progression through our
stages, and we do not know to which degree the understanding of societal
value systems is a help or even a condition for understanding the occurrence
of developmental processes. The general cognitive development of a child is
nowadays embedded in a social system in which cognitive functioning
becomes a most important aspect of life. It was not always like this. In the
old times the religious functioning of society was of much more importance,
because it ensured the continuity of the social order (Berger 1970).

Why then should a study of religious development across the life span be
of significance? Speaking in terms of methodology, there are two possibilities
for investigating the mechanisms of growth in religious judgment: interventional studies and assessment of natural development. Interventional
studies may stimulate transformations of thought and give substantial
explanations as to why those changes came about. Our intervention with
secondary school classes used a quasi-experimental design with two different
treatments, stimulating a decentration process and a metareflection of
results of interaction. (The findings of this large-scale investigation are
presented in my recent book, *Wieviel Religion Braucht der Mensch?* [How
much religion does a person need?].) The second way of investigating the
mechanisms of growth is through observation and/or analysis of natural
development; a basis for analysis can, for instance, be provided by biographic
interviews.

Stage Transformation as Life Event: A Model

We have conducted a first fundamental study attempting to investigate
relations between religious stage development and life experiences. For this
purpose our interviewing procedure included several steps. We first assessed
the current level of religious judgment by means of our standard interview
(Paul Dilemma). The next steps were retrospective. We hypothesized that
a subject at a given stage has passed through a number of religiously relevant
crises, leading to stage transformations. Theoretically, we thus expected
some kind of correspondence between critical life events and structural
transitions. We hypothesized the following four-step model with regard to
structural transformation (see von Brachel and Oser 1984): (1) The subject's
cognitive structure, equilibrated so far, is confronted with problems of such
a kind that these difficult issues cannot be dealt with adequately anymore.
The structure changes to a state of disequilibration, indicated by cognitive

contradiction, by the person having a feeling of inadequacy and of insecurity concerning patterns of thought. A temporary reaction can be by way of defense. (2) An increasing disintegration of the former cognitive structure is taking place; new elements are recognized, calling for processing and integration. Inconsistencies in the person's cognitive functioning result, because problems are resolved by utilization of different structural patterns. This is indicated by the fact that the person stresses the relativity of opinions and wavers between various beliefs, opinions, and approaches to problem resolution. (3) A period of integrating new elements follows. The former structural elements gain a new valence and change their relative position. The new elements are considered more valuable, the person makes a shift in focus, stresses the importance of the new knowledge, separates, and tries out the new modes of thought. (4) Finally, the new structure is transferred to other issue areas and in this process is further tested and strengthened.

Remembering: Five Patterns of Restructuring Former Religious Orientations

Our research sample included forty-eight subjects, equally distributed as to sex and religious orientation; the age groups were 11/12, 15/16, 19–21, 24–26, 37–45, and 55–62. Since we plan a longitudinal follow-up study, the results of the investigation have not been published yet. However, I would like to present some summarized findings and a case example from the preliminary report (von Brachel and Oser 1984). It is worth noting that we experienced the well-known difficulties of retrospective research. Some of our individuals claim that their thinking did not change at all since the days of their childhood. Individuals remembered distinct former styles of thought to different degrees. Nonetheless, what was remembered was of high significance for us: not one subject described religious orientations that would not fit into our stage scheme; and no subject reconstructed a stage of religious thought that was above his or her current stage.

It was possible to distinguish five patterns of reconstructing former religious orientations (which we describe in terms of stages) and critical events or periods of life:

(1) Reconstruction of many stages and transitions

These subjects tend to be on a higher stage. They tend to work in a profession promoting a conscious confrontation with matters of religion and morality. They tend to describe their life history not in terms of incisive crises but rather in terms of "intellectual growth." These subjects also tend to be older and Catholic.

(2) *Reconstruction of one prior stage and transition*

This is a very common pattern among our sample. These subjects tend to be on stage 3; the transition in mind refers to issues of autonomy; contextual influences play a significant role. These subjects tend to be younger. The transition tends to be more marked with respect to Catholics than to Protestants.

(3) *Reconstruction of one prior stage but not of a transition*

This is a second standard type, occurring on stage 2 as well as on (a laicized) stage 3. These subjects tend to be older. Their life history displays conventional features and doesn't allow for too much intellectual exposition. This type can be found among Protestants more often than among Catholics, especially on stage 3.

(4) *No reconstruction of former stages and transitions;*
   "I always thought like that."

These subjects showed reluctance to be questioned in a way that they experienced as intruding on their private life. Moreover, they expressed a very normative viewpoint: "Being in a crisis" is socially undesirable. This type can be found among subjects in "well-established" circumstances (where it seems part of the life-style to dispose of a clearly ordered view of the world), as well as among middle-class persons who have distanced themselves from both the church and religious issues.

(5) *Low stage, no transitions reconstructed,*
   but many crises in life

These subjects are characterized by marginalized circumstances of life. They tend to be older, more often female than male, and more often belong to the lower social classes.

One of our hypotheses had been that a person who had gone through various structural transformations would be provided with a high competence in problem solving and actually would have coped successfully with a number of crises in life.

There is no clear evidence concerning this hypothesis, at least not on a general and abstract level of analysis. Subjects obviously distinguished between "life crises" and "transformations of thought (structures)." They associated the latter with "new thinking," "becoming more mature," etc., whereas the notion of crises in life is related to "difficulties," "emotional problems," etc. Typically, subjects did not see a pronounced relationship between those two dimensions. This allows different interpretations: maybe structural transformations actually are not connected with situational factors; maybe a process of redefinition has taken place (omitting influential factors; attribution of only positive — "noncrisis" — factors on a transformation that subjects came to interpret as progress).

Two Case Studies

For a closer look at life histories and at cognitive development, I will present some interview excerpts. As a first example, here is a portion of what a woman told us who believed that she did not change much during her life. This Protestant woman is 18 years of age. Her current stage of religious judgment is 4(3).

Interviewer (I): What do you think your answer to this story (Paul Dilemma) would have been in former times?

Subject (S): I think it would have been the same. Not in each detail, but as a whole. There have been quite a few things to add to my thinking, by things that I'm doing, maybe in the course of my religious education. There have been influences at home, too. But essentially, I would have answered in a similar way, I hope.

I: You said spontaneously that Paul should keep his promise, to stay true to his own character. That's been the most important reason you mentioned. And you stated that religiosity gives strength for self-realization. Do you think you would have argued like this, say, five or ten years ago?

S: Even ten years ago, I'm quite certain. Possibly then I wouldn't have been very well able to express it. On the other hand . . . looking back has something dangerous about it. But no, I would have given the same answer at least: He should keep his promise.

It is clear that this person believes in an unchangeable inner foundation of (her) religious judgment; she does not think that there have been major transformations of thought during her life history. On the other hand, she does remember influential and even shaping factors in her life:

S: There's been much that rested on experiences, primarily.

I: I beg your pardon . . .

S: On experiences. Friends. That it's useless to tell things just to get a better image. That it doesn't pay to lie, because then you cheat yourself.

I: Do you mean that in those days your moral reasoning was habitually much more concrete? Would you have used words like "self-realization"?

S: Being true to oneself, that emerged in the relationship to friends . . . but not on the other thing. As to God and such, there have been no changes. It took a long time, indeed, until my relation to God . . . I always did pray, with my mother, and such. But she never said to me something like, "If you do this, God will punish you." Such stories I never have heard. Same thing as to sin. Nobody told me those stories. So I wasn't impressed when the teacher talked about the Bible; that wasn't important to me, and it isn't important nowadays. What's important to me is my direct relationship to God. I perceive God in terms of other human beings who also want to realize their own potential. But I do believe that religious education has an influence. In my family, God perhaps only plays a role in our prayers, you know. It's always been the direct way, not via Jesus or Maria. Well, I guess that's typically Protestant, this direct reference to God. That never bothered me, anyway. I believe that's one form of faith, among a lot of different forms.

This person is aware of the connection between the inner development and educational influences. But she cannot spell it out clearly. This is a result that we found in many cases.

■

Let us now listen to another person who is aware of the religious development he has gone through. He is Catholic, 20 years of age, and currently reasons at about stage 2.

I: Could you tell me whether you always thought that way, or if, and how, your thinking has changed?

S: Well, formerly, about the time I was a fifth-grader, I certainly would have been very sure that it was God's intervention and not just an accident. Education plays a role, doesn't it? In those times we had more religious education and used to go to church every weekend. And we prayed with our mother every evening. It isn't that way anymore.

I: Could you say more precisely how you would have seen the situation (part of the Paul Dilemma questioning) in those times?

S: I would have thought that God's hand came down from heaven, invisible, and manipulated something at his car, his brakes, so that something fouls up and he has an accident.

I: So you would have imagined a direct intervention?

S: Yes, kind of.

This young man shows a clear knowledge that in earlier times he conceived religious issues in a distinct way, and he is able to present an explanation for his changes in views:

S: With time you see more clearly the injustices in the world, don't you? You are confronted with other people who don't attend church, who don't believe in God, and they still enjoy their lives. You begin questioning yourself.

This man has an intuitive awareness about what caused his cognitive transformation. The old scheme did not assure a personally satisfying comprehension of the world anymore. Contrary to his stage 1 beliefs, there apparently could be well-being without belief in an omnipotent God; and there could be injustice in spite of the supposedly almighty God.

The interviewer now asks him to explain the character of this transformation:

I: If you look back, how long did this change in thinking take? Did it happen suddenly, or did it take a longer period?

S: Yes, a longer period. Two or three years.

I: And how did you feel during this time? Did you reject your old way of thinking strongly? Did you think, "What a dummy I have been to believe in all that"?

S: No, there was only slow change.

I: Some kind of dissociating yourself?

S: I think so. I didn't go to church once a week anymore; I concluded religious instruction. Slow changes.

I: So there hasn't been a strong kind of crisis?

S: Not at all. It happened automatically, in a way.

This subject had an eminent interest in the dissolution of the old—restricting—structure. He knows that step by step he superseded his prior religious world view, without being able to locate the transition in particular life events. At the time of the interview the former structure had made way for a new cognitive-religious conception, which still was in a phase of construction and stabilization.

It is a fascinating enterprise to study transformational processes across the life span. Even if the biographical interview method, which of course is not more than a substitute for longitudinal observation and questioning, cannot definitely support the strong claims of the theory (that if a person is at stage 4, there must have been three periods of structural transformation), I am convinced that this kind of inquiry provides at least partial possibilities for uncovering elements in structural transformation that may serve to explain some of the laws governing religious development—regularities in the very process of restructuring modes of thought, influences of outside social realities. Surely there is still much work to do, but we no longer start from a level zero. Nipkow's beautiful book *Ohne Gott Aufwachsen* [Growing Up without God], among others, provides a basis for further research. This author introduces the social context as an important determinant of the transformation process, and the concrete content of this determinant is not the same as it was thirty or fifty or a hundred years ago. The social differentiation of life spheres, according to Max Weber, included religious systems, and this changed the conditions affecting individuals' growth in religiosity. Our study is just another small contribution to an understanding of what is actually going on when people develop toward religious maturity in our "postmodern" times.

A Reply to My Critics

From the time of the first publications outlining the theory of religious judgment, various critiques have been put forward by a number of authors. I would like to discuss some of those critical arguments that I find most relevant.

1. *This theory neglects the affective aspects of personal religiosity* (see Ebert 1984, 462; Fraas 1983, 105; 1984, 81; Grom 1981, 133; Schweitzer 1985, 321). This viewpoint implies the existence of two different and separable intrahuman systems: the cognitive domain and the affective domain. These critics seem to subscribe to a notion of polar systems in psychology.

I do not subscribe to such a conception, on theoretical as well as empirical grounds. Theoretically, my stance is like James Rest's, stated with regard to morality: "dividing reality into thoughts, behavior, and emotions does not provide theoretically clear units of analysis: What is an emotion disembodied from cognitive referents? What is a behavior without intention or thoughts without any feeling component?" (Rest 1983, 559). Empirically, we find just that: there is no such thing as reasoning without feeling. In our interviews subjects show real emotional involvement: they struggle with the situation intensely; they are insecure about what to think and what to say; they refer the situation back to their own experiences; they often refuse to follow through frightening thoughts, etc. Especially in our Job (Hiob) Dilemma interviews, we often have the experience that subjects get completely (and that means by its very nature, emotionally) involved in their own religious discourse. One woman remembered rough times in her own life history. With tears in her eyes she talked about how her husband died. From that experience on, she was no longer able to believe in divine grace and justice. In cases like this, religious judgment is obviously shaped by critical life events, particularly by experiences of contingency in which a person gets involved, whether willingly or not, and which are experienced in terms of both cognition *and* emotion.

It is important that there is also a methodological answer to the above critique. Our aim is to measure the structural aspects of religious consciousness. You cannot study at the same time and by the same research procedure both the (presumably) universal dimensions (i.e., cognitive structures) and the differential dimensions, which certainly are relative to a subject's state and history (i.e., motivations, emotional dispositions). Stated differently and arguing in terms of a concept of distinct psychic systems, it is hard to conceive a research methodology that at the same time takes adequate account of both the cognitive and the affective aspects of a given psychological issue. If we wanted to measure the affective aspects of the subject in the first place, we would supposedly proceed like Hinder (1986, 182). This author shows that in moral-dilemma interviews subjects are more involved when they have to justify a "pro" decision to the Heinz Dilemma (pro-stealing) than when justifying a "contra" decision; pro-deciders use more exhaustive arguments for their justifications. Hinder assessed this by way of letting the subject fill out a questionnaire (after the interview) designed to bring out the degree of involvement with the dilemma.

But the critique (neglect of affective aspects) does of course address a general problem of the Piagetian approach. Piaget considered emotions to be the functional "motor" of the structures. He believed affective powers to be narrowly connected with structures of thought. On the other hand, Martin Hoffman's empathy theory is an example of a more balanced consideration of affective and cognitive factors. According to Hoffman (1986), five levels of empathy can be distinguished, each in a particular way associated with forms of cognitive processing.

2. *The theory does not pay regard to the dimension of the unconscious* (Englert 1985, 355; Fraas 1984, 81; Mette 1983, 213). These authors notice a neglect of psychoanalytic thinking in the study of religiosity. They argue that some religious processes take place in the sphere of the unconscious — for example, the formation of the image of God that supposedly corresponds to the image of the parents. The critique also insists that a structuralist approach is unable to take hold of the religiosity of the very young child, who has not yet developed the mental and verbal capabilities necessary to answer the questions in a religious dilemma interview.

Partly, I do accept this critique. One must advocate complementary approaches to the phenomenon of religiosity. We need a variety of methods to get close to the core of religiosity, and actually in our 1984 book (Oser and Gmünder) we suggest an interdisciplinary approach ourselves. The structuralist approach enables one to grasp the structural complexity of religious consciousness. Neo-psychoanalytic approaches (Rizzuto 1979), on the other hand, may be able to explain why some people have a frightening image of God while others have an image that engenders security and positive emotions.

Whereas I accept the idea of integrating structuralistic and psychoanalytic thought on a general level, I see diffulties on a methodological level and on a theoretical level. Speaking in terms of methodology, the fact that our approach does not account for young children's religious judgments cannot be considered adequate proof that the structural approach is in principle unable to capture children's thought. Closer at hand would be an attempt to find appropriate ways of methodology. Damon (1977) demonstrated, for the moral realm, that this task is solvable. We do not claim that our work is finished yet. On a theoretical level I see serious problems in the kind of hermeneutics many psychoanalytic authors employ. I do accept that early parent–child relationships model or shape the relationship perceived between a person and the Ultimate Being. But I do not believe that all early social relationships are phenomena characterized by constraint and implying neurotic features; rather, I agree with Rizzuto (1980) that mother and father can provide positive experiences for a later formation of a representation of God, and I think that not enough psychoanalytic investigations have focused on this point of view, which may prove to be a more adequate description of early development (see Fromm 1979; Ringel and Kirchmayer 1985; Rizzuto 1979; see also Bucher and Oser 1987a).

3. *The notion of an "Ultimate Being" has not been defined with sufficient exactness* (Fetz and Bucher 1986). A further criticism refers to the concept of an "Ultimate Being." Fetz and Bucher (1986) argue that this notion is used too broadly and that not every entity, though it may serve as an ultimate for a subject in a situation of contingency, can claim the designation of being religious. This too-broad use is claimed to be exemplified by Achermann's study on the "religious judgment of atheists." The authors suggest a consultation of the phenomenological approach to religion (Otto 1963; van der Leeuw 1933), and they propose to reformulate "religious judgment" as "judgment of (solely) contingency mastering" whenever the Ultimate Being is not an entity that can be described in religious terms. Fetz and Bucher argue that without this differentiation, the notion of religion would be unclear and would lack precision to such an extent that it would be impossible to empirically distinguish religion from other symbol systems.

This is a weighty reproach, and there have been times when it made me very uneasy and reflective. But then one of the first lectures that I attended in theology (Introduction to the Old Testament) came to my mind, and I remembered the professor saying that the prohibition against making images of God was the strongest and deepest thought in early Judaic theology. It was pointed out that Yahweh was with the people and that this "being with" brought comfort and inner strength.

More to the point, in my opinion, Fetz and Bucher confound ontological features (*Sosein*) and personal relationship (*Mitsein*), two fundamental modes of dealing with the Ultimate. According to our work, the religious subject expresses a high self-confidence in the mode of being with (*Mitsein*), and the Ultimate Being can only be perceived indirectly as, so to speak, a foundation (a basis for making feasible) for this "being with." Bonhoeffer's dictum "A God who exists, does not exist" means to say that no one can express anything about the Ultimate Being unless it be in terms of his or her relationship to this Ultimate Being, his or her love and fear, hope and despair. Belief is always a matter of interaction, and belief cannot happen but in a concrete situation. (The statement "Whenever I offer bread to this sick person, God becomes visible in this world" covers all that can be said about God.)

The most significant criteria for this relationship have been indicated before: (a) the subject's activities: coping with difficult situations, making meaning, interpretating religious revelations, and praying; (b) the seven polar dimensions: immanence vs. transcendence, holy vs. profane, hope vs. absurdity, etc. If we make use of these criteria in the context of Fetz and Bucher's argument, it becomes clear that nobody can believe, for instance, in alcohol, drugs, or television as a kind of Ultimate Being. The human person experiences the Ultimate Being only through her or his relationship and not by means of definitions and descriptions of this Ultimate Being.

I can accept the criticism stated above insofar as we discuss religious issues. I do not consider it as useful with regard to religious judgment, which is ultimately an expression of a relationship in a context that concerns me intensely. Thus, what we obtain in our research are not descriptions of an Ultimate Being but rather descriptions of how and why subjects relate to this Ultimate Being in concrete situations. Fetz's own work refers to a completely different issue: Fetz (1985; Fetz and Oser 1985/1986) asked subjects where God lives, what God is doing, how the world came into being, etc. These are components of the "So-Sein" ontological aspects of an individual's view of the world. It is not an accident that religious aspects play a certain role within this world view. Fetz's schema of three stages—archaic, hybrid, and differentiated world view—outlines the development of ontological consciousness in a descriptive sense: God is perceived as an element in a knowledge structure.

The theory of the development of religious judgment takes another viewpoint. We analyze the interactive quality; we investigate how the person conceives his or her relationship to the Ultimate Being as a vital force in coping with the vicissitudes of life. It has not been our premise but an empirical finding that subjects are often not capable of describing their representation of God. They may be able to recall their childhood image of a personal God, reminiscences of a good father, a positive feeling, and a general sense of an ordering force built into their thinking, but these are metaphors for something which seems to be less important than the relationship that emerges when subjects talk about what they are *doing* in their religious, often secret, hidden, inner lives.

4. *The "Paul-Dilemma" does not involve a relevant religious conflict, but rather asks moral questions (of keeping vs. breaking a promise). This is the reason why some stages of Oser's scale are actually moral and not religious stages* (Grom 1986, 70; Neuenzeit 1985, 203; Schmidt 1984, 34). It is easy to respond to this criticism with three arguments. First, many other dilemmas were used in our research, as well as for stimulating religious consciousness. Our first study utilized eight dilemmas (Oser and Gmünder 1984, 183ff.). In many of our more recent investigations we employed three different dilemmas: the Paul Dilemma, the Hiob (Job) Dilemma, and the Chance Dilemma. In other studies we, in fact, only used the Paul Dilemma, but not arbitrarily so: we know that the cross-situational consistency is quite high — 97.21 percent when allowing for one stage difference; 88.35 percent within two-thirds of a stage.

Second, what stimulates the religious judgment in the interviewing situation is indeed at least partly the dilemma itself, but more importantly and to a high degree, the probing questioning. Probe questions refer to the seven polar elements and to the religious activities described earlier. If we do not use the word "God" in the dilemma story and do not refer to an Ultimate Being during in-depth questioning, we find that many subjects tend to resolve the dilemma without apparent religious reflection. But introducing God is like changing to an entirely other "mother structure," comparable to using another language game, offering another instrument of grasping the world. The reason for this is ultimately and fundamentally independent from other structures. We come back to this point later.

Third, the dilemma is nothing more than a stimulus for bringing to the surface the deep structure of religious modes of dealing with the world. The dilemma entails a disequilibrium, and we ask the subject to reconstitute the equilibrium, to solve the dilemma, to make sense of it by carefully considering the options and by weighing the conflicting arguments in one's mind. The subject reconstructs his or her pattern of religious thought him- or herself. The dilemma acts only as a trigger.

There are limits to the explanatory power of any kind of research. We cannot absolutely warrant that our method uncovers the deepest underlying structure of religious consciousness, the "structure of structures" that guides a person's thought in every context of life. Research can come fairly close to real life, but there will always be a gap. That is why reliability and validity measures are of absolute necessity. Additionally, the limits of research possibilities are not only determined by methodological reasons. Researchers have to adhere to ethical standards. Who should put forward such standards if we do not do so ourselves — those who work in the field of studying religiosity (or morality)? We simply must not interrogate people in moments of severe stress or grief, of a serious sickness (unless the sickness itself is the theme of the interview), at times when a beloved person passes away (maybe even not at times of being blindly in love), in the intimacy of their prayer.

5. *Not every stage of religious judgment that is achieved later in the life span is a higher and "better" form of religiosity. Particularly, stage 3 is not "better" than stage 2* (Fetz 1984; Fetz and Bucher 1986; Englert 1986, 266; Schweitzer 1985, 324). In a further criticism, Fetz and Bucher (1986) pose the question of whether stage 3 is a more religious stage than stage 2; these authors arrive at a negative conclusion. Often, the subject's reasoning at stage 3 denies and contests the existence of a divine being, and in accordance with atheistic thought, he or she insists on a solipsistic autonomy of the human being who has no need anymore to believe in God or in a transcendental and ultimate reality. The world is now regarded as autonomous, as independent of God. This point of view, often expressed by adolescent subjects, has a striking similarity to functional critiques of religion (Feuerbach, Nietzsche, Freud).

It is not easy to reply in a few words. Our data show that the atheistic subjects at stage 3 often believe in something unknowable. Their atheism frequently is characterized by a negation of the particular image of God that dominated their childhood. In many cases some other entity has taken the place of God, for example, nature, matter, the human spirit, universal love, a cosmic power, etc.

Stage 3 does not necessarily take an "atheistic" form. In whatever form it comes along, I think that it is a very important part of religious development. Obviously, the developmental drive toward this stage may mean to move away from the traditional religion and certainly from the church; but in the long run it renders possible a freer form of religion and the liberation from religious dogmatism and authoritarian orientation. In some cases the development ceases at this point, resulting in a subject's termination of his or her membership, of religion as a sociocultural system or (which does not make much difference) in a change to a merely superficial affiliation to the notion "religiosity"; we can even regard as religious the standpoint of persons who classify themselves as atheists or agnostics. When applying a broad concept of religiosity (Robertson 1973, 52ff.) there is no problem in speaking about a religious stance also in these cases; but if we identify religiosity with church membership and attendance at divine service, then the development especially to stage 3 can of course in some cases not be called a specifically religious development.

Thus it is my impression that there are two questions involved: (a) the validity of stage 3 and (b) the limits of the term "religiosity" with respect to persons displaying atheistic attitudes. Both questions have to be answered also on empirical grounds. Up to now, I see no proof that stage 3 does not really exist, that is, is not valid: if we compare adolescents' detachment from home and parents to their detachment from God and the belief of their childhood, there are, in terms of relationships, similar processes involved. The young person rejects his or her childhood dependency, refuses being led by the nose, being controlled and being the object of his or her parents' criticisms. Young people want to make up their own minds. Nonetheless, typically they do not think that this means discontinuing every contact with their parents for the rest of their lives; they know that the time will come when they can interact with them on an equal basis (Fasick 1984). Typically, there is no necessity to reject parental authority totally. This is a complicated period of balancing autonomy and relationship. To become a more autonomous and more integrated person inevitably means to rethink what has been considered valuable before, to learn to stand on one's own feet, to try out limits, and to experience possibilities — to go as far in one's own thinking and problem solving as one can go.

Insofar as this comparison of social relationships and Human–Ultimate Being relationship is legitimate, I cannot understand this particular criticism. The seeming immaturity of much of adolescents' behavior and experimenting with life is a necessary ingredient of a developmental progression leading to adult maturity. Why should not the same reasoning apply to developmental changes in adolescent religious thinking? Reports of teachers with much experience in religious education of 12- to 17-year-olds do answer this question in the affirmative. Insofar as stage 3 is typical for religious reasoning in the teenage years, it clearly provides a preparation for the emergence of stage 4. Given that stage 3 can include various contents (orientations related to different life histories and backgrounds), I do not doubt that this period is a necessary condition for the much more comprehensive thinking of a stage 4. I see neither logically nor empirically convincing counterarguments.

6. *The problem of structure and content is not solved yet, and that is the reason the theory cannot claim universal validity* (Fetz 1984; Bucher 1986, 201; Garz 1987; Grom 1986, 70; Schweitzer 1985, 323). A further critique concerns the problem of distinction between religious contents and religious structures. In our book (1984) we claim a universal applicability of our theory, and, as a presupposition to that, we postulate the necessity and the possibiltiy of separating religious contents from religious structures. As already indicated, we have collected data from various cultural and religious groups: Indian Hindus and Buddhists, Christians and Immanists in Rwanda, etc. Although these subjects believe in different Ultimate Beings (Brahma, God, Immana,) their answers to our dilemma questions can be reconstructed as being structurally the same. Furthermore, we found, in terms of the stage scheme, significant age trends in all samples. These data can be interpreted as indicating the universal validity of this theory. But further research is obviously needed. In particular, the relationship between modern Western

thought (Enlightenment, decline of myth, secularization) and the logic of the religious stage hierarchy has to be analyzed more thoroughly. In my opinion the differentiation of world views on account of the experience involved in living does not, contrary to Habermas (1976), necessarily lead to a secular and atheistic world view. Concomitant with the differentiation of spheres of life (*Lebenswelt*) there is a differentiation of the religious belief, of a person's faith. Like moral development, religious development is in itself a continuous differentiation and integration of cognitive forms. Additionally, we cannot but be part of history, and history was guided by religious judgment: the religions represent systematic changes in conceptions of society. It may even be that the general process of differentiation has a major focus in religiosity.

The structure–content gap requires formal definitions of the structures. Only by formalization can a strong claim for universalization and generality of features be justified. But there are limits to formal descriptions of the development of thought, in some domains more than others. As to the moral domain, several authors make a distinction between "soft" and "hard" stages of sociomoral reasoning development (Kohlbert et al. 1983; Garz 1987; see chapter 6 below). Garz subsumes the whole sphere of religious development under the headline of a soft stages concept. I reject this position. Even if the content–structure separation does not work to an absolute degree, the core of this development is universalizable. The scheme also includes a normative developmental model (autonomy and integration) and a renunciation of self-concept. The only open point is stage 5, which shares the same destiny as Kohlberg's stages 6 and 7, namely, the unavoidable necessity that different philosophical or theological core models are needed to understand the most complex, mature, and wise states of subjects' religious consciousness.

The gap between structure and content also poses a problem to the technical side of research. A reconstructive methodology endeavors to find the shared structural elements in as many statements as possible. This implies that theory construction must be open for progress and revision. The interactive "bootstrapping" model of theory construction and research is somewhat irritating from the standpoint of more simple falsification concepts in sciences, but it is necessary from the standpoint of generating a valid psychological model.

Conclusions

In summing up I would like to stress the fertility of many of the points of critique discussed here. Although I do not subscribe to these criticisms as a whole, there are many concrete objections I do accept. I do readily admit that a structural developmental theory can only capture a part of the religious consciousness; I do insist, however, that this part is rich and powerful and that a structural developmental approach is the appropriate means of uncovering most relevant issues of religious meaning making. I did design the research program described above precisely with the purpose of answering some of those questions. There is much more to be done; for instance, the availability of more extensive longitudinal data will permit a major step in theory validation.

Part 2

Developmental Theories and Education: Historical and Theological Perspectives

3

Developmental Views of the Religion of the Child: Historical Antecedents

Friedrich Schweitzer

IN THEIR RECENT VOLUME *Faith Development and Fowler*, Craig Dykstra and Sharon Parks suggest that the specific appeal of faith development theory is largely due to our contemporary cultural situation (Dykstra and Parks 1986, 3ff.). According to their observations, the pluralism and the enormous influence that psychology has exerted on contemporary forms of self-understanding have to be seen as the plausibility structures on which faith development theory rests. Dykstra and Parks do not take this observation as a final clue for rejecting such a theory as invalid. Nevertheless, their argument entails a far-reaching relativization of this theory. In the light of their observations, this theory could easily be considered just another faddish expression of contemporary culture.

Although I consider Dykstra's and Parks's observations as partly valid, I suggest that we must look further if we are to gain an adequate understanding of the historical and cultural backgrounds of contemporary views of religious development. More specifically, we have to look beyond the empty field that dialectical theology created for the psychology of religion between the 1930s and the 1960s. This empty field is not the real starting point of a developmental view of religion. Rather, it is but an interlude in a longer period of history which contains the origins of such a view. If we are to discover the motives and forces beyond this understanding of religion, we will have to look at this history as it develops over the centuries. In what follows, I will attempt a first view at the history of the developmental understanding of religion before modern psychology became prevalent. I will, however, limit my observations to the history of religious education. I will not be able to include in any comprehensive way the philosophies and psychologies that have influenced religious education. And even with this limitation, I can hardly offer more than a glimpse at the very complex historical development.

Most of all I will focus on what can be considered the historical precursors of today's cognitive-developmental approaches to religious education. Especially in the third part of this chapter, I will describe three models of religious education which were designed in the eighteenth and nineteenth century to deal with the religious development of the child. This historical background and the rationale behind these models can make us aware of some of the historical and philosophical legacies with which today's cognitive-developmental approaches to religious education must come to terms.

Is There a Discovery of the Religion of the Child?

Since the publication of P. Ariès's influential book *Centuries of Childhood* (1965), there has been much discussion about the "discovery of childhood" and the "invention of youth" (Musgrove 1965). While it seems questionable to consider childhood and youth as social inventions, which amounts to denying the biological basis of maturation and of the physiological processes that govern it, there is nevertheless agreement about the crucial importance of the new understanding of childhood and youth as it developed in the eighteenth century (see, e.g., Herrmann 1982).

This basic understanding also holds true for the history of religious education. John Locke's *Some Thoughts Concerning Education*, published in 1693, and even more, Jean-Jacques Rousseau's *Émile*, published in 1762, were the hallmarks of a new understanding of the child, in education as well as in religious education. But even if Locke and Rousseau set landmarks in the history of religious education, they cannot be considered the inventors of a childhood religion. A brief look at the educational ideas of the sixteenth and seventeenth centuries can bring this out.

How was the child seen in religious education before the eighteenth century? Was there any awareness of the development of the child? And, if yes, how was development connected to religious education? If one looks at the educational writings of M. Luther, J. A. Comenius, and A. H. Francke, who can be considered major representatives of the educational thinking within the Protestant Church of the sixteenth and seventeenth centuries, the following four observations seem warranted:

1. There is a vague conception of the special importance of early experiences and of the learning processes in the first years. The child is seen as more accessible as well as more vulnerable to educational influences than

older people. Luther writes: "It is difficult to make old dogs obedient and old rogues pious for which the preaching office works and must work in vain a lot. But young, little trees are easier to bend and to direct while a number of them also get broken through this" (Luther 1530/1969c, 580). From this point of view, the aim is to build up lasting habits that can serve as a foundation for learning in later years. (This is stressed especially by Comenius; see Comenius 1965.)

2. There is a tacit knowledge about the gradual development of the children's cognitive and emotional capacities, but this perception of the order of development is continuously fused with the order of things and the order of knowledge which is taught. This is even true for Comenius, who described the course of life as a sequence of eight schools, from the school of prenatal-becoming to the school of death (1965, 223ff.). Those schools are not based on human development in the modern sense. Rather, they are taken from an *a priori* scheme that is geared to the restoration of the likeness of God which the human being has lost. Even when Comenius speaks of "capacities," he is referring more to the extent of knowledge which a child has already acquired at a certain point than to a child's maturational readiness (Schaller 1967, 256).

3. The limited capacity of children is of most concern in respect to the children's understanding of what they are taught. It is at this point that Luther most clearly stated the need to adapt oneself to the child. He writes: "as we are preaching to children, we also have to babble with them" (Luther 1530, WA 30, 1, p. 143). This point is more than accidental for Luther. There are fundamental theological reasons that convinced him of this point of view. Suggesting a game as a teaching and learning aid for children, he writes "And nobody should consider himself too clever and despise such a childish game. Christ as he wanted to direct humans had to become human. If we are to direct children, we also have to become children with them" (Luther 1526, WA 19, p. 78).

With Francke it can be seen that the awareness of the difficulties that children might have with understanding, for instance, biblical texts was more than an abstract or general awareness. Referring to such difficulties, Francke quotes Psalm 147:10, "His delight is not in the strength of the horse nor his pleasure in the legs of a man" (1957, 35). Francke obviously realized the danger that children might come up with a "nonsense conception" of what such images as the "legs of a man" mean. But although Francke showed such a clear awareness of the limited capacity of the children's understanding, he nevertheless maintained that it is just a matter of explaining things: Repeated often enough, the real meaning would be retained.

4. Religious development is not an organizing principle of religious education in the writings of Luther, Comenius, and Francke. It is treated as a subordinate factor to which instructional methods have to be adapted. In

general, religious development was not discussed as an anthropological issue of its own value and importance. It was referred to rather in passing. Rarely it was made the major focus of a chapter or even a paragraph.

The most important exception to this is Luther's response to the question of child baptism. Here the nature and development of the child became a central issue and were discussed at length within an anthropological and theological framework (see Asheim 1961, 202 ff.).

Summing up these short remarks about the views of religious education in the sixteenth and seventeenth centuries, it can be said that while there definitely was some awareness of the distinct character of a child's understanding, religious development never was a central or even organizing principle of religious education. Religious development was treated as a subordinate factor. This conclusion is also in line with what we know about the reality of religious education in those days. Religious education meant for the most part learning biblical quotes by heart and mechanically repeating the catechism (which is the repeated criticism of numerous authors of the time).

The new awareness of the child's religion has to be seen against this background. It is not an "invention" or a "discovery" in the sense of finding something new that had been completely unknown, but it is a new and vigorous realization of the central importance of religious development in childhood as well as of its distinct character. When I refer to the "discovery" of the child's religion in the eighteenth century, it is this realization that is meant.

The Eighteenth-Century Discovery of the Child's Religion

Against this background of the religious education in sixteenth and seventeenth centuries, it is most of all the voice of J.-J. Rousseau which stands out. Rousseau's view is still provocative today. In his *Émile* he says: "Every child that believes in God is necessarily an idolatrist or at least an anthropomorphist. Once phantasy has envisioned God, it is very rare that reason will understand him." Therefore Rousseau suggested that it would be best not to have any religious education before the age of 14. In his opinion "it would be better to have no conception of the Deity at all, rather than having one which is low, fantastic, offending and not worthy for God."

According to Rousseau's observations, the child's "mind is too short" to grasp the idea of infinity. They take everything to be infinite as they are lacking a measure. When one tells them about "the power of God," they consider God about "as strong as their father" (1981, IV, 265, 268f.).

All this is said in respect to Emile, that is, in respect to boys. Girls like Sophie, Emile's future spouse, are to be given a different education. While according to Rousseau religion is even more beyond the girls' capacities, they nevertheless should be told about religion early on. With them, there is no need to wait, because women "are not able to decide themselves" and must therefore "accept the decision of their fathers and husbands." The combination of "wisdom and piety" is impossible for women. Rousseau's prejudice is obvious. It is interesting to note, however, that it is only for women that Rousseau suggested a religious education that is based on the development of the child. From Emile's childhood, he wanted to omit religion altogether. In the case of Sophie he wished for a children's catechism. Such a catechism would have to be written by "a man who is familiar with the development of the child's mind." And it would "only be good if the child answers the simple questions spontaneously" (1981, V, p. 409–11).

These quotes from Rousseau's *Emile* show that by 1762 the religion of the child had become a central focus of discussion. Rousseau probably was the first to come to the radical conclusion that religious education must not take place (for boys!) before adolescence, but he was not the first to systematically consider the limited capacity of the children's religious understanding. A couple of years before the turn of the eighteenth century, John Locke had already made a similar point in his *Some Thoughts Concerning Education*. There Locke criticized all attempts at explaining to children the idea of God in any detail. "False" or "unintelligible notions" were the only result Locke could expect from such a religious education (1823, IX, p. 129).

Locke's critical evaluation of religious education was geared against teaching the Bible to children indiscriminately. The "promiscuous reading of it," Locke says, "is so far from being of any advantage to children . . . that perhaps a worse could not be found." "For what pleasure or encouragement can it be to a child, to exercise himself in reading those parts of a book where he understands nothing?" (ibid., p. 148).

According to Locke, large portions of the Bible are not "suited to a child's capacity" but are "very disproportional to the understanding of childhood." Therefore Locke comes to the conclusion that only such principles should be presented as "are suited to a child's capacity and notions." For Locke, such principles can be found in the stories of Joseph and his brothers or in the stories of David. In addition to these stories, Locke suggested certain "moral rules" which he considered "easy and plain," as, for instance, the Golden Rule of Matthew 7:12 (ibid., p. 149).

What we find with Locke, then, is a first attempt at systematically selecting materials and contents suited for a religious education which does justice to the children and their development. Locke's basis for this attempt was his sensationalist philosophy and psychology as set forth in his *Essay Concerning Human Understanding*, published in 1690. (It is interesting to note as an issue for further research that Rousseau, who overcame the limitations of sensationalism in his ideas about education in general, did not follow this path in religious education.)

Taking the arguments of Locke and Rousseau together, we can discern two aspects which seem to have worked as the major presuppositions for the eighteenth-century discovery of the child's religion (Rang 1959): (1) a new focus on experience as the primary source of all knowledge and understanding; (2) a new interest in a genetic understanding, which grew out of sensationalist philosophy and psychology. The genetic perspective results in an anthropology from below, which was to replace the anthropology from above held in previous centuries.

The new awareness of the religion of the child as it developed in the eighteenth century has been the starting point for an extensive educational discussion. Since then, various attempts have been made to integrate this new understanding into educational models. Three such models are especially prominent and I will describe them in more detail.

These models are selected because they appear to be the historical precursors of today's cognitive-developmental theories. Moreover, these models offer an opportunity to widen the scope of the present discussion about a religious education based on developmental theories. The models should, however, not be taken as a comprehensive account of the history of religious education in the eighteenth and nineteenth centuries. A more complete account would have to include many other theorists and a number of different models as well. J. H. Pestalozzi, for instance, set forth an early version of the psychoanalytic understanding of religion. For him, religion is based on the trust which is or is not experienced within the family (1932). A discussion of psychoanalytic approaches to religion and of their historical precursors would therefore have to focus on Pestalozzi. In this paper, which looks at the historical background of cognitive-developmental approaches, Pestalozzi will only be touched upon.

Three Models of Religious Education

The Rationalist Model

This model was developed in Germany roughly in the last thirty years of the eighteenth century by an educational movement called the Philanthropists. It was strongly influenced by the ideas of Locke and Rousseau. However, J. B. Basedow and C. G. Salzmann, the main representatives of this movement in the field of religious education, did not follow Rousseau in his complete neglect of religious education in childhood. Rather, they tried to design an educational introduction to religion.

In the case of Salzmann, on whom I want to focus here, this meant to take "stories of good children" rather than biblical materials as the starting point for religious education (Salzmann 1897). These moral stories were to convince the children of what they would encounter later on in the Bible. It was Salzmann's hope that the Bible would be more credible and convincing if the children would already be convinced by the time they first encounter the Bible. Salzmann writes:

> One should rather teach the children from early on to judge things from the right point of view, according to their true value, and then give them the Bible and introduce them to the special teachings of Christianity— how willing they will be to believe a book which only teaches them things of whose rightness they have already been convinced. (1897, 154)

Thus the rationalist model reacts to the new understanding of the child's religion by dropping and leaving out all religious contents that might be hard to understand or might be subject to children's fantastic distortions. What is left then for religious education as the only content that is considered appropriate is a morality based on natural religion. There is hardly any room left for revealed religion in this framework. Revelation is only to confirm what has already been learned beforehand. At best it is to function as a substitute for reason at those points where the human mind is suffering from occasional "adumbrations" (Saltzmann 1897, 206).

The rationale of this model of religious education is to keep reason clear of all childish distortion. The children are only given what they will understand in an adult way—or, as we would have to say, what children were supposed to understand in such a way. As we know from the work of Piaget and Kohlberg, there is not only a religion of the child but also a morality of the child, and this morality is no less of a distinct character. But the discontinuity of moral development seems to have been less obvious to these educators of the late eighteenth century. To them morality and a natural religion that was based on reason alone seemed to offer a viable way for an education in line with the new understanding of the child's religion.

This moralist reduction of religion is, however, not to be understood primarily as a consequence of the educational approach. Rather, it was a consequence of and a reaction to the religious crisis that had taken hold of the adults themselves in the days of the Enlightenment. To them, the adults and educators, the Bible had become an object of doubt, and it was they who were looking for new ways in education that might overcome this doubt—in favor of religion, although in rationalist reduction.

Salzmann writes: "It seems to me that it is also dangerous for religion and virtue if one relies only on the belief in a certain story or on the truth of certain ideas which lie beyond our sphere. We are living in doubtful times. The credibility of the biblical story, the rightness of our dogmatic system, is contested from all sides." He continues, saying that the old method "was maybe good when belief in the Bible was soaked in with the mother's milk and when almost nobody would even think of questioning its divine origin. . . . But these times are gone for good. And the credibility of Scripture is discussed just like the credibility of every human book . . ." (1897, 153, 158).

From here it becomes clear that the rationalist model was not meant as a reduction of religion. It was not just a secular attempt at dropping religion from education. Rather, this model is expressive of the new search for autonomy and for autonomous religion. Belief is no longer to be based on the authority of others or on the authority of tradition. Rather, belief seems only possible now on the basis of one's own experience and of one's own understanding.

This autonomy also is what defines being adult or mature in the understanding of the Enlightenment. This autonomy is fought for against the dependence in which the human being is kept by outer or inner forces. It is this idea of autonomy on which the modern understanding of freedom and sovereignty of the people is premised. If one takes account of this cultural and political context of the idea of autonomy, it becomes quite clear that we are not only dealing with a time-bound idea in religious education. What we encounter here is a central aspect of modern society: individual autonomy as a presupposition of democracy.

If the connection between the idea of autonomy on the one hand and modern society on the other hand holds true, the conclusion seems warranted that the attempt to integrate the idea of individual autonomy into religious education has to be seen as a step of epochal significance. There is no way back behind this threshold of modern times. The question we have to ask, however, is if the Enlightenment idea of rationality is not based on an anthropology that is far too narrow. The idea of rationality on which this anthropology is focused carries with it at least the danger of turning into a type of rationality that is positivist and technical (This danger is generally realized today; see, e.g., J. Habermas in philosophy or J. Moltmann in theology.) As we all know today, such a rationality is detrimental to both— the human beings and the nature around them. What we need to do then today in religious education is to search for ways of how we can achieve, maintain, and support individual autonomy without falling prey to a positivist or technical version of reason.

An autonomy that goes beyond a narrow understanding of reason is, however, not premised on dropping all religion from education. The modern idea of freedom can be understood not only as leaving behind the religious tutelage of Christianity but also—and more adequately—as an expression and historical consequence of Christian anthropology. If this is true, if individual autonomy and Christian faith can go together, the educational separation of reason and religion in the sense of revealed religion is by no means necessary.

More refined versions of the rationalist model, such as J. H. Pestalozzi's

Investigations about the Course of Nature in the Development of the Human Race (1797), come closer to this point of view. Similar to Rousseau and the Philanthropists, Pestalozzi maintained that religion starts as "error" and is continued by social "deception." But for Pestalozzi, religion can be refined as "truth" once the individual moves beyond the stages of "corrupt nature" and of social corruption. Superstition and religious ideology are considered necessary antecedents of true religion and morality: "Therefore a superstition based on error and a zealous faith based on deception are nevertheless necessary for the human race on various stages of its existence in an essential way." Why are they necessary? "Generally both provide first nourishment to the germ of morality and of the true religion" (Pestalozzi 1938, 152). (It should be noted that Pestalozzi's views on religion changed in various ways during the course of his life.)

The Romanticist Model

In 1799, about forty years after the publication of Rousseau's *Émile*, F. Schleiermacher made his famous appeal to the "cultured despisers" of religion (Schleiermacher 1967). This appeal was also directed against the attempt to drop religion from education in order to replace it by morality and reason. In his speeches "On Religion" Schleiermacher insisted on an understanding of religion as "intuition and feeling." For him, religion is a phenomenon of its own right quite independent of morality and metaphysics. Therefore Schleiermacher can see "the longing of young hearts for the miraculous and supernatural," as he says, "with much devotion." Even if Schleiermacher realized that this longing is attached to inadequate ideas and that it remains in a "deception," he nevertheless considered it "most natural." Moreover, he maintained that this "deception" could "easily . . . be corrected" if there only were educators to cultivate religion (1967, 106f.). The "moral stories" as they were used by the followers of the rationalist model Schleiermacher considers boring and detrimental. According to him, these stories "violently suppress" the "religious potential" of the child. With an understanding that is limited to "ends and purposes," the children are "completely betrayed for their sense" (1967, 108).

With his critique of "ends and purposes" as the only direction of thinking and with his defense of a "sense" that strives for "the undivided impression of something whole," Schleiermacher opposed an anthropology that allows only for rationality. It is not clear, however, if Schleiermacher really aimed at overcoming and transforming this rationality or if he would have been content with reclaiming an area for "feeling," "intuition," and "sense" which could coexist side by side with rationality. If only the second was his intention it would nevertheless be a valuable contribution to the task of regaining a wider anthropology as the basis for religious education. But there would still remain the danger that religion is limited to a somewhat private sphere of religious feelings while everything else is dominated by a positivist and technical rationality.

The powerful but nevertheless limited contribution of the romanticist model is even more visible with Jean Paul, who published his *Levana* a couple of years after Schleiermacher's *Speeches*. J. Paul carries the romanticist model to its extremes. He considers the child's religion as the truest form of religion. He writes: It is "angels that are created not fallen beings. Therefore in truth the human being does not come up to the highest but rather comes down from there and only then goes back up" (Paul 1963, 57). According to J. Paul, there is "a whole religious metaphysics already dreaming in the child." Otherwise it would be quite impossible to teach religion.

Considering childhood as a prime time of religion, J. Paul criticized Rousseau for having missed the best time for religious education. He says: "When could the most holy take root in a more beautiful way than in the most holy time of innocence, or when that which is to be effective eternally than in that time which never forgets?" (1963, 58). Describing how children can be led into the world of religion, J. Paul writes: "Not through proofs. Each step of finite knowledge is climbed through teaching and by degrees. But the infinite which itself carries the endpoints of that ladder with its steps, can only be intuited at once, rather than added on. Only on wings, not on stages does one arrive there" (1963, 55f.).

"Only on wings, not on stages" — this poetic image could well serve as a summary of the romanticist model and its understanding of religious education. In many ways it is here that we find the first account of the richness of childhood religion. Like Schleiermacher, J. Paul offers a valuable and necessary defense of this religion against all rationalist attempts to debase it. Against the new clarity of the daylight which reason promises to shed even on the most remote and misty areas of human existence, the romanticist model insists that in-depth faith is a "flower of the night" (Paul 1963, 104).

Although this understanding of faith might hold true in many ways, and although we have to appreciate the romanticists' plea for a wider understanding of human existence as containing both, day and night, we nevertheless have to see the shortcomings of this model as well. Can the religion of childhood really serve as the model of all religion? Is it really true that the "deceptions" acquired in childhood can be "corrected easily" as Schleiermacher expected? It seems that the crisis of credibility which was the starting point for the rationalist model is no longer taken seriously here. This can also be seen from the limited attention which the romanticist model is willing to give to adolescence as a period of religious doubt. Schleiermacher, who gave a developmental account of the tasks of religious education, only specified such tasks for early and middle childhood. There seem to be no tasks for a religious education in adolescence (Schleiermacher 1966).

It seems clear then that the major deficiency of the romanticist model is its neglect of the conflictual nature of religious development. In this respect, this model is as one-sided as its precursor and counterpart which I have called the rationalist model.

It should be mentioned, however, that especially with the later works of Schleiermacher refined versions of his previous views are to be found. In his lectures on education in 1826, he comes to a very realistic attitude toward the child's understanding of God. There he writes:

> so it is true if one takes the concept by itself that children at this age are not yet capable of a concept of God. But if one therefore was to suspend the development of the religious principle until the concepts of God have reality then one could never start, there is always something inadequate in all concepts. (1966, 223)

Contrary to Rousseau, Schleiermacher answers the questions of when to begin with religious education by referring to the idea of development. He writes: "If we find the same progression in transitions towards truth in all matters, it is quite impossible that the religious domain should not be subject to the same law. We therefore have no reason to withhold the religious from children" (1966, 224).

The romanticist model gained some long-term influence, for instance, through the work of F. Fröbel, but it was not to become the dominant model of the nineteenth century. Rather, it was soon replaced by an idealist philosophy which, in the case of Hegel, for example, was focused on the historical objectivizations of the spirit. From this point of view, "subjective" religion was to be mediated with the "objective" religion of the church (see, e.g., Palmer 1844). Together with the religious revival movement of those days, this idealist philosophy brought about a new situation for religious education as well. A reappraisal of the traditions of the church took over from the Enlightenment ideas about religious development of the rational individual.

Nevertheless, the idea of development and of an education based on this development was not lost, but development was now seen as closely connected to instruction. Contrary to the romanticist model, which considered religious development as a spontaneous production of the child, the scholastic model to which I will turn now defines religious development only in terms of schooling and of an instruction based on a clear-cut curriculum.

The Scholastic Model

This model became influential in the second half of the nineteenth century through the followers of J. F. Herbart, the so-called Herbartians. Most of all with Tuiskon Ziller, the leading figure of this movement, we find the attempt to design a comprehensive curriculum that was to guide the religious development of the child. This curriculum was to start out in first grade with fairy tales, then continue with Robinson Crusoe and the patriarchs of the Old Testament, going on with German heroic sagas, then the kings of the Middle Ages and of the time of David, and finally the life of Jesus, the prophets, and the history of the Reformation (Ziller 1886, 20). It is easy to see that this grandiose plan is based on the assumption that there is a parallelism between ontogeny and phylogeny. It is Ziller's conviction that "the developmental stages of the human kind which have passed so far, are the ones which the individual also has to go through again and again" (1886, 16f.).

I will not focus here on this questionable equation of ontogeny and phylogeny, which projects Ziller's curriculum of cultural stages onto an evolutionary level and idealizes it. Rather, I want to look at the instructional method by which Ziller hoped to put his curriculum into practice. It is interesting that this method was to stay more or less the same even while the contents were changing with the age of the students. For Ziller, the decisive point always was the clear "articulation" of the lessons, which for him depended on the application of the "formal stages" of instruction (Ziller 1884). These stages are the legacy of J. F. Herbart's associationist psychology: preparation, presentation, combination, summary, and application — this was the perennial procedure that was to guide the students through the developmental curriculum of cultural stages.

The Herbartians' belief in method is their crucial weakness, at least in my eyes. If religious development is pressured into this didactical procrustean bed, it is turned into a matter of textbook knowledge. It is "schooled up" as I. Illich would say. Religious development is separated from all experience in life. It is reduced to the development of a certain mind-set or way of thinking. The result is a scholastic version of religion — a type of religion that is meaningful only within the special plausibility structure of the school. This is why I call this model the scholastic model of religious education. To be sure, as foreign as the didactical scheme of the "formal stages" has become to us, much of what goes on at school is still based on such a conception of teaching. Religious education at school is often "schooled up": it does not stimulate or allow for experiences that are relevant for religious development. The critique of the scholastic model that a number of reform-oriented educators set forth in the early twentieth century is therefore still valid.

Nevertheless, Ziller's idea of designing a curriculum that corresponds to the development of the child is an ideal that is still waiting for its realization. Many experiences and many questions that arise in the course of religious development are not addressed in religious education, and many other topics that are addressed are taken up at the wrong point of time or are presented in a way that makes these topics boring or inaccessible to children and youth. In respect to such inadequacies of teaching, I see the lasting contribution of the scholastic model and its idea of a developmental curriculum.

With the scholastic model we have come to the point in history when modern developmental psychology came into the picture and when S. Freud and J. Piaget started out with their work. Rather than following the further development of religious education in the twentieth century, I want to offer some conclusions—first, concerning the relationships of religious development and education, and, second, concerning the developmental theories of J. Fowler and F. Oser.

Conclusions

From the historical outline I have given, we can first conclude that the inclusion of a developmental perspective in religious education is not an invention of the 1970s or of structuralist psychology. The interest in such a perspective is not limited to twentieth-century psychology or culture but goes back at least to the eighteenth century. Even in the sixteenth and seventeenth centuries early forms of this interest can be found.

Second, the reasons for the inclusion of a developmental perspective in religious education are a mix of theological, philosophical, psychological, political, and educational considerations. Of special importance are the following aims: (1) a thorough understanding and personal integration of religious teachings (Luther, Francke); (2) the restoration of the human being in the likeness of God within the whole of creation (Comenius); (3) coming to terms with religious doubt by reconciling rationality and religion (the German Philanthropists); (4) a nonreductionist anthropology and education over against a rationalist philosophy and culture (Schleiermacher, J. Paul); (5) the design of a curriculum that does justice to the distinct character of the child's religion and development (Ziller). Some of these aims are time-bound and appear to be dated. Others are of epochal importance and continue to be valid. Some of these aims are directly connected to the interest in religious renewal as it was characteristic of Reformation theology as a whole. Others carry the hallmarks of modernity as well as its burdens.

Turning now to the developmental theories of Fowler and Oser, we have to ask how these theories look against the historical background that has been described in this paper. How do these theories, when they are taken as educational models, compare to the three models of religious education in the eighteenth and nineteenth centuries?

It seems to me that the cognitive-developmental theories of religious development cannot be simply equated with any of the three major models of religious education I have described. Rather, they seem to share the weaknesses as well as the strengths of all three models. I cannot describe this here in detail, but I want to point out at least some of the characteristics that the structuralist theories share with the educational models of the past. It will become visible then that these contemporary theories carry with them the legacy of the historical development and that they will have to come to terms with this legacy if they are to be taken up in religious education today. Stage theories of religious development are connected to the rationalist model in a fundamental way through their adherence to Piaget and Kohlberg. Both Piaget and Kohlberg focus on the aspect of logic in their studies of human development (see Kohlberg 1984; cf. Schweitzer 1987a). For them, the stages of cognitive and moral development are defined by the degree to which these stages come close to or are different from a logic that is fully developed. The theories of religious development of Fowler and Oser accept this rational way of constructing a stage hierarchy based on logic. At the same time, however, they attempt to widen our understanding of development. In this sense they follow the romanticist model, going beyond rationalism: Fowler postulates a "logic of conviction," which he differentiates from the "logic of rational certainty" (Dykstra and Parks 1986, 19ff.). Oser challenges the assumptions of other theorists who limit religion to an early irrational stage of development (Oser and Gmünder 1984, 20f.). Thus, both Fowler and Oser argue for a more inclusive understanding of development that goes beyond the rationalist model, but at the same time they stick to this rationalist model and keep the rationalist methodology. They define development by matching it against a highest stage which, at least for Oser, is defined by communicative reason in the sense of Jürgen Habermas (Oser and Gmünder 1984, 102f.). Such a definition comes dangerously close to dissolving religion into reason.

The danger that hierarchical stage theories entail for education is that the lower stages — and especially the stages of early childhood — appear primitive and deficient. Such a view implies that the perspective of adulthood is dominant while childhood is considered only a pre-stage or preliminary form of real life. This can be seen, among others, from labels such as the term "pre-religious," which are projected onto the child. But childhood is not just a pre-stage of life. According to Christian theological anthropology as well as educational philosophy, childhood is a stage of life of its own dignity and value (Weber 1979). Its value and meaning cannot be measured by its contribution or relationship to adulthood.

Saying this, I do not want to idealize childhood. To stress the dignity and value of childhood does not mean that we can give up autonomy as an aim of education. Therefore, the stage theories of religious development should not only be criticized for their normative focus on adulthood; they should also be appreciated for their attempt to include autonomy as an aim of religious education. Moreover, so far as Fowler and Oser are trying to show that religion and autonomy are not mutually exclusive but can be reconciled in religious development, their theories have to be considered as possible answers to an epochal question of modernity. Their attempt is to show how being religious and becoming adult can go together (Nipkow 1987a; Schweitzer 1987a).

But the theories of religious development run still another risk, which in this case they share with the romanticist model. When Oser claims that there is a "domain" that "after taking away all logical, ontological, moral, social, cultural forms and particles is specifically religious" (Oser and Gmünder 1984, 62), he might well end up with a much elusive phenomenon which is limited to individual privacy. To put it bluntly: What is left here to religion is what no one else is willing to claim.

Oser's definition of religion is, so to speak, too convincing because it sets up religion over against everything else. Therefore it runs the risk of having nothing left over for religion — an empty notion of religion. Compared to this, Fowler seems to run the opposite risk: for him, religious development includes everything, from the cognitive to the social and moral and finally to the symbolic. But in the end it is hard to say for Fowler what religion really is if it is not to be just everything taken together (see Fernhout 1986).

Another legacy belongs again to the rational model: the focus on progress. Development is seen as unidirectional. It goes toward the light which is greater the higher one comes. But what if faith, as J. Paul says, really is a "flower of the night"? Such flowers are not found by those who want to climb only where daylight gets ever brighter. Rather, a nocturnal search is needed here or, to say it less metaphorically, a focus on the vicissitudes of life, which are moving forward and backward, up and down, sometimes in one direction but more often in circles or even in a painful muddle.

Finally, the pitfalls of the scholastic model are also present here. They are at hand where religious education takes the form of discussing religious dilemmas (Oser 1987, 18). A discussion of hypothetical dilemmas does not allow for the experiences children need for their development. Here we have to keep in mind the difference between psychological interventions and long term educational work. If one wants to prove psychologically that religious development can be stimulated by teaching, a short-term intervention using hypothetical dilemmas may be sufficient. But for an education that is interested in the development of children and youth, it seems more important to create educational institutions that can serve as developmental environments over time. In this respect religious education could learn from the experiences with interventions in the field of moral education. Here Kohlberg came to question what he then called the "'psychologist's fallacy': that what makes a theory good for assembling and organizing psychological research data is what makes it good for defining the aims and methods of education" (Kohlberg 1981a, xii).

This fallacy would also be at work if one was to use any of the psychological stage models as a curriculum. Psychological stages can define only a general horizon of educational expectation. They can serve as hermeneutical aids for a teacher, but whenever the effort is made to use them as schedules by which to set the time for starting points and end points in religious education, they turn into hindrances for religious education.

4

Stage Theories of Faith Development as a Challenge to Religious Education and Practical Theology

KARL ERNST NIPKOW

A CRITICAL APPRAISAL of James Fowler's and Fritz Oser's theories from an educational and a theological perspective cannot be restricted to Fowler's main publication of 1981 and Oser and Gmünder's book of 1984. Rather, we will have to draw on what has been published by both authors since those years and pay attention also to the general discussion about the topic. This is all the more necessary since even the most recent collection of essays about Fowler (Dykstra and Parks 1986) reflects the voices of a conference held already in March 1982, that is, at a time before the steps that Fowler has since taken to refine and enhance his work could have come into view.

Regarding Fowler, we are witnessing a process by which his original developmental theory, besides being updated in the coding *Manual* (Moseley, Jarvis, and Fowler 1986) and enriched by the linkage to R. Kegan's stages of selfhood (Fowler 1987a), is explicitly being brought into the theoretical framework of a concept of practical theology (Fowler 1983; 1985; 1987c, 294) and applied to the fields of adult education (1984a) and pastoral care (1987a).

While Fowler's pivotal new emphases lie on the side of a theological contextualization, Fritz Oser and his associates seem to be more directed toward a continuing elaboration and empirical validation of their research approach itself (Oser 1988). In addition, they have contributed remarkably to the application of their developmental stage theory to the theory and praxis of religious education in classrooms (Oser 1988; Bucher 1987a; Bucher and Oser 1987b), a field that Fowler neglects because of his different professional background, which explains his prime interest in ecclesial formation of children, youth, and adults for faith and vocation.

Why these introductory remarks? The diverging ways in which these authors demonstrate how to apply their theories practically significantly affects the understanding of their theoretical and empirical positions. At the same time, to bring their work under theological analysis presents diverging problems. The structural-developmental approach itself can less easily be maintained if it amalgamates with Erikson's and Kegan's categories of ego psychology, on the one hand, and with the usage of Christian or religious theological language, on the other. Such blendings tend to blur the boundaries between the three perspectives.

Faith Development Theories and the Frame of Reference for Religious Education

Stage Theories as a Mirror of Modern Religious Individualization and Pluralization

Elsewhere I have delineated at greater length the arguments for a theory of religious and Christian education within a threefold frame of reference, circumscribed by *society, church, and the self*. My approach is grounded in the existence of three basic forms of religion in relation to Christianity today: *public religion, ecclesial religion,* and *personal and private religion* (Nipkow 1987a; cf. Rössler 1986). Correspondingly, my concept of religious education has three starting points. They refer to the functions of religion in modern Western societies (Nipkow 1975, vol. 1), the social challenges and the educational mandate of the Christian churches in this situation (Nipkow 1975, vol. 2), and ministry with individuals in their life span and intergenerational relationship (Nipkow 1982, vol. 3). Within this frame, the task of what I have tentatively called "the lifelong help (sponsorship) for personal identity," that is, a growth-related, developmental focus — the focus of the present book — is only one among others.

There are many parallels between the frame of reference just mentioned and Fowler's comprehensive understanding of practical theology. His faith development theory as such, however, as is the case with Oser's theory of religious judgment, seems to be primarily the theoretical reflection of the historical process which has led to the third form of religion mentioned, the type of individualized (not necessarily individualistic) personal search for meaning. This individual journey may take the shape of a specific religious profile, but it need not. The "shared center(s) of value and power" (Fowler 1981, 17) can be very manifold (cf. Berger 1979). The following characteristics of the present structural-developmental theories illustrate in an impressive manner our metatheoretical attempt to locate them, from both historical and sociology-of-knowledge perspectives, at the side of modern "subject-orientation."

First, Fowler's key term, "faith," while taken up from a specific religious background, is now employed to cover all contemporary ways of leaning into life and devoting oneself to what may have a final, absolute, "intrinsic excellence or worth" for an individual (Fowler 1987a, 18). Whether or not "faith" is an ontological "human universal" (Fowler 1984a, 50), used in this manner it is a "construct" that reflects the post-Enlightenment "modernization of mind," involving the familiar processes of secularization, differentiation, individualization, and pluralization.

Parallel to Fowler's broad notion of "faith," Oser advocates an "extension of the notion '*religiosity*,'" by which one "can even regard as religious the standpoint of people who classify themselves as atheists." (see pp. 62–63 above).

A second striking proof of Fowler and Oser's resonance with modern, individualizing religious consciouness concerns the nature and aim of development, which, in particular with a blatant clarity in Oser's theory, leads to the accomplishment of human "autonomy" (Oser and Gmünder 1984; see also the subtitle of Oser 1988). The structure of independent, self-responsible "religious judgment" (Oser) and the focus on the human person in his or her activity of "construing meaning" (Fowler) show that the Piagetian heritage is not being revoked or abandoned at the higher stages. Rather, the notion of the "Ultimate Being" (Oser) is being interpreted as the transcendental condition of the very autonomy in question and therefore as the enabling ground of true human freedom. When describing his stages 4 and 5 (chapter 2 above; stage 6 in his 1984 book), Oser follows a philosophical and theological model that is typically to be found with those Protestant and Catholic theologians, such as W. Pannenberg and H. Peukert (see Oser and Gmünder 1984, 103, 104), who apologetically try to reconcile a post-Christian Kantian transcendentalist pattern of thought with a notion of God by which the biblical God becomes a regulative idea, a term for a "metaphysical *a priori*" that operates as a logical means, that is, a necessarily valid truth content, for the construing of an ultimate meaning and of a truly human praxis.

In other words, Oser sees his stage theory as a description of the relationship between the Ultimate Being and the human individual as a "growingly integrative relationship" and "conjointly" a "growingly autonomous way of being" in this relationship. For him it traces a "developmental logic" of a process toward a form of religiosity that can only be conceived of under the conditions of the modern changes of religion and resulting in a liberal religious self-understanding. Within this historically new framework, Oser's image of the end point emphasizes a specific philosophical-theological option, which is not the only compelling one, as he himself knows and has often openly expressed. At the background of a universalist ethics of communication, modern autonomous consciousness is being reconciled with the idea of an Ultimate Being in terms of transcendental logic. (Oser's personal intentions are directed toward a more substantial notion of God in Christian terms with a relationship between the Ultimate Being and the individual that implies the experience of faith as a "gift." In his commentary on this paper, however, Oser also admitted that at the present state of his theory this character of "gift" might be "devaluated" by the "*a priori* constructivism.)

In Fowler's view, it is somewhat different, as stage 6 is to imply a fundamental *metanoia*. But it is not before stage 6 that the self as the point of reference of all previous stages is being left behind. Only "with this stage the self is no longer the prime reference point from which the knowing and valuing of faith are carried out. Figure and ground are reversed: where previously the self was apprehended as a figure interposed upon the (back)ground of Being, now self is relinquished as epistemological and axiological center" (Fowler 1987a, 75).

A third conspicuous feature by which the affinity of contemporary stage theories to the process of modern pluralization is disclosed is the interesting fact that for Fowler's theory, at least as far as stage 5 is concerned, the given underlying process of individualization and pluralization itself becomes at the same time the explicit normative aim. Stage 5 is characterized by the open-minded *understanding of the plurality of truth claims* as they are expressed in different faith attitudes (Moseley, Jarvis, and Fowler, 1986, 152–55).

If what is said is true, the challenge of stage theories for (religious) education, although they may understand themselves as being grounded in structural-formal, that is, content-free assumptions, is instead a content-laden issue. The seemingly universalist, ahistorical constructs of structural theories, if held against the framework of the evolution of the modern mind, reveal a historical specificity. Notwithstanding all cross-cultural validations which seem to prove the trans-situational and universalist nature of stage theories, their affinity with the historical process is rather striking and deserves at least further careful consideration.

Neither the structural-developmental psychology nor the neighboring ego psychology (Kegan 1982) is therefore neutral. No theory of social sciences can be regarded as something that is without a peculiar cultural, philosophical, and political impact caused by those factors that are invested in its theory building itself. If speculative elements are taken into account, as is the case with both Fowler's and Oser's descriptions of their less empirically validated higher stages, such theories transport a specific message. Both Fowler and Oser are well aware of this character of their theories beyond positivism as value-free science.

Oser's theory communicates and supports the aim of a developmental education toward religious autonomy, which in its more mature form is linked to and truly made possible by the autonomous, free relationship to universal intersubjectivity mediated by the idea of an Ultimate Being as the idea of absolute freedom. Fowler's theor·· postulates and finds, in a comparable although not identical way, a pattern of personal growth that makes him praise as his end point a journey to growing self-awareness together with the awareness of an ever-widening network of social relationships and commitments. It is noteworthy, however, that Fowler does not view rational autonomy as the end point of faith development, but rather sees the Conjunctive stage as representative of a post-Enlightenment reintegration of symbolic and unconscious elements with a chastened autonomous rationality. The educational and theological assessment of stage theories has to begin very early, with regard to the theory constitution as such. What are the consequences of the discussion to this point for general and religious education? The following section offers two answers.

The Impact of Stage Theories for Self-responsible, Deep-structural Learning and Development-oriented Curricula

From both theological and educational perspectives we can underscore the great importance of the cognitive-structural approach with its interest in the subject and in "structural learning" for an education to critical consciousness. The discovery of the individual as self-responsible to God in the Reformation and the secular idea of the self-responsible moral self in the Enlightenment join each other in the conviction that the human being has to be acknowledged as a person whose dignity lies in his or her calling to give a response of his or her own.

Therefore, first, already the child has to be taken seriously as an active and critical partner in all educational interventions. Stage theories require that we listen very carefully to what children, youth, and adults do with what is transmitted to them in their constructions. None of the other accounts of learning as they are to be found in learning theories (excluding the psychoanalytical approach), be it imitation learning (see A. Bandura) or receptive learning (see D. Ausubel)—not to speak of classical and instrumental conditioning—shows the same affinity with emancipatory educational goals as does deep-structural learning. In a time when a conservative rollback of education is taking place in many respects, as is the case in Germany in the present Catholic religious educational policy, and partly the Protestant too, religious educators need the support of empirical research that demonstrates the limits of the mere transmission of religious information.

Information alone does not reach the interiority of persons, where the independent organizing of knowledge takes place. To understand this one must take into account the structural transformation of information in self-structuring insights.

The second major point refers to curriculum. Up to now, our curricula in religious education in schools in West Germany follow scarcely any developmental research findings on any large scale. The reception of L. Kohlberg, F. Oser, and J. Fowler is still in the beginning (regarding more recent assessments, see Kürzdörfer 1987; Nipkow 1987b; for a well-balanced introduction into all developmental issues, see Schweitzer 1987a). A more systematic account of the structural-developmental approach—besides others—in the field of instructional theory (didactics) has been tried with the concept of "elementarizations," hereby following the twofold interest in the promotion of significant personal learning and in a more appropriate allocation of content matter in the curriculum (Nipkow 1983b, 1986, 1987c). But this attempt also needs further elaboration.

In a last perspective, the insights into the "conjunctive" structure of faith at stage 5 in Fowler's view and the research on the development of "thinking in terms of complementarity" (Reich 1987; Oser and Reich 1987a) might prove their great importance for two fields that at first sight seem to have nothing to do with each other.

Ecumenical learning, a new challenge to Christian education (see for the West German history of the concept, Becker 1987), follows the leading idea of "conciliarity," which implies among other things the acceptance of "the principle of equality of *different* forms of the church" (Kirchenamt der EKD 1985, 45) and simultaneously the open-minded search for the *one* Christian truth in Jesus Christ that surpasses each of its denominational embodiments. "Conjunctive" faith fits the requirements of "conciliar" thinking and acting.

A similar but not the same situation is given where religious and scientific world views, separated in former times, now begin to come together again today in newly converging approaches: evolution, cosmos, and creation as open systems (I. Prigogine; see the survey in Link 1987). Whether or not an incompatibility between religious faith and the new sciences is perceived depends on one's stage of cognitive development. In adolescence, youth mostly stumble across irreconcilable contradictions between "creation" and "evolution" (Nipkow 1987a, 10). It has been shown (Reich 1987) that thinking in terms of complementarity "can alleviate crossing the critical phase." Among other things such thinking manages to coordinate conflicting statements and to arrive at an overarching synopsis (Reich 1987).

Oser and his associates are convinced that the more-developed forms of religious thinking have a lot to do with the capacity for complementary thought patterns.

The Necessary Socio-Political and Historical Contextualization of Structural-Developmental Theories for Educational Purposes

While what has been said can be of great help in religious instruction and curriculum planning, the focus on the individual and personal growth remains insufficient. This has to do not only with individualism. (Fowler at more than at one place has given a very critical account of individualism, when he, like Daniel Yankelovich [1982], criticizes the shift from an "ethic of self-denial" to an "ethic of self-fulfillment" [Fowler 1984, 8].) It has to do, above all, with the limitation to the personal and the neglect of the social and historical, to which structural stage theories are subject by their nature. This must be taken critically into account.

Developmental theories are concerned "with personal rather than social or systemic change" (Fowler 1987a, 107) — or with historical change, as I would like to add. To interpret their ahistorical setting as a moment of historical evolution is, therefore, a first step in providing for the broader frame of reference needed in any education, religious education included. In my own approaches to religious education this deliberation has made me start with an economical, political, and social analysis of contemporary Western late-capitalist societies with their inherent systemic antagonisms (Nipkow 1975, vol. 1; in this volume see the contribution by J. Hull). Viewed against such a background, theories concerning individual growth, if they are not historically contextualized and interpreted, run the risk of serving the purposes of the functional ego, the major concern of which is self-organization, self-integration, and self-equilibration.

The fact that progress from one stage to another can be defined by a dramatic change in "social perspective taking" — a crucial structural aspect for both Kohlberg and Fowler drawn from R. Selman (Fowler 1987a, 68) — and by a closely related widening of the "boundaries of social awareness" (75) clearly shows that the social dimension is by no means simply missing in this work. In his reply to his critics in his symposium paper, F. Oser reminds us that he also, with his stage 5, "actually focuses on social responsibility." Surely a principled, post-conventional, universally open moral responsibility, as well as a faith development that includes personal autonomy and critical consciousness, is a necessary condition for what we intend. But in order to fight effectively against the functionalization of the developing self and, at the same time, to prevent religious belief systems from being employed as mere social and psychological instruments, our approach must go beyond these qualities.

The issue is not a question of asserting that these theories, as Oser puts it, "abandon any considerations of the social dimension of religiosity." They do, of course, include them, but they are handled as issues of *personal* development only, not of *systemic* relevance. To lay open the concrete mechanisms by which specific religions, as in the case of the Christian churches, are being instrumentalized and allowing themselves to be instrumentalized in an educational system of a country, requires, first, sociological analyses and a hermeneutic of suspicion. Second, such a task demands from the churches themselves a continuous theological self-clarification. In this sense, the frame of reference for religious education takes on a triadic shape, consisting of three dimensions: self, society, and religious institutions with their theological self-understanding.

It is my impression also that it is difficult for structural-developmental theories to question the basic theoretical assumptions to which they owe their constitution. Although John M. Broughton's harsh critique of Fowler's theory is in most respects not at all convincing, one of his observations remains valid. He contends that "faith development theory cannot offer a challenge to, or even an interpretation of, modernization," since it is itself a derivative of the modern process of individualization and pluralization and, "as a consequence, it necessarily describes and prescribes an individual development that systematically converges with and unintentionally promotes the production of modernity" (Broughton 1986, 108).

The striking proof of this inherent theoretical dilemma is to be found in the stance of James Fowler himself. By his practical theological efforts he demonstrates that religious and Christian education have to follow more than the developmental track only. Broughton does not take any notice of Fowler's vital theological and political interests by which he avoids just that naïveté and blindness that Broughton is faulting him for. Fowler's recent attempts to embed his faith development theory in a concept of practical theology rest on clear theological criteria concerning "God's liberating and transforming praxis" (Fowler 1984a, 84–92; 1987a, chap. 3). Thereby, Fowler manifests his very strong commitment to a "public church" (1987a, 22; 1987c, 298; 1985), a church with high public responsibility, in correspondence to God's praxis. Furthermore, in following J. B. Metz, Fowler focuses his special critique on a conformist Christian bourgeoisie (Fowler 1985). It is also true, however, that all this has found entrance into Fowler's life work by virtue of his role as a theologian, not by virtue of his role as a developmentalist.

In conclusion, therefore, religious educators will have to ask which kind of developmental theory will be more resistant to becoming theoretically misinterpreted and ideologically misused. The answer depends on if and how the historical and societal contexts are being made explicit. It would be an inappropriate expectation of a psychological theory to demand that it change into a critical sociological and/or theological theory. The more adequate way leads to the design of a broader overall psychological frame of reference as a result of interdisciplinary efforts.

Faith Development Theories at
the Intersection of Psychology and Theology

If it is so that in Fowler's recent publications we meet a colleague who is seriously engaged at the intersection of psychology and theology, this fact deserves a special appreciation. Yet the question arises, how both fields can be put into an appropriate relation. Further, which kind of theology is it that has been linked to his stage theory? Oser is also aware of the normative theological implication of his own approach, in particular with respect to the terminal point of development.

Faith development "provides a descriptive and normative framework" for guiding persons (Fowler 1987a, 119). Where do the norms come from? According to Oser, the answer lies with the formula coined by L. Kohlberg, that "development is the aim of education" (Oser 1988), which in the case of development in stages means education toward the next higher stage. Fowler, however, with his contextualizing of faith development theory in practical theology, contends that the processes of stage transition and reconstruction should be regarded as "by-products" of the interaction of persons with their life experiences and their encounters with kerygmatic and educative contents (Fowler 1987a). Practical theologians and Christian educators are challenged by three major implications of the developmentalists' approaches: (1) the anthropological and epistemological axiom concerning the human being as actively organizing his or her experiences by structurally transforming his or her cognitive-emotive deep structures, (2) the hierarchical stage character of transformation, and (3) the end point of development.

The Epistemological Assumptions of Structural-Developmental
Approaches as a Problem of Theological Anthropology

According to modern structural-developmental theories, human beings have been involved, presumably from the dawn of history, in the process of organizing their experiences. The problem is not this fact itself, but the desirability of its implications. One can well imagine authoritarian political or religious systems where the individual as an active agent is not wanted. From the theological and educational premises shared in this chapter we have already supported the subject-oriented assumption that is basic to stage theories, provided that the frame of reference is enlarged. But what about the claim of Christian faith and experience that human life and its fulfillment before God come as a gift?

Fowler makes the exciting attempt to reconcile both perspectives. By the theological and anthropological idea of "vocation," understood as the "response a person makes with his or her total self to the address of God and to the calling to partnership" (Fowler 1984a, 95), he integrates the faith development theory into a theological perspective, which makes it possible to underscore the active nature of human beings. Deeply indebted to H. R. Neibuhr, Fowler displays his theological convictions predominantly in "covenantal" categories, which go back to Old Testament covenant theology and its derivatives in reformed theology. In this view, the human being, called by God and invited to a covenant of mutual obligation, becomes God's partner. No expression is used so often by Fowler as that of "partnership with God." In close proximity to Niebuhr, vocation and partnership are valid not only for the "partnership with God's work of ongoing creation" and with "God's governance" but also "in the liberative and redemptive work of God" (Fowler 1984a, 84–92; 1987a, chap. 3). Thus, a theology of the covenant (*Bundestheologie*) lays a strong emphasis on a person's active role. The same applies to the second pillar of his theological building, the belief in the inbreaking "kingdom of God," which prompts Christians to become its "pioneers" (1987a, 76). The affinity with and compatibility with action-oriented Piagetian psychology is obvious.

Another theological thought pattern links the psychological construct of "developmental structures" to the "structural order" inherent to the world as God's creation. For Fowler "we are prepotentiated, as it were, to generate the capacities necessary for us as a species to fulfill our vocations as reflective-responsive members of creation. We have as part of our creatively evolved biological heritage the generative deep-structural tendencies that make possible our development as partners with one another and with God" (Fowler 1987a, 54).

Where do "grace" and the holy "Spirit" find their place in this context? Similar to Karl Barth, but without explicitly mentioning him, Fowler perceives God's grace "as the presence and power of creative spirit" working within nature, being "given and operative in creation from the beginning" (Fowler 1984a, 74). An independent "state of nature," isolated from God, is, therefore, a "fictional concept," and "human development toward wholeness is . . . always the product of a certain *synergy* between human potentials, given in creation, and the presence and activity of Spirit as mediated through many channels" (ibid.). In this perspective, there can be no *ontological* separation between God and creation. By what we call "sin," only the *ontic* separation is being expressed. This refers to the lack of knowledge in our consciousness, and the lack of acknowledgment in our will, of what already exists from the very beginning: God's loving covenant with us.

In the last years the issue of natural theology has been given a thorough reappraisal by the Tübingen theologian Eberhard Jüngel. Drawing on K. Barth, the distinction between the "ontological" and the "ontic" is one of his attempts to regain a new theological access to and appreciation of God's love invested in creation (Jüngel 1980, 159f., 200f.). For religious and Christian education these reflections are of high importance. They lead us to a point where also developmental theories and Christian theology can meet.

On the one hand, this is true, but Fowler's descriptions of "man the meaning-maker" (Fowler 1987b, 15) can, on the other hand, easily be misunderstood. We should avoid making more of the Piagetian epistemology than it really offers on scientific grounds: genetic insight into certain "operations" and "transformations" of our mind, nothing more. Otherwise, if ideological generalizations are added, relating to the meaning of life as a whole and to the human person as the exclusive author of his/her life history, the individual is being put into a very problematic position of self-groundedness and absoluteness, a stance that Fowler explicitly resists elsewhere (esp. Fowler, 1984b).

Hierarchically Staged Development of "Faith" and of "Religious Judgment" as a Problem of Congregational Education

Why develop in stages? Different from Kohlberg and also more hesitatingly than Oser, Fowler shrinks back from simply reiterating the formula that to develop to higher stages is in itself a major aim of religious education and pastoral care. He underscores D. Levinson's opinion, which "asserts the dignity, the creativity, and the richness that each of the four major seasons of our lives makes possible" (Fowler 1984a, 48). Therefore, "it would be a mistake to think of the movement from one faith stage to another as analogous to climbing stairs or ascending a ladder" (57). Fowler definitely wants to avoid being unnecessarily locked "into a kind of 'higher'–'lower' mentality in thinking about the stages" (ibid.).

His first reason has to do with an affirmation of the worth of each person "In no way will we be suggesting that a person characterized by one of the less developed stages is any less a person than one described by a more developed stage" (Fowler 1987a, 57). In emphasizing "the importance of avoiding irresponsible categorizing of persons and groups" (1987a, 95), Fowler declares it to be "a paramount concern" of his "that the stages of faith and selfhood never be used for purposes of nefarious comparison or the devaluing of persons" (80). A second reason is of a *theological* nature. The stages "are not to be understood as stages in soteriology" (ibid.). No person must have constructed a given stage of development in faith or selfhood "in order to be 'saved'" (ibid.).

But do these warnings really solve the problem? Is it sufficient to say that "development takes time" (1987a, 81), that "transitions cannot and should not be rushed," and that much of the stage-theory-oriented "concern in pastoral care has to do with helping persons extend the operations of a given stage to the full range of their experiences and interactions" (ibid.)? Cautiousness alone does not reach the point, which lies in the fact that, notwithstanding all safeguards, a stagelike sequence, whether made up of "hard" or "soft" stages, *does* articulate a normative hierarchy. Fowler has "acknowledged" this "normativity" throughout his work (Fowler 1987a, 95).

This becomes particularly obvious when Fowler in his book *Faith Development and Pastoral Care* (1987a) describes *congregational membership* from stage perspectives. In depicting the lower stages Fowler very frankly lays open their limitations, if one sees them in the light of the possibilities of adulthood. Admittedly, in his stage descriptions there exists a balanced distribution of both strengths and weaknesses on all developmental levels except for stage 6. In particular, the gifts of childhood are vividly highlighted. But, the subsequent applications to congregational life and to specific religious groups make the problem quite clear: if what might be appreciated in childhood still dominates in adulthood, we have to remember Paul's advice to do away with "childish ways" (1 Cor 13:11).

At first, with reference to "Intuitive-Projective Faith" and "Impulsive Presence" Fowler detects "at the most primitive end of the fundamentalist spectrum some kinds of congregations which seem regularly to involve persons in collective manifestations of something very like the structurings of this stage" (1987a, 84). "Such groups (in particular certain occult ones) seem to provide religious sanction for the acting out of fantasies and impulses relating to violence, power, death, and miracle which show the primitive structures of unrestrained and unprotected early childhood" (ibid.).

A similar problem arises if "Mythic-Literal Faith and Imperial Selfhood" constitute the modal developmental level for the community, if, instead of regarding this stage "as a way station on a longer journey," it bears the characteristics of "a final destination" (1987a, 85). Fowler discovers this pattern in "certain fundamentalist and some Pentecostal communities" (ibid.). Adult church members who cannot move beyond a construction of God "in anthropomorphic terms on the order of a stern, powerful, but just parent or ruler," experience serious lacks, in Fowler's view. They will see God as punishing and rewarding humans in terms of their badness or goodness in a way a friend of Fowler once has characterized as a "quick pay-off universe." Clearly for Fowler this stage "lacks" things that are important from psychological, educational, and theological viewpoints (62). These include "the ability to understand its own interiority" and "to construct the interiority of other persons, as well" (ibid.). "This means that from within the patterns of knowing and valuing of the Mythic-Literal stage, persons are seen as rounded, moving, behaving surfaces" (ibid.), and God is constructed so, as well.

There is also no doubt about Fowler's opinion on "Synthetic-Conventional Faith and Interpersonal Presence." On the one hand these "kinds of persons ... constitute the most consistent corps of committed workers and servers in the church" (1987a, 88). On the other hand, Christians described by this stage are regarded as narrow-minded as far as the scope of their social awareness and political responsibility is concerned. "They have limited

ability to take account of the systems that shape, constrain, and sometimes oppress persons. They have difficulty in relating their faith to social, economic and political structures" (ibid.). Another descriptive passage relates to the sometimes "anti-intellectual" and "defensively conventional" frame of mind church members of this level will display, in particular in confrontation with groups who insist upon "critical and analytic approaches to matters of faith" (ibid.).

Thus, the argumentation leads to what Fowler calls "a stage level of aspiration" (1987a, 97) which has to guide and inform church leadership, pastoral care, and adult education. Such a level of aspiration, which for Fowler is "Conjunctive faith" (ibid.), can serve as a normative invitation. At any rate, says Fowler, "Conjunctive faith" should be taken seriously, if a congregation is striving to become a "public church" (94) that wants to act responsibly beyond a familylike narrowness of congregational life. Persons of the conjunctive stage "have the capacity to understand and relate to Christians of each of the other stages" (ibid.). They can foster a community of mutual tolerance and ecumenical learning. They have a capacity "to receive, and to dialogue at depth with, the faith witnesses of people from other traditions" (1987a, 94).

With this outlook we are confronted with an issue of considerable actuality and weight. Stage theories develop descriptive-analytical instruments and also normative ones. They allow theologians and religious educators to discuss the problem of religious "infantilism" or growth of faith (see 1 Cor 13:11) in new ways. If adults are still "locked in" at one of the childhood stages, "it gets more and more difficult to undertake transition to the next stage" (1987a, 97). Similarly, if a young adult carries the Synthetic-Conventional faith too long beyond postadolescence, further transition becomes difficult as well. Fowler speaks of "optimal correlations" (1981, 107; 1987a, 96) between stage development and age as points of orientation not only for those who bear educational and pastoral responsibility but also for oneself. For the first purpose, he suggests the promotion of "environments of developmental expectation" (116). For the individual member he goes so far as to propose "that we begin to offer periodic faith development and vocation inventories or checkups. Such an opportunity can be offered to new members who come to the community by transfer or by profession of faith as a part of their preparation for membership in this particular congregation of the Christian church" (118). How are we to comment on this?

On the one hand, the differences, as they have been described by Fowler, are existent, and, according to the clear witness of the New Testament, the task of growing up in faith is put before us "We shall become mature people, reaching to the very height of Christ's full stature" (Eph 4:13). Therefore, we are allowed to draw a line from faith development theory to a concept of congregational education. On the other hand, what has been outlined leaves us with open questions. The soteriological implications cannot be dealt with in some warnings only.

The reason for this lies in the interrelationship between the issue of personal faith certitude concerning "salvation" and the imperatives of stage expectancies concerning faith progress. These two aspects, which semantically are both covered by the same term, "faith," run the risk of being experienced as *one* inextricable context. When being confronted with an "environment of developmental expectation" or even being offered a personal "developmental inventory or checkup," the danger is great that the ground for faith certitude will shift from God's justifying deed in Christ to the individual's own efforts. Fowler recognizes that the average expectable level of development for adults in a given community may exert a certain coerciveness in two directions, if an adult is either below or moves beyond the mode. At both times, such a modal environment can make one "feel deviant and somewhat deficient" (Fowler 1987a, 97). We have to add, however, that the very idea of a necessary development itself can produce the same feeling, unless one can deal with this idea in the appropriate higher-staged way.

An appropriate comprehension of the difference between the soteriological aspect and the one that is implied in the structural-developmental notion of "faith" requires a complementary, if not dialectical postformal form of logic (Commons et al. 1984), as it is usually accessible not before stage 5 and, therefore, rather late in adulthood, if at all. The cognitive operations that are needed presuppose the capacity to simultaneously distinguish and relate both aspects to each other. The logical safeguards by means of which the theorist proposes to defend himself against a misunderstanding are dependent on the theorist's own level of structuring "faith," the existence of which, however, cannot be taken for granted with everybody else.

Casually, Oser remarks that one of his own hypotheses "had to be dismissed: that religious judgment does not depend on social class and educational training." That means that it does depend on them. Consequently, there are certain differences between the process of unconscious deep-structural development itself and the attempt to make an educational and counseling perspective out of it, although its rationale might clearly be the purpose of pastoral care. If the perspective of "growth of faith" is being suggested to church members, a deep-structural phenomenon will now seize one's own consciousness and become subject to a lot of new factors such as social class, educational training, learning capacities, and defense mechanisms.

Probably there will be different opinions about this topic according to the general cultural and religious climate—for instance, in American congregations compared with European churches—and the denominational heritage. Protestant traditions like Calvinism, Pietism, and Methodism with their emphasis on a visible religious change can be much more open to and sympathetic with a perspective of "growth" toward a distinctly proclaimed mature stature of faith as an endpoint, than can others, like Lutherans.

Why develop in stages? From his theological background Fowler does not hesitate with his answer. Again it lies with "the kingdom of God" and with "the partnership with God." Stages 5 and 6 urge and pull people to a point of final "perfection," not in a "moral" sense, nor in the sense of "perfect psychic balance or integration" (Fowler 1987a, 76), but in a religious sense insofar as our "selfhood" gets rid of "the burden of self-integration and self-justification." In this way, it is being transferred "radically into God, and therefore has a new quality of freedom with the self and with others" (ibid.). Thus, stage development obtains a role even in the crucial *metanoia* itself, on the way to man and woman as a new creature (98). The "Conjunctive" stage and the stage of "Universalizing faith" "constitute part of the eschatological pressure of God's coming kingdom" (ibid.).

The Issue of the End Point of Religious Development and Education

The problem of the previous section could arise, first, because the term "faith" has been introduced by Fowler without discriminating between a psychological and a theological definition. Second, although this term has trust and confidence as one of its fundamental features, it is more characterized, according to the nature of the structural-cognitive approach, by those aspects that make faith a cognitively operative, active agent and partner. Faith is "a way of construing, interpreting, and responding" (Fowler 1984a, 52). This definition of "faith" reveals a basic affinity between a theology of cooperating, covenantal partners, and a psychology of an actively interacting and progressing human mind. But what about a child's simple and firm trust in God, or a mentally handicapped adult's joyful feeling of belonging to God? Both, from a different understanding of "faith," entirely demonstrate faith's theological meaning. What is true completion or wholeness in a Christian perspective? What is the appropriate terminal point of "faith" development and education, if it is not to be defined at the sacrifice of other important or even constitutive elements of Christian faith?

The following is not meant to portray a Lutheran position as the only valid perspective. My interest is in becoming aware of possible theological alternatives for dealing with the concept of stages in general and the issue of the highest stage in particular (see G. Moran's intentions in this volume; see also Bayer 1980).

Martin Luther conceptualizes "stages" or "grades" of faith as *stages of growing temptation* and, correspondingly, *growing confidence in God* (Nipkow 1987a; 1987b). He distinguishes between three stages ("Treatise on

Good Works" [1520] in 1966, vol. 44, pp. 26–29). When living one's life without greater mischief, faith will not be tested very much. Therefore, faith will be "still slight and weak" and is on its "first" stage. What, however, Luther asks, if great afflictions are accumulated upon the soul, loss of health, property, reputation, and friends? Will faith still then remain "a sure confidence in God"? Now God is "hidden."

Luther's second stage refers to the verification of faith when it is confronted with God's hiddenness in human suffering. The difference between the first and the second stage is already "unmeasurable," says Luther. This is even more the case between the second and the third stage, the "highest," when the Christian feels God's wrath resting upon him/her and everything looks like God's complete withdrawal, like total God-forsakenness. In this view, progress of faith is a progress in the power of paradoxical confidence *sub contrario* (next to its opposite). Luther's stages allude to a progress of increased attachment and "faith intensity," but not, necessarily, of "faith development."

Can such a "progress" legitimately become an educational goal? Does it yield a sort of end point? I don't think so. Doubts of faith in the form of theodicy and of creeping atheism "befall" a person; it "happens" to someone as something terrible, and one has to be afraid of it. The way to the "top" in faith is a way to the "depth"— a pilgrimage to the "bottom." The believer cannot experience this journey as his or her intention or achievement.

It is the same with the way out of this darkness: if faith is raised to a new level in a wonderful revival, this also is nothing one can boast about as though it were an achievement. It is experienced as God's work. Furthermore, the dynamics of this "up" and "down" is a daily faith struggle, and God's full grace is a daily gift, too "All Morgen ist ganz frisch und neu, des Herren Gnad' und große Treu . . ."(Luther 1966) ("Every morning the Lord's grace and great faithfulness are entirely fresh and new . . .").

To draw the first conclusion, we now can make a distinction that allows us to contend for the right of both approaches—the developmental and Luther's theological approach. The decisive point is that we strictly relate "faith" in "faith development theories" to what it legitimately can only be referred to. If, on the one hand, God is acknowledged as the one and true sovereign in his work of redemption and liberation, he does not need higher stages of development on the side of human beings in order to give what he wants to give as *his* new life for us. Here is full *completion.* If, on the other hand, the perspective of *our* grasping, comprehending, and construing the meaning of what he alone can do, has done, and will be doing, is taken into account, it makes good sense to speak of "faith" as something that can change and develop—although, in my opinion, it always will remain *incomplete,* even on a "final" stage 6.

Second, even after making this sharper delineation between a theological and a developmental perspective, the task of conceptualizing the end point of "faith development" or of the development of "religious judgment" remains an open question. Faith, as far as it is a human answer, can take a different shape, as both Fowler and Oser already show. The final "image" cannot be found by deductive measures, but only by ways of interpretation.

In Fowler's theory, stage 6 reveals quite obviously a rather specific theological imagery. Stage 5 also reflects a certain option. Interestingly enough, this stage has been named differently as "polar-dialectical," "paradoxical-consolidative," and finally "conjunctive" (Fowler 1974a, 217; 1976b, 196–97; 1980b, 148–49; Fowler, Jarvis, Moseley 1986, 158, 177, 178, 182). Elsewhere (Nipkow 1988), I have tried to show that religious experience on this stage can assume a twofold nature. It may emphasize either a more paradoxical experience, being expressed in the postformal *dialectic of the paradox,* or it may be more of a conjunctive character, being expressed in what I have called the postformal *dialectic of reconciliation.* An illustrative example of the first is given in Søren Kierkegaard's meditations in *Fear and Trembling* (and in Luther, see above), whereas the second has theological and philosophical antecedents in J. A. Comenius and G. W. Hegel.

Again much depends on the developmentalist's and theologian's personal convictions as to which of the two dialectical structures will be brought to the fore. As far as I can observe, modern theological thinking tends more to patterns of a final reconciliation with rediscovered mystical tendencies. In Fowler's concept, the term "Conjunctive faith" — in alliance with the Niebuhrian view of radical monotheism — is also admittedly informed by "the idea of God as the *coincidentia oppositorum* — the "conjunction of opposites," developed by Nicholas of Cusa (Fowler 1984a, 64; 1987a, 71). While thus, with Fowler, "the coupling of a strong mystical dimension with transforming social action" (see the "pioneers" of the "kingdom of God," 1984a, 72) qualifies the end point of faith development, Oser tries to lead Piaget's idea of equilibration to a definition of the end point by the employment of the logic of transcendentalist reconciliation. The higher the stages the more perfect the equilibrium; this is the basic underlying rationale, "the developmental logic," according to Oser.

To sum up, structural-developmental theories, as well as the aims of Christian and religious education, cannot do without normative discussions. It would be a "naturalistic fallacy" to make the attempt to solve our problem empirically. The struggle about the true images for our life and for education respectively needs the open discourse of all, the permanent efforts to promote a philosophical, theological, and political consensus. With their analytical and their inherent normative character, stage theories are a powerful challenge to achieve this goal.

Part 3

What Critics Are Saying

5

The North American Critique of James Fowler's Theory of Faith Development

SHARON DALOZ PARKS

THIS CHAPTER PRESENTS a review of the North American critique of James Fowler's work since the publication of *Stages of Faith* (1981) and prior to the publication of *Faith Development and Pastoral Care* (1987). Fowler has joined the conversation between theology and the social sciences by formulating an understanding of personality development which interprets and accounts for the continuously evolving relationship between the individual, his or her community, and the power of the ultimate reality they share. This theory is a response to the central enlightenment insight, namely, the fact of the composing mind. The central passion of this theory is to illumine the character of the composing of our "ultimate" or most comprehensive environment, and the convenantal symbols and relations upon which all human being and becoming depend. As good critique embraces the strengths as well as the limitations of a given perspective, I will briefly outline the significant contributions of this work, and then I will identify the primary clusters of debate that have arisen within this growing body of scholarship.

Don Browning of the University of Chicago begins his review of James Fowler's *Stages of Faith* by observing:

> It may be that in our time theology will be revitalized, not by the systematic and foundational theologians, but by the practical theologians, theological ethicists, and religious educators. Although James Fowler's *Stages of Faith* is not actually a book on theology in any sense of the word, it does have enormous relevance to practical theology and through it to the entire body of theological reflection. Its immediate relevance is to the practical theological disciplines of pastoral care and religious education. But it would be a great pity for this book to be relegated to those readers professionally or existentially interested in those endeavors. It is a book of

much broader scholarly interest; it is a work that should be of equal
interest to the professional theologian and the secular inquirer into the
structure and dynamics of human nature. (Browning 1983, 124–27)

Building on Browning's observation, I want to suggest that theology is
revitalized in the practical and direct response of theologians to the pain,
yearnings, and possibilities of the cultural-historical currents of a time and
a people; and faith development theory, as pioneered by James Fowler, is
serving as just such a response. As such, since it has been cultivated in North
American soil, the strength of faith development theory may be manifest in
its capacity to address key tensions and yearnings in North American culture; likewise, its limits may be prescribed by the myopia inherent in any
single culture's view.

The capacity of this theoretical perspective to contribute to a conversation
of international interest is found, in part, in its power to reflect the deep-
ening awareness of many within North American culture of the phenomenon
of globalization that is now upon us. All of those seriously engaged in
intellectual reflection must increasingly take account of a growing conviction of the interdependence of all life—reflected in the ecumenical, economic, and ecological realities that fundamentally shape the anxieties and
hopes of our time. These realities, concentrated most vividly in the threat
of nuclear destruction, relativize traditional forms of authority, including
religious authority. Yet simultaneously the limits of relativism and secularization become increasingly apparent. Even the more sophisticated and
cynical recognize the need for a common faith—a new *public paideia*—by
which a culture (which now must be reconceived in global terms) may renew
its common life. It is in this context that faith development theory finds its
resonance and makes its most significant contribution (see Fowler 1984b).

Faith development theory responds to this contemporary situation in
three primary ways: (1) It offers a way of speaking of faith and holding traditional religious (and secular) symbols, stories, and practice that does not
foreclose the conversation about ultimate values and commitments within a
pluralistic world. (2) It manifests the conviction that even faith—the centering ground of human trust—can change, undergo transition and transformation, and retain its integrity. (3) It does so in a manner that potentially
illumines the relationship between the individual and his or her context, thus
holding the tension (increasingly felt particularly in the individualistic milieu
of western culture) between the claims of the individual and the individual's
necessary dependence on the wider human community.

Central to the dynamics described above is an enhanced consciousness of
motion, change, and transition—experienced as both global in scope and
personal in impact. The metaphor of *development,* dominant in Western
culture and connoting movement, growth, and ongoing transformation, has

the power to resonate with both a deep source of traditional conviction and the sense of contemporary reality within the American (immigrant) soul. At the same time, the understanding of faith in which this theory rests—faith as a broad human phenomenon not exclusively bound by cultic religious control—both opens up the religious imagination and serves as a solvent of the secular resistance to religion. In short, faith development theory offers a dynamic language for an understanding of faith and religion that provides one way of addressing the reality of change and pluralism in a secularized world. Yet its concern for the quality of mature faith counters the conventional dogma of relativism to which an ideology of pluralism is all too vulnerable, and thus it has the power to appeal to the religious-theological mind seeking integrity within pluralism. (The metaphor of faith development itself and the story of human becoming that it describes correspond to the growing emphasis on metaphor and faith language within religious-theological discourse, which increasingly finds its voice in the language of "meaning" and "story" [narrative].)

While these are primary dynamics that undergird the appeal of this theory, there are other, more hidden forces also at play. Western culture is slowly becoming aware that theological thought in both its religious and secular forms has been dominated by attention to "transcendence" at the expense of an adequate recognition of "immanence." In its attention to the "subject" of faith and in its capacity to name the manifold ways in which faith is mediated through the whole environment—both ultimate and intimate—of the individual, faith development theory has the power to serve as a corrective to this imbalance and thus as an awakener of the theological imagination. This is not yet taking form in any obvious way, but I do believe that a part of the intuitive appeal of faith development theory (as well as some of the most vehement resistance to it) is to be found in this potential address to foundational theology.

On the "practical" side, there is a growing awareness that practical theology is only loosely constituted as a discipline and remains flabby as long as it is constituted by artificially reified subdisciplines—preaching, liturgics, pastoral counseling, religious education, spiritual formation, program administration, and social concern. Both practitioners and theorists in these fields have been quick to see the implications of faith development theory for their various domains; yet perhaps more significant is the power of faith development theory to foster serious conversation among them—as demonstrated by the address of this conference to both "pastoral care" and "religious education."

If we may hypothesize for the moment that among these reified subdisciplines "religious education" is the rubric that most adequately embraces the whole of the pastoral task—that of leading and being led out toward more adequate forms of faithfulness—then it is to be noted that faith development theory is serving this central activity of the church by offering a theory of educational "readiness" and is doing so with a rigor or discipline that the church needs. Further, it compels attention to the significance of adult religious education, while simultaneously recognizing the power and significance of childhood. Again, in its psychosocial conviction it corrects a too-exclusive focus on the education of the individual and a naïve evaluation of the educational power of the total—interpersonal, social-cultural, and physical—environment.

It is this same psychosocial conviction that fuels the potential contribution of faith development theory to ethics. This potential has been represented most forcefully by the work of Ronald Marstin (1979), who builds on Fowler, but it is reflected also in some of Fowler's own most recent address to the issues of vocation, the public church, and the formation of a *paideia* that can serve to re-vision public education (Fowler 1984b).

Returning to a broad cultural perspective, we note that the appeal of faith development theory is located also in its capacity to link religion with psychology. Psychology has become *a* dominant, if not *the*, way of ordering meaning, composing narrative, and orienting the individual to ultimate reality in the personalistic culture of North America. However, the limits of psychological interpretation are being felt both in pastoral care and even by a growing number of "secular" clinicians (as well as in the conventional culture at large). Faith development theory offers a perspective that both affirms psychological insight and points beyond it. Faith development theory affirms psychological insight in its attention to the formation of personality as manifested through the internal development of structures or capacities which order the relationship between the self and his or her sense of ultimate reality. Yet at the same time, faith development theory points beyond established psychological practice in five primary ways: (1) The Piagetian paradigm is finally an interactive model that not merely bears a psychological truth but presses toward a psychosocial conviction. (2) Faith development theory is preoccupied less with the person's past than with the potential of the human life (as a consequence it is concerned less with the diagnosis of pathology than with the patient's direction of growth). Thus, (3) its tendency is to protect the person's meaning-making, faith activity— thus holding a bias against any chemical intervention that would blunt the energy, motion, and spirit of the person. (4) It draws attention to the fact that growth and therapy occur in a context—the context of an ultimate environment—and that the character of nurture and healing is dependent on the adequacy with which persons and communities and their educators and healers construe the character of the reality in which they dwell. (5) Finally, as we shall see, the linkage of faith with developmental psychology directs attention to the relationship between structures of personality and the contents (symbols, stories, and doctrines) of faith and thereby fosters a crucial discussion among both theologians and clinical psychologists.

Points of Debate

It is not difficult to locate the primary points of the debate that cluster around faith development theory. A review of the critical literature reveals clearly five primary foci of resistance and concern. They are: (1) the definition of faith; (2) the description of stage 6—Fowler's vision of "mature faith"; (3) the adequacy of the theory in relation to particular religious beliefs; (4) the adequacy of the account of affect, process-motion, the unconscious, and the imagination; (5) the adequacy of the theory vis-à-vis a critical sociopolitical analysis, especially a gender analysis. It is the first two of these that have dominated the discussion to date.

Critique of Fowler's Definition of Faith

Fowler uses a broad generic definition of faith. As Harvey Cox has said in his now oft-repeated response to Fowler's definition, "There is something in this definition of faith to offend everyone." It seems that it is at once very easy and extremely difficult for North Americans to hear this definition of faith. It may, indeed, be the case that as "the applicability of the word *faith* widens . . . the breadth of its meaning narrows . . ." (Moran 1983, 122). If so, it is also the case that former meanings must be surrendered or at least modified in order to accommodate broader categories for understanding faith experience. Thus the dimension of the soul that seeks the enlargement of present understandings and arrangements appears intuitively and appreciatively responsive to this perspective. Those, however, with much at stake in traditional definitions are immediately troubled and resistant (after all, "faith itself" is at risk). These are, on one hand, those whose religious conviction defines faith in terms of a gift to which the human is simply receptive, a phenomenon not only beyond human control but also beyond human responsibility. This is faith understood as so radically transcendent as to just "happen" (Huebner 1986, 516), and it is generally defined in (Christian) religious terms. It appears, on the other hand, that those representing a more secular stance sometimes reflect an equal investment in retaining faith as exclusively transcendent. While the first seem to have a stake in defending the agency of God, the second seem to have a stake in protecting the irrelevancy or irrationality of God. The first would prefer to confine a discussion of faith to the subject of "grace." The latter would prefer to confine faith to religious categories safely deposited on the margins of society and to label as merely "ego" the meaning-making, covenantal activity in relation to the ultimate that Fowler, following on Smith, Niebuhr, and Tillich, describes as faith.

Alongside this diffused but firm resistance are more particular and nuanced critiques. For example, if faith is life-grounding trust and commitment to centers of power and value beyond personal control, why doesn't Fowler identify "trust" as one of the seven aspects of developing faith? (See Fernhout 1986, 85; Moran 1983, chap. 6.) Or why are aspects such as "willing" and "humor" not as fundamental and as systematically central? (See Loder and Fowler 1982, 138.) Can one discuss faith in Fowler's terms without including a more profound account of the experience of fear, the void, suffering, dread, and awe? (See Wallwork 1982, 374.)

Other critiques of Fowler's definition of faith press in the direction of more precision in definitions: If there are distinctions to be made between faith, religion, and belief, what is their relation? Gabriel Moran affirms both Smith's and Fowler's concern for the reduction of faith to belief understood as mere intellectual assent to abstract propositions. He argues, however, that if faith is relational (as Smith and Fowler affirm), then, if faith is to find institutional (relational) form, there must be a relationship (and tension) between faith and belief. Hence, he would argue, Smith should not have said "That religious people are expected to believe in something is a modern aberration," but rather (as Moran would formulate it), "That only religious people are expected to believe something, and that religious people are expected only to believe something is a double modern aberration" (Moran 1983, 124).

In this same vein, many others press for a yet richer articulation of the relationship between faith structures and contents. Fowler has set the stage for this work and charted a course by which it may proceed. But I believe that it is fair to say that, for example, the consequences of the relationships between a given faith content and the differing stage structures has not yet been explicated. If faith development theory is to realize its potential for revitalizing theology, this work will have to become integral to the faith development project. (This work is likely to require the theory to provide thereby a more explicit articulation of the transcendent and immanent dimensions of faith, their interrelation, and the present imbalance of attention to these dimensions in theological discourse.)

Finally, Fowler's definition of faith is critiqued as being too exclusively linked with "knowing" (see esp. Fowler and Keen 1978, chap. 3). It is observed by one critic that there is a difference between having a center of supreme value and making a psychic commitment to that value (Wallwork 1982, 375). Fowler's emphasis on cognition may reflect not only Piaget's preoccupation with cognition but also the split in most of Protestant theology between head and heart, mind and body.

A related issue is voiced by a few who raise the question of the relation of knowing and action-participation in the domain of faith. In his press for a more articulated role for "obedient action" in faith, Dykstra offers a useful model by which the whole critique of Fowler's definition of faith may proceed. He urges Fowler's critics to recognize that there have always been many definitions of faith, and one must be as careful as Fowler is in saying *"if"* faith is this, *then . . ."* (Dykstra 1986a, chap. 2). Such a discipline would assist considerably in clarifying the discussion of faith prompted by Fowler's work.

Critique of the Universalizing Stage of Faith

The whole first five stages in Fowler's scheme have not begun to receive the force of critique directed to his last stage, Universalizing faith, stage 6. The most caustic of these critiques is fostered by the awareness that all theory is to some degree "biography writ large." Thus it is remarked that stage 6 is "elegant, attractive" but also that it seems "antipluralistic and condescending" and "too highly shaped by the lifeworld of the theorist" (Hoehn 1983, 79), or that it "sounds like a professor with a coherent view of the universe" (Keen in Fowler and Keen 1978, 103)—a reflection of an ethos of idealism and intellectualism represented by writers and speakers who conceptualize well (Ivy 1982, 272).

More systematically, questions are raised regarding the shift in methodology that occurs at stage 6. Each of the earlier stages is composed from a range of sources, rooted firmly in the empirical research method of the semiclinical interview, but stage 6 is composed quite differently. Fowler claims only one interview in which stage 6 appears; he draws rather upon theological insights and biography, identifying stage 6 exemplars among well-known figures such as Gandhi and Mother Teresa. Thus, it is argued, stage 6 does not appear as an evolution of the psychosocial structures described by stages 1 through 5; that is, the examples used do not necessarily demonstrate the attainment of all that Fowler states—a qualitatively new form of all seven aspects of faith as he has described them (Egan 1982, 114; see also Downing 1986). Moreover, the distinctions between form and content become blurred without adequate explication.

Additional critiques of stage 6 cluster around the two following questions: (1) Does the fascination with stage 6 preclude adequate attention to the rich implications of stage 5? (2) Does fascination with stage 6 serve to detract attention from the need for further empirical research in the faith development of those who are aging beyond "mid-life"?

Since developmentalists know that we tend to hear only one stage ahead of "where we are" (and Fowler is yet only in his forties) it must be supposed that there may be stages of faith beyond Fowler's stage 5 which, while not tied to maturation, may be fostered by the aging-maturation process. In other words, although in constructive-developmental theory maturation is not a determinative factor, Fowler's stages up through stage 5 are influenced by biological maturation as a "necessary but not sufficient condition" for the development of a given stage. If we are looking at faith across the life span as well as the development of mature faith, are we to suppose that the conditions for the "maturity" of faith are in place by middle age — as supposed by the description of stage 5 and stage 6? (see Buchanan 1987). Might we find more stage-6 persons and might a stage-6 description be significantly recomposed by exploring these questions further as the theorist(s) themselves continue to age-mature? Has Fowler prematurely foreclosed the process of faith development? Some critics have suggested that Fowler's description of faith development should stop with stage 5, leaving the future open. It can be anticipated that these questions will be pressed harder as the aging population in North America expands.

Fowler has responded to these suggestions, in partial measure, by stating that "The goal . . . is not for everyone to reach the stage of Universalizing faith. Rather, it is for each person or group to open themselves, as radically as possible — within the structures of their present stage or transition — to synergy with spirit. The dynamics of that openness . . . operate as lure and power toward ongoing growth in partnership with Spirit and in the direction of Universalizing faith" (Fowler 1984c). But, it might be asked, if we are not to hope that everyone might become "mature in faith," is some elitism at work here? We will return to this later.

In fact, Fowler might have done better to leave the questions of development beyond stage 5 open to further research which could remain in continuity with the methodology supporting the first five stages. It must be recognized, however, that it is absolutely incumbent upon Fowler to declare his vision of mature faith — which is precisely what his stage 6 does. Theories of human development do, finally, "stand on their heads." The direction and goal of the trajectory envisioned do serve as the primary influence upon what the theorist sees and identifies as significant along the journey. To be responsible as a theorist, Fowler has had to be clear on this matter. But we may ask whether or not his vision of mature faith needs to have been titled stage 6.

Fowler has described mature faith in terms of both structure and content, but the strongest critiques of stage 6 have been directed consistently at its content. In *Stages of Faith* Fowler described stage 6 in language heavily dependent on Judaic and Christian imagery — the kingdom and the sovereignty of God. Further, the example of Jesus has been implicit in his choosing of exemplars: Dietrich Bonhoeffer, Mahatma Gandhi, Dag Hammarskjold, Martin Luther King, Thomas Merton, and Mother Teresa. With the exception of Mother Teresa, all are males dead before their time, having in some way given up on their life in the affirmation of a larger good, and with the exception of Mahatma Ghandi, all stand within the Western Christian tradition. This definition of stage 6 seems to trouble critics primarily because it is an affront to the openness to pluralism which the theory fosters. Fowler's discussion of the "absoluteness of the particular" does not seem to appease this sense of dissonance. (There are also questions as to why at only this stage are the distinctions between structure and content collapsed or the relationship between them now joined? And can there be a fuller account of sin and evil in this highest stage?)

It should be observed that in *Becoming Adult, Becoming Christian* Fowler's explicitly Christian language is more muted in his discussion of stage 6; he quotes at length a passage from Gandhi that incorporates passages from the *Bhagavad Gita*. Further, he claims that he could have used examples from Buddhist, Jewish, humanists, and militants as well. This stance may ameliorate some of the critique of stage 6; however, it is my perception that until there is empirical validation in continuity with the methodology underlying the first five stages, "stage 6" and the question of mature faith will continue to be a primary and crucial point of theoretical debate.

What is now interesting to note is that the two primary critiques of Fowler's work are directed at the openness of the definition of faith and the closedness of the description of stage 6 — mature faith. Some critics address both issues with equal concern. At the risk of appearing to deal too superficially with the issues raised within each of these two primary sets of critique, I want to suggest that the tension between these two points of critique may reflect a deep ambivalence within the North American soul. Is it perhaps the case that consistent with its democratic traditions, North American culture responds to the call to an enlarged vision of human community (and therefore resists Fowler's seemingly provincial definition of stage 6)? Yet North American culture simultaneously fears the loss of familiar forms of faith — and the loss of privilege these forms support — (and therefore resists likewise Fowler's profoundly inclusive definition of faith).

Critique from the Standpoint of Particular Traditions

A representation of the critique of Fowler's work in North America must recognize that, particularly in relation to the issue of faith and its content, critique takes form in part along denominational lines. Many Roman Catholics, prepared by traditions of both natural law and spiritual formation, have responded readily to faith development theory. Unitarian-Universalists have found the theory to be useful in describing both their history of having often "come out" of other denominations and instructive as a map for moving from a more relativistic stance to engagement with the contents and commitments of faith.

The response of other Protestants has been more measured. Protestants tend to hold the suspicion that faith development theory in its attention to the potential of the faithful life is too soft with its anthropology, not taking the pervasiveness of sin and "the Fall" seriously enough. However, among the mainline denominations, the United Church of Christ, Disciples of Christ, and Methodists have responded significantly to this theoretical perspective, the latter encouraged by John Wesley's teaching about sanctification. Presbyterians have been the last of the Protestants to be engaged by this perspective. "Lutherans and Calvinists particularly have been slow to embrace this sort of work because with some conviction and some reason they believe that in some ways Christians can claim the word *faith* in a unique and singular way, and that others have to use the category of religion" (Fowler 1984c).

Although some evangelicals are drawn to this perspective because it promises pragmatic assistance in terms of evangelism and formation, there is, again, resistance to the generic use of the term "faith." In this instance, the resistance is to the relativizing of the notions of scriptural and ecclesial authority and of the claim that there is no salvation apart from the self-disclosure of God in Jesus Christ. As faith development theory is insistent upon a broader notion of faith, these are inevitable and important points of theological debate; they are important, however, not simply in relation to faith development theory, but because these issues also stand at the heart of the North American struggle with the religious and political pluralism of the contemporary world.

Critique of the Accounts of Process, Affect, the Unconscious, and Imagination

We may observe that a theory has already demonstrated a good deal of power when critics press for it to include "everything." Any theory can only assist us in seeing *some* things—no theory can see *all* things. The question of what must be included in a theory of faith development must be considered against the backdrop of the finitude inherent in any theory. Nevertheless, critics are quite right in insisting that some features are required if a theory of *faith* development is to approach adequacy.

Though Fowler has described how faith might be educated or sponsored when understood from a developmental perspective and has described the relation of conversion and faith development, it remains the case that Fowler's work is regularly perceived as attending more to stages that appear static than to the motion described in Piaget's understanding of equilibration.

Likewise, though Fowler insists that in faith "the rational and the passional are fused," his stage descriptions are heard in terms of their power to know rather than to feel, their power to describe the development of cognition triumphing over their power to describe the development of emotion and affection (trust, love, loyalty, righteous anger, etc.). This sort of critique takes its sharpest form when one critic suggests that what emerges in Fowler's description of development is stages rather than persons (Gorman 1982, 105–6). These are critiques that Fowler shares with most constructive-developmental (Piagetian) theorists. Both of these issues, however, have been addressed significantly by the work of Robert Kegan (1980; 1982). Fowler has begun to incorporate the insights from Kegan's work (see Fowler 1987a, chap. 4). Kegan has pushed Piaget's theory of cognition to a theory of ego and meaning making as its central activity. Kegan describes stages as secondary to the motion that people are—the motion of life itself which is manifest in both cognition and affect. This work invites all developmental theory to move in a more dynamic direction, and since in 1980 Kegan affirmed Fowler's work as not adding something to this paradigm but articulating a religious dimension at the heart of the paradigm, it is puzzling that Fowler did not heretofore incorporate Kegan's insight.

Fowler also shares with other constructive-developmentalists the vulnerability to a yet inadequate account of the role of the unconscious in the formation of faith. While other developmental theorists may be able to leave this to the domain of other theoretical perspectives, this is more difficult to do when one is dealing with faith as the rubric in which the whole of a person's formulation of reality is embraced. Fowler is quite open to this conversation and has used the metaphor of the "deep self" and its power in relation to his description of the formation of stage 5; he has also pointed to the importance of work such as Ana-Maria Rizzuto's appropriation of object-relation theory in relation to the formation of our sense of God (Rizzuto 1979). Yet he has not yet used projective tests or other such measures in his research as some critics have suggested he should do. In my own work I am encouraging the development of methodologies appropriate to the constructive-developmental paradigm which enable us to interview the "shadow side" of faith. But at the present time faith development study remains limited in its power to tap the well of soul less accessible to the verbal self.

Likewise, though Fowler devotes a short chapter in *Stages of Faith* to the subject of faith and imagination and has identified the "role of symbols" as one of the seven aspects of faith, he is still repeatedly asked to give a more adequate account of the role of imagination in faith—a critique he has resisted (Fowler 1986b, 289). Yet, as I have suggested elsewhere (Parks 1980, chap. 6; see also 1986b, chap. 6), when the *process* of imagination is linked more profoundly with the *process* of faith development, then the way is opened to address several of the primary critiques addressed to faith

development theory simultaneously: the necessary relation between structure and content; the process versus stage orientation of the theory; the role
of the "unconscious"; the relation of affect to cognition; the role of fear,
suffering, and the void.

Critique from a Critical Social-Political Perspective

Those who bring a critical social-political perspective to faith development theory do not have to look far to find a fitting subject for their
reflection. The word "faith" may be problematic for some, but the word
"development" is the first point of sensitivity for those aware of its use by
economists. It evokes a class critique on a global scale when economic
development in "underdeveloped nations" has been equated with the imperialism of North American and Western European interests. Some have
suggested that to use this word is already to defeat everything that faith
development theory might best serve, reflecting rather than correcting the
ritualization of progress which dominates our achievement-obsessed society
(Huebner 1982b; Loder and Fowler 1982, 137–38). Moran, on the other
hand, has suggested that the issue of human development is too important
to give over either to the psychologists or the economists — or even to the
ecologists; he suggests that the word be enriched rather than abandoned
(1983, 1–27). (I have suggested that the word *transformation* might be used
in addition to or even preferably to "development," though it does not
necessarily connote positive growth; see Parks 1986a, 156.) Faith development theory must, in any case, continue to examine critically its central
metaphors as a part of its theological task (Way 1982).

John Broughton has delivered the harshest critique from a social-critical
perspective. A constructive-developmental psychologist himself who is seeking to be radically informed by critical social theory, he questions whether
developmental stages are confounded with existing social hierarchy (1986a,
97). He is concerned both with class structures and with gender role arrangements. Specifically, faith development theory is oriented to "knowledge";
faith is described, in part, as a "knowing." The study of the sociology of
knowledge, represented, for example, by the work of Foucoult, recognizes
that knowledge is power and recognizes that the question of who defines and
controls that knowledge is crucial. Accordingly, Broughton asks for greater
clarity regarding the adequacy of faith development theory to distinguish, for
example, between the person of "more mature faith" at Fowler's stage 4 and
the politically submissive citizen. (This is a form of critique that might also
be placed within the press for further elaboration regarding the relationship
of structure and content, faith and imagination.) Since faith development
theory is self-consciously normative as well as descriptive work, this sort of

critique—particularly those based on an analysis of class, gender, and race—must be taken with utmost seriousness. This work has only begun to emerge (beyond that of Fowler's desire, from the beginning, to be sensitive to these perspectives—especially class and race).

The clearest, most elaborated critique of this sort is coming from a gender analysis. At an informal level, a few male critics have asked, "Even if it is presumed that faith development theory and the theories in which it is rooted represents a male bias in its vision of maturity, is it the case that males must attain the 'illusion of control' represented by Fowler's stage 4?" (Dykstra 1982b). Or is this vision of development reflective merely of the development of the illusions of white male mastery and privilege, which is only modified in the direction of a more profound mutuality *after* stage 4 and the secured achievements of the successful mid-life male? (Buchanan 1987).

The most substantial analysis and critique challenging the normativity of developmental models in general come from women's research and analysis. In constructive-developmental theory, this work has been pioneered primarily by Carol Gilligan, whose research has identified "a different voice" in the study of moral development, a voice that reflects on moral decisions from an orientation to responsibility and care rather than in terms of rights and the limitations of powers (1982). This work has dramatized the differences between the story of human development understood in the terms of individuation of the self and that understood in terms of relation and the formation of a responsive self dwelling in the context of an interdependent reality.

Gilligan's work is sponsoring the work of others. Mary Belenky and her associates, in their important book *Women's Ways of Knowing*, have extended Gilligan's insights, identifying the role of "coming to voice" as salient in the development of women and describing the significance of the distinction between separate and connective knowing (Belenky et al. 1986).

In relation to faith development theory *per se* Maria Harris has argued for alternative metaphors to better describe the experience of women, and she suggests the metaphors of "sabbath" and "completion" (1986, chap. 5). Carol Ochs has critiqued the development or journey metaphor, which dominates the literature of spiritual formation in general, suggesting as an alternative the metaphor of the walk, which may connote a less prescriptive sense of form and goal (1983, chap. 9). In my most recent work I have begun to argue not for an alternative to the development-journey image but rather for the recognition of the necessary relationship of the metaphors of home *and* journey, dwelling *and* pilgrimage. These metaphors have been artificially separated and reified by historical and political arrangements and must be rejoined as companion metaphors in the story of human development, particularly if the story of female development is to be included—but also if the story of male development is to be complete (Parks 1987).

Fowler is well aware of Gilligan's work, which he has discussed at length both appreciatively and critically in *Becoming Adult, Becoming Christian*. Yet when he follows this discussion with a fresh description of the stages of faith development, the dynamics of the individuating self (in contrast to the connective self) continue to dominate the description—even when examples from women's lives are used.

If we pursued this line of critique, we might begin by returning to Fowler's description of stage 6—mature faith, observing that not only are his examples predominantly males dead before their time but they are also those whose relationships with women may be perceived as problematic. Further, these men may be perceived as defined over against community rather than participating in the daily creation and sustaining of vital living community. Fowler characterizes them as having undergone a unique "negation of ties" (1984a, 73)—language which women do and *do not* identify with our deepest impulses toward faithfulness. Paul Philbert has commented:

> Fowler's conception of the end-term of development as probably leading to lonely prophetic martyrdom rather than to mutually enlivening community raises some underlying questions.... Are there sociohistorical allegiances controlling the individualistic focus of these stages which will only reinforce the competitiveness and isolation characteristic of our present [North American] world? ... [h]is last word on development portrays a strangely isolated hero. How ironic that a vehicle which serves so well as a metaphor for the integration of challenging concepts of growth still divides us at the very foundational level of imagination which Fowler likes to name *faith*. (1982, 122).

Until such time as stage 6 exemplars are identified by methodology in continuity with the other stages, might persons such as Nelson and Wini Mandela also be candidates for stage 6?

In the light of sociopolitical analysis, other imagery must also be examined such as "Sovereignty of God" and "Kingdom of God" (Fowler has shifted recently in light of feminist critique to the use also of the language of "commonwealth of love"). Some of this necessary reexamination has begun to emerge also from the perspective of race and class. (See R. Moseley's forthcoming book *Becoming a Self Before God: Process and Paradox in Religious Transformation;* see also G. Baker-Fletcher 1987; K. Baker-Fletcher 1987.)

But perhaps sociopolitical critique finally most forcefully compels us to recognize, first, that it is not easy for any of us as individuals to think in adequately inclusive modes and, second, that therefore perhaps the impact of gender, race, and class analysis will not have its full effect until the composing of theory itself becomes a shared enterprise.

Conclusion

For this account to be complete one additional critique must be noted. Some have called for a closer conversation between faith development theory and its natural related literatures—for example, Baldwin, Goldman, Elkind, and Allport. These are theorists in psychology and specifically the psychology of religion, and the point is appropriately made. Yet within a decade, James Fowler has fostered a conversation which, though it takes form at the crossroads of religion and psychology, it is not confined to that sphere. Faith development theory now engages not only psychologists and theologians but also ethicists, historians, clinicians, educators across the life-span—both parochial and public—spiritual directors, pastors, social theorists, social activists, and many others. Not all of these conversations yet take place in full depth; but it is not too much to say that something significant in human experience and human hope has been touched by this work. Therefore, it will continue to require our most vigorous and faithful critique—in North America and wherever its influence stirs the faithful imagination.

6

Hard versus Soft Stages of Faith and Religious Development: A Piagetian Critique

F. CLARK POWER

BOTH JAMES FOWLER and Fritz Oser began their research on faith and religious development within the Piagetian framework, attempting to describe a sequence of stages that would meet such standard criteria as invariant sequentiality and structured wholeness. In the course of their work they found that they had to accommodate the model to the unique features of the religious domain. My aim in this chapter is to appraise to what extent they have managed to remain within the parameters of Piagetian stage criteria. I do so not in the spirit of distinguishing the orthodox from the heretical but in order to gain a better grasp of the issues involved in the study of research on religious development.

The Kohlbergian Context for the Hard-versus-Soft Distinction

The hard-versus-soft stage description is one that Kohlberg introduced (Kohlberg and Armon 1983; Kohlberg and Higgins 1984; Kohlberg, Levine, and Hewer 1984; Kohlberg 1986) in an effort to sort out similarities and differences between his own theory of moral development and theories that were either modeled on his own, such as Kegan's (1982) and Fowler's (1981), or that shared many of its developmental assumptions, such as Perry's (1968) and Loevinger's (1976). Although the distinction originated rather late in Kohlberg's work, his interest in the question of defining Piagetian stages dates back to his doctoral dissertation (Kohlberg, 1958). There he distinguished between the Weberian "types," which he identified in his original,

116

cross-sectional research, and true stages, which he believed could be described only in longitudinal research. When his subsequent longitudinal research revealed anomalous cases of regression, Kohlberg was forced to make significant modifications in his conceptualization of the stages and in his method of assessing them (Colby 1978). Kohlberg (1978) summarized the thrust of those modifications as his adoption of a more thoroughgoing Piagetian structuralism.

As Kohlberg redefined his stages, he discovered that moral development continued into adulthood, a finding that contradicted his earlier position that the only development to occur after adolescence represented Eriksonian functional rather than Piagetian structural change (Kohlberg and Kramer 1969). In a paper aptly entitled "Continuities in Childhood and Adult Moral Development Revisited," Kohlberg (1973a) maintained that the processes Erikson identified in the formation of identity were relevant not only to functional stage change but to structural change as well. This integrative approach made him a Piagetian pioneer in life-span developmental psychology; but, as Gibbs (1979) noted, it also opened his high stages up to charges of ethnocentrism (Simpson 1974; Vine 1986), and ideological and gender bias (Gilligan 1982; Sullivan 1977; Schweder, 1981). Gibbs (1977, 1979) believed that Kohlberg could have avoided such charges had he stayed within the confines of orthodox Piagetianism and refrained from postulating the existence of postconventional Stages 5 and 6. According to Gibbs, Kohlberg's postconventional stages were not really stages at all but metaethical positions that adults develop in response to existential concerns for meaning and identity. Ironically, Kohlberg's application of the hard-versus-soft stage distinction in criticizing other developmental theories emerged directly out of his response to this challenge to his own higher stages.

In assessing Fowler and Oser's theories I will focus on the following questions, which reflect several of Kohlberg's concerns: (1) Do the stages describe action related rather than reflective reasoning? (2) Are they truly universal? (3) Are they logical structures of organization or principles of psychological unity and stability? (4) Are they irreducible to other stage sequences? Although Gibbs (1979) and Döbert (1987) among others have faulted Kohlberg's stages on Piagetian grounds, I know of no other life-span theory of social cognitive development that comes closer to the Piagetian ideal. Thus, for the purpose of comparison I will use Kohlberg's theory to illustrate a hard-stage approach.

Operative versus Reflective Reasoning

Perhaps the most basic hard-stage criterion is that the stages describe organized systems of action. For Piaget, thought itself is fundamentally the subject's action of the world: "In order to know objects, the subject must act upon them, and therefore transform them: He must displace, connect, combine, take apart and reassemble them" (Piaget 1983, 104). Piaget understood the very process of development as a continuous constructive activity in which the subject coordinates his or her actions and thereby grasps the interrelations among objects. His stage sequence begins with the directly observable, physical actions of the infant in the sensorimotor period (e.g., sucking, grasping, looking, and listening) and progresses through later periods in which such actions as combining, ordering, and putting into one-to-one correspondence become interiorized and can be carried on mentally.

In keeping with Piaget's notion of stages as structures of coordinated action, Kohlberg argued that the justice operations of equality and reciprocity are the organizational principles of the moral stages. He attempted to demonstrate this theoretically by showing how responses to moral dilemmas have common deep structures of justice underlying surface differences in content. Although he conceded to Gibbs that persons reasoning at the postconventional level often posited metatheoretical notions about the nature of morality, he asserted that at the core of post-conventional reasoning is a normative justice structure, oriented to solving the action-problem presented by the dilemma itself. As evidence for this claim he (Kohlberg 1984) noted that stage 5 moral judgment is more predictive of moral action than any other stage.

Before focusing on whether Fowler and Oser's stage models meet this first, hard-stage criterion, I will briefly discuss my interpretation of their respective conceptions of faith and religion. I have previously argued (Power and Kohlberg 1980) that religious faith may be thought about in two rather different but complementary ways, as either a largely tacit trust that reality can sustain the human quest for meaning and worth or as an explicit acknowledgment of a transcendent or ultimate principle. Faith in this first sense, what we may call tacit faith, constitutes a horizon for all human experience. It subsists mathematically or preconceptually in the sense of confidence and purposefulness with which we undertake the tasks of daily living. Because it is a largely unconscious dimension of experience, we cannot approach it the same way we can approach conscious problem-solving activities, required by a Piagetian conservation task, for instance, or by a Kohlbergian moral dilemma. Nevertheless, faith may be investigated indirectly insofar as it is a condition for developing patterns of human action and reflection.

I am inclined to regard Fowler's faith stages as descriptions of this tacit faith, since at least up to stage 6 they do not focus on nor presuppose any explicit acknowledgment of an ultimate reality, understood as a theistic God, pantheistic cosmos, or state of nirvana. Because the stage sequence is not based on the transformation of religious or even metaphysical concepts, Fowler's designation of his stages as stages of faith has appeared arbitrary to some of his supporters (e.g., Kohlberg and Power 1981) as well as to his critics (e.g., Broughton 1986; Fernhout 1986; Wallwork 1980). In spite of his inclusion of questions that involve specifically religious topics and his theological interpretation of the process of ego development as directed by and integrated through the influence of the Ultimate, he has not yet described the stages of faith in a way that manifests the necessary relatedness of the Ultimate to the entire process.

A second way of thinking about religious faith is exemplified in Oser's work on religious reasoning. His approach attends to explicitly theological concerns which arise in thinking about the relationships of God to the world or more generally in confronting what Ogden (1966), Tracy (1975), and Toulmin (1950) have called "limit experiences" of the finitude and inexplicable gratuity of our existence. Limit experiences involve suspending everyday cares and concerns in the awareness of questions of ultimate significance. Insofar as one acknowledges God or the Infinite, one makes one's generally tacit faith in the meaning and worth of human activity. Linking faith to limit experiences in this way does not mean that the Ultimate only has significance at the borders of life. Limit situations lead to the awareness that the Ultimate is the ground of all experiences. The stance we take in these limit situations informs our mundane activities in the sense that being conscious of the basis for our faith we can face life with a renewed sense of courage and meaning. Note that the kind of religious reasoning that is evoked in limit situations need not be related to any particular belief system or creed and may constitute a purely rational or natural law theology.

With this distinction between implicit and explicit faith in mind, let us return to the issue of whether Fowler and Oser's stages describe first-order problem solving or second-order metatheoretical reflection by asking how they go about investigating their respective notions of faith. Fowler's interview consists of a number of life review questions followed by a set of questions that inquire into subjects' abilities to reflect on the foundations of decision making rather than resolve any particular problem in their environment. For example, question 4, in section 3 of the Faith Development Interview (Moseley and Fowler, 1986) asks: "When you have an important decision to make, how do you generally go about making it?" In order to answer such a question, persons must focus their attention not on resolving an external problem but on their own processes of decision making.

Another set of questions from section C addresses the moral domain: "Do you think that actions can be right or wrong? If so, what makes an action right in your opinion? Are there certain actions or types of actions that are always right under any circumstances? Are there certain moral opinions that everyone should agree on?" Such metaethical questions about the nature of morality should be distinguished from normative questions that involve decisions about the morality of specific actions (Frankena 1973). A similar point may be made with reference to the religious questions, for example, question 3 in section D of the interview states: "Do you consider yourself a religious person and what does this mean to you?" To ask someone whether they would consider themselves religious demands, first, a metareligious definition of religion, and, second, a self-reflective appraisal of one's identity as religious in light of that definition.

One of the advantages of asking subjects to define what they mean by religion and morality is that the interviewer does not impose his or her own preconceptions. It is a strategy that Gilligan (1982) has used quite effectively in demonstrating that there are gender differences in how persons define what is a moral problem. However, such an approach does not allow a direct focus on how persons actually go about solving problems. The reflective thrust of such questions demands metatheoretical reasoning and heightened self-consciousness, competencies that may presuppose but go beyond logical operations on external objects and their relations (cf. Broughton 1983).

Oser's interviewing methodology is far more suitable for observing reasoning in action insofar as it utilizes Kohlbergian-type dilemmas. The most frequently cited of Oser's dilemmas is the Paul Dilemma. It involves a quasi-moral decision about upholding a contract made in duress. It qualifies as a religious dilemma because the promisee is not a human person but God, and the duress is experienced in the broader context of what I have called a limit situation. At the heart of the dilemma then is the question of how human action is to be coordinated with divine action.

Although this dilemma seems resolvable by making an action-choice either to go to the third world or to pursue a marriage and prosperous career in Switzerland, much more is involved. As older, higher-stage subjects recognize, their choice symbolizes their sense of vocation and approach to such theological problems as determinism versus free will and primary versus secondary causality. Young persons scored at the first two stages do not yet grasp these implications; and their responses are straightforwardly action-oriented and analogous to those made in response to Kohlberg's moral dilemmas. They accept the terms of the dilemma as they are presented; however, the more mature subjects wrestle over the construction of the dilemma. They ask whether it is meaningful to make promises or ever pray to God and whether it is appropriate to interpret historical events as unambiguous manifestations of God's will. Such questioning is far removed from the action-choice demanded by the dilemma, as it involves second-order, metatheoretical speculation about the relationships of the finite and natural to the infinite and supernatural.

The Universality of Stages of Faith

Related to the notion that Piagetian stages represent the organization of action is the claim that they are universal. In my opinion, such a claim entails at least three conditions: (1) that individuals in any cultural context spontaneously address the problems defining the developmental domain; (2) that the resolutions of these problems be considered universally normative; and (3) that the same stage structures and developmental sequence be present in all cultures without variation. All three of these conditions appear to apply to such basic categories of thinking as space, time, causality, and justice, categories that Kant had assumed to be *a priori*.

What can be said for the universality of the stages of faith and religious development? First, both Fowler and Oser's approaches seem to address universal problems of meaning and value. As yet they have not found cultural contexts in which individuals have not been able to relate to their questions. Yet not all individuals feel compelled to deal with the issues they raise. Both Oser and Fowler have found that many individuals simply do not think about the problems posed by limit situations in religious or metaethical terms. We may criticize them as being unauthentic or unreflective. Yet note that the demand to think about issues of ultimacy is rooted in the existential exigencies of personal development and self-transcendence and not in the adaptational exigencies of interacting with the physical and social environment.

Related to the issue of whether religious problems present themselves spontaneously and unavoidably is the question of whether faith development is normative or merely optional. Kohlberg's efforts in moral education were based on the conviction that a higher moral stage is a better stage and is "required" from a moral point of view. The imperative for faith and religious development appears to be somewhat different. In my opinion, it is rooted in the dynamics of self-awareness and authenticity. In this respect, Fowler is quite correct in maintaining that progress to the higher faith stages involves a sense of personal commitment that is absent in Piaget's accounts of equilibration. This sense of commitment not only helps to explain the dynamics of higher-order development but is essential to both Fowler's and Oser's descriptions of their terminal stages, which express belief in a personal God. Such a belief entails freedom and love and therefore involves more than a complete and balanced logical system. Because of the voluntary dimension of faith and religious development, I believe that Fowler and Oser are rightly hesitant about making the same kind of normative claims for their theories as Kohlberg or Piaget do for theirs.

Finally, we must consider the thorny problem of defining stages of faith or religious reasoning that will be valid for members of various world religions as well as for agnostics and atheists. As yet neither Fowler nor Oser has conducted extensive cross-cultural research, although Oser (this volume) reports that a pilot study of Islamic and Hindu subjects suggests the cross-cultural validity of his early stages. If Fowler and Oser are to succeed in defining universal stages, then I believe that they will have to modify the descriptions of their final stages, which are currently formulated in Judeo-Christian theological concepts. While such theistic concepts may be extended to the Hindu and Islamic traditions, I do not see how they can be to the Buddhist tradition, let alone to agnosticism and atheism. Given the theistic embeddedness of these higher stages, it may be more appropriate to think of Fowler and Oser's stage theories as describing the religious development of theists within the Judeo-Christian tradition. As such, more attention might be given to Vygotsky's (1962) approach to the process of developmental enculturation. Such an approach takes far more seriously than does Piaget's the influence of the particular historical and social context on development.

Structural Wholeness

Of all the criteria for hard stages, Kohlberg focused most on the notion of structural wholeness. In his view, soft-stage theories blurred crucial distinctions between logical and psychological principles of organization, structure and content, and competence and performance. With regard to Loevinger's theory, for example, Kohlberg (Kohlberg, Levine, and Hewer 1984a) noted that she thought of structure in a weak sense as a hypothetical entity that accounted for integrative functioning of the personality, like the psychoanalytic ego. Accordingly, she treated interview responses as diagnostic indicators or signs from which a stage could then be inferred. In her scoring manual she assigned items to stages on the basis of a probabilistic relationship of content to structure. This procedure allowed her to include among her scoring criteria material related to ego functions, motives, and affect.

Kohlberg insisted on more stringent criteria for the items in his scoring manual because he viewed structure as a "system of transformational laws governing operations" (Kohlberg, Levine, and Hewer 1984a, 242). He believed a structure as such is real and can be abstracted straightforwardly through a careful reading of the interview data: "The responses of subjects to the dilemmas and their subsequent responses to clinical probing are taken to *reflect, exhibit, or manifest* the structure. They are the realizations of 'archetypal' structure in actuality, under special conditions" (p. 407).

In my opinion Fowler's understanding of structure is much closer to Loevinger's than Kohlberg's, and his stage descriptions are "soft" by design. Moseley, Jarvis, and Fowler (1986) define the structure of faith as "a complex unity comprised of the interactions of several components or competences"

(p. 8). The scoring rules for assessing the faith stages stipulate that all the components or aspects should be scored so that together the "elusive core structure" might be identified. The aspects relate to distinctive ways of thinking about the interview material. Each aspect has its own organizing principle, although the organizing principles tend to overlap from aspect to aspect, as I will illustrate.

The first three of these aspects, Form of Logic, Social Perspective-Taking, and Form of Moral Judgment, are derived from the hard-stage theories of Piaget, Selman, and Kohlberg. Research by Wallwork (1980) indicates that there is a necessary but not sufficient relationship among them. The remaining four, Bounds of Social Awareness, Locus of Authority, Form of World Coherence, and Symbolic Function, build on and extend the first three in interesting ways. For example, Aspect D, Bounds of Social Awareness, describes a widening pattern of affiliation as individuals move from a familial to a peer group and finally to a universal sense of belonging. Although this logic of this aspect appears to be one of increasing inclusivity, upon inspection it turns out to be a logic of perspective taking applied to the issue of defining group boundaries (in-group and out-group) as the following criteria for coding a response as Stage 4 indicate: (1) Stage 4 judges who is included and who is alien on the basis of ideological compatibility. (2) Stage 4 tends to see other individuals as part of a system or a group rather than as individuals.

Insofar as the faith stages have cognitive structures, they are manifest in the structural stage descriptions of each aspect. That is, the logical principles of organization appear to extend only within the boundaries of the discrete aspects and not to the *structure d'ensemble*, the faith structure itself. The use of similar criteria to assess different aspects may intimate a kind of logical coherence, but no such inference should be drawn given the redundancy in the scoring system. Without a logical "master structure" Fowler's faith stages lack unity in the rigorous hard-stage sense. Nevertheless, as Kohlberg, Levine, and Hewer (1984a) admitted, this may not be such a bad tradeoff, since "the strength of hard stages is limited by the need to subdivide into discrete domains those worldviews that are in an ethical and religious sense unified" (p. 238).

In addition to lacking a hard-stage principle of structural organization, Fowler (Mosely, Jarvis, and Fowler 1986) includes quite a bit of affective and performance-related material in his scoring criteria, as the following examples show:

A)   Stage 1 will often test authority in concrete ways (p. 76).
B)   Stage 2 is apt to be harshly judgmental in its characterization of other different from himself (p. 89).

C)   Stage 3 will often select authority figures on the basis of charisma
      (p. 124).
D)   The person at stage 4 will usually be able to consider and analyze the
      viewpoint of another, but often in a defensive manner with an eye to
      maintaining his or her own viewpoint (p. 140).
E)   Stage 5 will often be self-critical rather than defensive in its
      perspective-taking (p. 161).
F)   Perspective taking at stage 6 will be concrete. . . . Perspective taking
      at stage 6 can also be expressed as a "felt sense" of solidarity with others
      (p. 185).

Note that the probabilistic relationships of the above criteria to logical structures is communicated through the qualification "Stage x will *often* . . . , will
usually . . . , is *apt* to be . . . , *can* be. . . ." These criteria represent per-
formances that usually follow from a structural stage-related competence
but need not necessarily be so related. They are in Kohlberg's terms "signs"
rather than manifestations of a structure.

Oser's stages generally meet Kohlberg's requirements that the stages be
logically organized responses to meet a face validity test for structure. Unlike
Fowler, he does not attempt to assess stages through content or performance
criteria. His stage descriptions are based on theological competence rather
than on religious feelings or action. For example, he describes the logic of
the first stage as based on the principle of unilateral divine determination.
His scoring criteria list expressions of that principle in various contents:

1)   Man acts because God forces him to act.
2)   His acts are one-dimensional and blindly responsive.
3)   God's interventions are comprehended as reward or punishment (Oser
      1980, 295).

Perhaps the most significant structural shortcoming of Oser's theory is
that his data are derived from dilemmas that exclusively focus on religio-
moral questions, such as those presented by the Paul Dilemma. His research
to date does not address whether individuals use the same stage of reasoning
to resolve a variety of religious problems in addition to those touching on
moral issues. By narrowly delimiting his range of inquiry he avoids one of
the most difficult issues in cognitive developmental studies: the synchronic-
ity of the stages across different problem areas (see Fischer and Silvern,
1985). Oser cannot claim to have identified genuine stages of religious
reasoning until he determines whether individuals employ the same structure of reasoning in dealing with diverse issues in the religious domain.

A second, less significant problem of structure is presented by the way
Oser deals with atheism and agnosticism. Although he is sensitive to the
content-versus-structure distinction, he nevertheless appears to link atheism

and agnosticism with stage 3. He describes the achievement of stage 3 as an ambiguous recognition of the autonomy of the human. At this stage, atheism becomes possible since human events can be explained in purely secular terms. Those who maintain a theistic perspective must rely on a kind of voluntaristic faith since they lack a stage 4 systemic perspective that locates a limited sense of human autonomy within the context of a divine plan. All of the higher stages, beginning with stage 4, describe ways of maintaining a conscious relationship with God that are consistent with the understanding of human autonomy at that stage. By such criteria all atheists and agnostics would be scored at stage 3. Yet there are vast differences in the kind of justifications persons give for their agnosticism and atheism.

In his original speculations about the problem of atheism Oser (1980) hypothesized that the structural definitions of the religious stages should be open to include atheistic positions at all the stages (Oser and Gmünder 1984). However, when he did study atheists, he did not stage score their reasons but developed a separate typology of their arguments. Instead of attempting to reformulate his interview and descriptions of the religious stages to include nontheistic efforts to deal with the problems of meaning, he has continued to explore the structures of the divine–human relationship exclusively.

Perhaps if Oser had broadened the domain of religious judgment to include atheism and agnosticism his loss of focus would have cost him the possibility of identifying any transformations in religious judgment according to logical criteria. Nevertheless, Oser's theistic definition of the religious domain leaves open the possibility that his stages are embedded within a more comprehensive structural framework. (Fowler's faith stages appear to provide such a comprehensive framework, but in their generality they fail to elucidate the religious relevance of atheism and agnosticism. For example, at the Tübingen conference on Religious Development and Education, Fowler maintained that in scoring expressions of atheism he would determine whether they were self-chosen [stage 4] or conventionally accepted [stage 3] positions. By treating atheism as he would any other kind of belief system [e.g., feminism or an ideology of nuclear disarmament], Fowler misses its distinctively religious or theological significance. Oser, on the other hand, focuses on atheism as a denial of God based on an appreciation for the autonomy of the world.) Obviously more research must be conducted with nonbelievers before this issue can be settled.

The Integrity of Faith and Religion

From a theological perspective the most serious implication of the hard-versus-soft stage distinction is that if faith and religious development are seen as reducible in structure to logical and/or moral development, then God too will be viewed as an epiphenomenon of human consciousness. There is, of course, precedent for this kind of reductionism. The theories of psychological and cultural development since Comte have typically viewed religious thinking as a primitive stage which eventually must give way to more secularized scientific and ethical stages. Durkheim (1965), for example, thought that the experience of moral obligation depended on a sense of the moral law as evoking both respect and attraction, elements traditionally found in relationship to God. He postulated that the rationalization of morality, which began when religions gave priority to social over cultic prescriptions, eventually led to the insight that the moral law was rooted not in God's will but in an evolving society.

Kohlberg (1973b) took a very different view of the relationship of morality to religion by arguing that moral development in some sense culminated in religious insight, which he discussed as a metaphorical "seventh stage" of moral development. His expressed intention in describing a seventh stage was to point out that stage 6 moral principles, although they represented the apex of moral development, were incapable of resolving such profound problems as why the innocent suffer. Not only did he recognize the limitations of moral reasoning, but he speculated that persons with the most highly developed moral consciousness experience the greatest need for religious consolation, since they grasp the existential import of the question Why be moral?

Although Kohlberg affirmed religion as a nonreducible human concern, he was in fact, I think, skeptical that anyone could construct hard religious stages because of his understanding of religion as "suprarational." Note then that at least in Kohlberg's mind the designation of stages of faith and religious reasoning as soft stages did not necessarily carry with it the further implication that religious experience was reducible to another domain. However, in a paper we wrote together (Kohlberg and Power 1981) we discussed certain soft-stage theories of religious development proposed by Baldwin, James, and Dewey that we felt were open to this implication. These theorists held that those concepts, such as God and the kingdom of God, were essentially imaginative reconstructions of the ideal moral self and the ideal society. While they recognized the impact of religious socialization, they assumed that children would assimilate the received tradition into their own developing moral structures. They did not think that religious experience would in itself promote development unless it were translatable into moral categories.

In contrast, Kohlberg and I have maintained that a domain of religious development can be identified that is related to other cognitive moral domains, but nevertheless may be defined in terms of its own problems, experiences, and ways of thinking. Because at least Western theistic views are based on a personal understanding of God, we have hypothesized that moral development is a necessary but not sufficient condition for religious development. This is no more of a reductionistic hypothesis than the one made by Kohlberg that Piagetian logical development is a necessary but not sufficient condition for religious development.

The theoretical justification for such a hypothesis may perhaps most easily be grasped by considering Oser's Paul Dilemma. As I noted earlier, there are at least two moral problems embedded in this dilemma: (1) Should Paul keep his promise to God? (2) Should God expect Paul to keep a promise made under duress? In answering this dilemma most religious believers would probably insist that God be regarded as at least as moral as any ideal human agent. The fact that God is above humanity means that additional metaphysical deliberations would have to be introduced. These presumably would not contradict God's essentially moral nature but would build on it. Because the concept of God "borrows" from moral concepts through analogy, as from the known to the unknown, we would not expect an individual's construction of the divine–human relationship to be at a higher stage than his or her construction of purely human relationships.

The empirical data on the relationship between the moral and religious stages have been inconsistent. Oser and Gmünder (1984) found a substantial number of subjects had higher religious than moral stage scores, although about twice as many had higher moral than religious scores. However, there are three other studies that report results more clearly supportive of the necessary but not sufficient hypothesis (Berkowitz et al. 1987; Giunti 1984; Power and Kohlberg 1980). I believe that the necessary but not sufficient hypothesis would stand up if Oser's scoring criteria were more explicitly formulated to reflect that relationship. Nevertheless, as compelling as the necessary but not sufficient hypothesis may be, the irreducibility of the religious stages can be maintained without it. Although Oser's first two stage descriptions show great affinity with the parallel moral stages, they increasingly diverge at stages 3 to 5, when their distinctively religious logic becomes salient. Thus I am inclined to accept Oser's claim that the religious stages are autonomous or are, as he sometimes calls them, "mother structures." Nevertheless, given the high correlations that are found between moral and religious stages, further empirical evidence should be marshaled in support of their differentiation.

Because they are so inclusive, Fowler's faith stages run two somewhat different risks of losing their distinctive identity. The first I have discussed in another context: it is the risk that his stages may be interpreted as ego stages or as stages of world views. The problem here is that the connection between Fowler's empirically based descriptions of his stages and his theology of faith development is too tenuous. The second risk is that the faith stages may be reducible to the aspect components, several of which are elaborations of hard stage sequences.* The best evidence for the integrity of the faith stages comes at Stages 5 and 6, when there is a clear identification of the stage structures with metaphysical and religious themes. Perhaps longitudinal analysis will help Fowler and his associates to identify the precursors of these developments so that the religious and metaphysical elements of the lower stages will become more salient.

Conclusion

Fowler's and Oser's theories offer two alternative approaches to the investigation of faith from a cognitive developmental perspective. According to the criteria put forth by Kohlberg, Fowler's theory of faith development epitomizes the soft-stage model. Its strength is its inclusivity. In it we find a concern for the passional as well as the rational and for performance as well as competence. It is a theory that shows that there is a coherence to our reflections on ourselves, society, and nature that would be missed by an exclusive focus on strands of hard-stage development.

In contrast to Fowler's theory, Oser's account of the development of religious reasoning comes closer to meeting many of the hard-stage criteria. The strength of his approach lies in the careful way he has delineated the domain of religious reasoning and in his use of the dilemma methodology to elicit structures of operative religious judgment. By sacrificing breadth for precision Oser has made an important contribution to our understanding of the logic behind the ways in which the divine–human relationship is constructed and transformed.

Although Oser comes closer to providing a hard-stage model than Fowler, I have tried to show some of the ways in which he too has fallen short. In my opinion, the problem with using the Piagetian approach for the study of religious concepts has to do with the nature of the subject matter. God or the Ultimate is not an object like any other finite object, and the Piagetian methods used to study relationships among objects, whether they be physical or social, must be modified to take account of this. Oser has, in my judgment, made some of those modifications, and his theory can tell us a great deal about the development of theistic ways of thinking. Yet I believe that his account of religious development or explicit faith must be situated within the larger account of implicit faith that Fowler provides, because faith goes

---

*Editor's note: John Snarey's recent paper on construct validity in the faith development theory (Snarey 1990) provides data that contradict this suggestion by Power. Snarey's study of faith development among sixty nonreligious kibbutz members provides convincing empirical data for claiming that the faith development stages represent unitary, integrated, and nonreducible constructs.

beyond theology. Similarly, Fowler ought to take Oser's concerns for studying the consciously religious dimension of human meaning-making if his theory is to gain acceptance in the wider and more secular psychological community as a theory of faith and not ego development or life philosophy. Thus, while I think that the study of faith must be done through a soft-stage analysis, I also believe that some of the rigor of the hard-stage approach can and should be retained as a way of pushing the study of faith toward greater clarity about its methods, stage descriptions, and claims.

7

Cognitive Developmental Studies of Religious Thinking

A Survey and Discussion with Special Reference to Post-Goldman Research in the United Kingdom

NICOLA SLEE

THE COGNITIVE DEVELOPMENTAL TRADITION in the psychology of religion is represented by an extensive research literature, dating back to the beginning of the empirical psychology of religion, which deals with the incidence and development of religious ideas, concepts, language, and thought in childhood and, more recently, adulthood. However, while there have been a number of forays into the literature (e.g., Strommen 1971; Riccards 1978), the field has never been thoroughly or systematically documented. Doubtless this is due in no small measure to the state of the research literature itself, which is unwieldy, uncoordinated, and largely unpublished, or, if published, not easily obtainable.

The present article undertakes this neglected task of documentation and provides a broad overview of the research literature. The survey begins by noting the origins of the cognitive developmental tradition in American studies of the late nineteenth and early twentieth centuries. The adoption of the Piagetian paradigm in the 1950s and 1960s and the impact of this paradigm on subsequent research and theory are then traced. The survey concentrates on studies conducted in the United Kingdom which have made explicit use of the Piagetian paradigm. Special attention is paid to the impact of Ronald Goldman's research on studies both in the United Kingdom and wider afield in Europe, Scandinavia, and North America. The impact of the more recent writings of James Fowler and Fritz Oser on British research is also noted. Finally, an attempt is made to summarize the achievements of this research literature and to highlight important issues for current debate.

A Survey of the Studies: Early Studies

Although it is possible to trace a developmental perspective on the religion of the child back to the eighteenth century and even earlier (see Schweitzer's historical review in chapter 3 in this volume), the origins of a genuinely empirical developmental psychology of religion stem from the late 1800s. Pioneering American studies at the end of the nineteenth century and the beginning of the twentieth (e.g., Hall 1891; Barnes 1892; Tanner 1906; Leuba 1917; Case 1921; Bose 1929) provided the first detailed evidence that childhood religious thought is characteristically distinct and essentially developmental in nature. These studies were themselves part of the new and burgeoning science of developmental child psychology established by Binet in France, Preyer in Germany, Spencer and Romanes in England, and Hall, Dewey, Baldwin, and Watson in America (for the history of developmental psychology itself, see Cairns 1983). Based on a range of documentary, clinical, and interview material, these early studies drew attention to the vivid anthropomorphism and literalism of the child's religious imagery and thought, to the paucity and the limitations of the child's knowledge and understanding of rudimentary religious stories and dogmas, and to the logical confusions attending their attempts to make sense of such material. Research also highlighted the surprisingly late achievement of abstract and symbolic religious understanding, although there is much variation regarding the age at which such thought is held to become possible. Above all, this research literature began to establish beyond doubt the uniqueness and particularity of the child's religious thinking, the strangeness and remoteness of the child's mental world from the universe of thought inhabited by the adult, and to interpret the distinctiveness of the child's religion in terms of a genetic perspective. Applying Darwin's evolutionary theory to the development of human rationality itself, these studies postulated an evolutionary process of religious development characterized by a series of qualitatively distinct periods or stages of religious development occurring at various ages and making possible new capacities of thought and believed to recapitulate, in broad terms, the evolution of the human race (e.g., Dawson 1900; Sully 1908; Ames 1910).

Following this early stimulus to developmental research in the psychology of religion, there was a period of fragmentation from the 1920s on for several decades, as early evolutionary and recapitulation theories fell out of favor and American psychology came under the influence of the new behaviorism. Although a flow of research studies continued through the 1930s and 1940s (e.g., MacLean 1930; Nagle 1934; Loomba 1942; Mathias 1943; Harms 1944; McDowell 1952; Dawes 1954), the field lacked a compelling and coherent theoretical perspective to give significance and direction to the work. (Note that Cairns identifies such a period of fragmentation within the wider developmental psychology in these years.)

The First Piagetian-based Studies

Against such a background, there was clearly a need for a new impetus in the research field. Such an impetus was provided during the late 1950s and early 1960s by the research literature and cognitive developmental theory emanating from Geneva and associated with the name of Jean Piaget. Researchers in North America and Europe began to adapt the Piagetian research methodology and the theory of structural stages to the analysis and interpretation of religious thinking (e.g., Godin and van Roey 1959; Godin and Marthe 1960; Elkind 1961, 1962, 1963; Goldman 1964; Thouless and Brown 1965; Lawrence 1965; L. B. Brown 1966, 1968; Long, Elkind, and Spilka 1967). A major result of this paradigmatic shift in research was a move away from analysis of the *content* of religious concepts toward analysis of the *activity* and *processes* of thinking itself, particularly in the context of logically or religiously problematic situations or stories. These Piagetian-based studies discerned many of the features of thought highlighted by the Genevan research, such as egocentrism, animism, artificialism, and so on, operative in the child's religious thinking. More broadly, the basic pattern of religious thinking development traced by these studies corresponds closely to the Piagetian account of cognitive development. Many studies detected a series of stages, broadly corresponding to the Piagetian stages, through which the child's religious thinking passes, but tending to occur at somewhat later ages than the Piagetian stages typically occur.

Few studies elaborated an explicit rationale for the employment of a Piagetian paradigm, but in hindsight it is possible to postulate a number of reasons for its adoption which at the same time help to account for the profound impact of Piagetian research and theory on religious thinking research and theory. First, the theory was able to integrate and consolidate within a comprehensive model of development existing disparate and apparently unrelated research findings that had previously lacked general significance and explanation. The anthropomorphisms and literalisms, the limitations and confusions of childhood religious understanding, and the late achievement of abstract religious concepts were now to be seen as functions of the child's total cognitive development and were found to have parallels in other areas of thought. Integral to this first function of the theory, the Genevan account of the development of cognition also appeared capable of genuine explanation of the characteristics and development of religious thinking. The theory offered a dynamic and genetic account of cognition which explained the nature of childhood thought by reference to the processes and structures of the cognitive operations available to the child at successive levels of development. A third feature of Piagetian theory, which accounts for its adoption by researchers of religious thinking, was its apparent testability. The theory of stages has been widely accepted by researchers as an empirical hypothesis capable of verification or, at least, falsification. The method for testing the theory has been adopted from the Genevans themselves. The Genevan semiclinical interview and the application of stage criterion-referenced analysis to the protocols have both been amenable to the testing of stage hypotheses in religious development. Finally, a significant reason for the adoption of a Piagetian paradigm in religious thinking is undoubtedly its deemed applicability to educational practice. Despite Piaget's own reticence about the pedagogical implications of his theory, the apparent applicability of the stage theory to the planning of curricula and teaching strategies has rendered the theory peculiarly attractive to researchers and educationalists alike.

Ronald Goldman

While these studies began to establish the viability of a Piagetian approach in the examination of religious thinking, it was Ronald Goldman's (1962, 1964) study of a small sample of English school children that conclusively clinched the paradigmatic shift in religious thinking research and related educational theory. During the twenty years following the publication of Goldman's study, it has continued to be identified as one of the foremost texts in religious thinking research (e.g., Langdon 1969; Francis 1979; McGrady 1983; Greer 1983; Hyde 1984). The work has attracted interest and debate and influenced research as far afield as North America, Australia, and Scandinavia. Goldman's study was by no means the first English study to utilize Piagetian insights and theory for the examination of religious conceptual development, but it was the first Piagetian-based study to attract wide attention in this country. (A number of unpublished studies during the 1950s had made use of Piaget's theory to investigate religious concepts [e.g., Dawes 1954; J. E. Johnson 1955; Bowden 1958], and Goldman draws heavily on these studies both in developing his own research and in interpreting his findings.)

Goldman's study was motivated by a sense of profound dissatisfaction and disillusionment, shared by many of his contemporaries, with the state of religious education in England. The 1944 Education Act and the Agreed Syllabuses of Religious Education set up by the Act, designed to rejuvenate the religious and moral life of the nation, to "christianize" the new generation of postwar school children, manifestly had not achieved what they had set out to do. Studies conducted in England in the late 1950s and early 1960s (e.g., Institute of Christian Education 1957; Hilliard 1959; University of Sheffield Institute of Education 1961) suggested that, far from promoting the religious sensibilities of children, the diet of Bible study and church history required by the syllabuses was resulting in boredom, confusion, and even rejection of religion by the majority of pupils. Goldman set out to examine the causes of this "failure of the 1944 Education Act" in the psychological development of the pupil.

Arguing that the Piagetian categories of preoperational intuitive, concrete operational, and formal operational thinking are applicable to the development of religious thinking, Goldman applied Piagetian stage criteria to data collected from interviews with subjects aged 5 to 18 years (unless otherwise stated, ages quoted refer to chronological ages) in which a series of questions on three biblical stories and three pictures was asked. From the application of stage criteria, Goldman concluded that the child's religious thinking is essentially developmental in character, passing from an early intuitive stage through concrete religious thinking to abstract religious thought, although the pace of development is slower in this area than in others, abstract thought not being achieved till mental age 13 or 14. Goldman went on to conclude that most Bible material, being essentially symbolic and abstract in nature, is unsuitable for use before the onset of abstract religious thought. It was inevitable, Goldman argued, that the Bible teaching of the Agreed Syllabuses was meeting with such widespread failure. The attempt to inculcate biblical understanding was doomed from the start by the inherent limitations of the child's cognitive growth. Goldman and his colleagues went on to develop an alternative to the syllabuses of the 1940s and 1950s in the form of a thematic life-centered approach which sought to establish in early childhood the primary "secular" concepts upon which later secondary religious concepts could be built in adolescence (Goldman 1970). The educational climate in Britain was ripe for change, and Goldman's research was the required catalyst.

Post-Goldman Research

Goldman's major impact on the educational scene and on subsequent research can be attributed as much to the pertinent timing of its publication as to its intrinsic merits. For all that, its influence has been both profound and diverse. Here we are chiefly concerned with Goldman's impact on research, and for the sake of clarity it will be helpful to distinguish a number of different categories of post-Goldman research, each of which exhibits Goldman's influence in increasingly broad terms. First, replication studies will be considered; this body of research is, by definition, closely dependent on Goldman's theory and methodology. Second, a group of studies can be identified which, although not strictly replication studies, have attempted to test the generalizability of Goldman's findings to novel populations and situations by adapting Goldman's original research design. These studies tend to be more critical of Goldman's research and seek to refine and develop his findings in significant respects. Third, studies that reflect Goldman's influence much more broadly by the adoption of a Piagetian paradigm will be considered. These studies vary in the extent to which they submit Goldman's approach to critical scrutiny. Finally, a group of studies that display what might be termed a "negative influence" will be considered; these are studies that have deliberately chosen to examine aspects of religious thinking ignored by Goldman and thereby to correct some of the inadequacies of Goldman's original study. In particular, these studies have tended to concentrate on the development of religious language comprehension and use. (Goldman's study has given rise also to an extensive secondary literature of critical analysis and debate; see Slee 1986a.)

Replication Studies

Strictly speaking, there have been very few replication studies of Goldman's original study, employing the original interview schedule and Goldman's methods of analysis. In Scandinavia, Martinsson (1968) used Goldman's design and replicated the results. In the United Kingdom, Morley (1975) administered Goldman's test to slow learners aged between 11 and 16 years and concluded that educationally subnormal children pass through the sequence of stages designated by Piaget in their religious thinking, as Goldman had found, but at a much slower pace. Indeed, except for some isolated answers at the abstract stage, Morley found that "none of the educationally subnormal children could be said to have reached the final stage of abstract thought," nor was there any suggestion that they might eventually reach this stage. In North America, Miller (1976) claimed to replicate Goldman's findings in a study that sought to test the relationship between stages of moral development and stages of religious thinking, but his sample in fact achieved the stages at a much later age than in Goldman's study. Thus, Miller suggests a first fragmentary and literalist conceptual stage from ages 8 to 11 years, followed by a concrete stage during ages 12 to 14, with abstract religious thinking appearing only at age 15.

By far the most extensive attempt to replicate Goldman's results, however, has been undertaken in the United States by Peatling (1973, 1974, 1977a, 1977b) and his associates (Peatling and Laabs 1975; Peatling, Laabs, and Newton 1975), although Peatling's research does not represent a true replication in the technical sense, since he has developed his own paper-and-pencil test which differs in significant respects from Goldman's original research design. Peatling developed a criterion-referenced multiple-choice test, *Thinking About the Bible,* consisting of a series of questions on the three Goldman narratives, with a range of four possible answers for each question representing four levels of religious thinking designated Very Concrete, Concrete, Abstract, and Very Abstract. *TAB* was originally administered to just under two thousand subjects aged between 9 and 19 years, but the test has subsequently been administered to thousands more subjects in cross-cultural samples. On the basis of the cumulative research evidence from cross-cultural samples, Peatling concludes that "religious thinking is developmental in an almost classical Piagetian sense" (1977a, 105), by which he appears to mean that there is a clearly discernible developmental sequence from intuitive through concrete to formal operational thought. However, Peatling also suggests that the transition between concrete and abstract religious thinking is much more complex than Goldman's account reveals. Whereas Goldman's sample achieved a fairly rapid transition, Peatling found evidence of an extended five-year intermediate period occurring between 10 and 15 years mental age. Like Goldman, Peatling sees his research as having far-reaching implications for religious education. He cautions against the use of biblical material in early schooling, suggesting that "the use of legendary/ mythical material must be reassessed far more realistically than it has yet been" (1977a, 105).

The use of *TAB* by other researchers in a number of different cultural contexts has produced perplexing results. While studies have confirmed in general terms the developmental progression found by Peatling, significant variation has been detected in the responses of different populations and some studies challenge Peatling's findings concerning stages of religious thinking. For example, pupils attending Lutheran schools were "consistently behind" Peatling's original Episcopalian sample in both a preference for abstract religious thinking and a rejection of concrete religious thinking (Peatling and Laabs 1975), while Methodist adults achieved much lower scores on Peatling's Very Abstract scale than was hypothesized (Peatling, Laabs, and Newton 1975). These results are interpreted in terms of the conservative religious teaching received by the Lutherans and Methodists, which Peatling suggests has slowed down cognitive development. Tamminen (1976), Greer (1981), and Kay (1981) administered *TAB* to samples of Finnish, Irish, and English school-aged pupils, respectively. Each study confirmed a general progression through Peatling's scales, but there were a number of important discrepancies. In particular, neither Tamminen nor Kay found evidence for cognitive stages; rather, the results suggested a quite even progression of development. Moreover, each of these studies detected the operation of a number of theological and psychological factors operative in *TAB* which cast doubt on the reliability of the instrument as a measure of cognitive preference (for a full discussion and critique of *TAB,* see Greer 1983).

Studies Designed to Test Goldman's Conclusions

Other studies, while not strictly replicating Goldman's original design, have attempted to test the generalizability of Goldman's findings to novel populations and religious content by adapting the test. These studies have been concerned to examine the influence of a number of variables on the process of development originally discerned by Goldman and thus to sharpen and refine Goldman's stage theory. In the United Kingdom, several such studies have been undertaken. For example, Whitehouse (1972) adapted Goldman's design to a novel biblical story in order to eliminate the miraculous element prominent in Goldman's test design which Godin (1968) had suggested might be a source of bias. Whitehouse found no significant difference in the results to support Godin's suggestion. The sequence of thought from intuitive through concrete to formal thought was clearly marked, although there was a wide spread of both chronological and mental ages in children's passage through the stages.

Murphy (1977a, 1977b, 1978, 1979), highly critical of earlier research findings and, in particular, of simplistic accounts of a fixed sequence of developmental stages, designed a series of tests to examine more closely the nature of the development of religious thinking. He used both interview and questionnaire methods to test subjects aged between 7 and 11 years on their understanding of a range of biblical parables. Murphy's results showed a developmental increase in the child's level of understanding of the parables, but the research also highlights the influence of other factors on cognitive performance, such as the content, language, and style of the parable and the method of investigation used. Murphy concluded that primary school children before the onset of formal operations manifest the ability to grasp the allegorical meaning of parables, as well as to employ religious language meaningfully; that understanding differs according to the nature of the material being used and the method of investigation; and that children's understanding of much biblical material is limited not by the lack of formal operational thought but by the inability to sequentially order events in time. Murphy sees his research as providing evidence for the inadequacy of a stage developmental model to account for the complex, multidimensional processes of religious thinking, although Greer (1980) has argued that Murphy's results are, in fact, quite consistent with stage theory.

In the United States, Hoge and Petrillo (1978) examined which of a number of factors hypothesized by Goldman were the most reliable predictors of the level of religious thinking, and tested Goldman's claim that "a gap between concrete religious thinking and higher level cognitive functioning in other areas tends to produce faith rejection" (p. 139). They administered a revised edition of TAB to a sample of Roman Catholic, Baptist, and Methodist students in the tenth grade (mean age 16.0 years) in order to test the level of religious thinking and a variety of other measures to assess the facilitators of religious thinking hypothesized by Goldman. Using path analysis to isolate the main determinants of religious thinking, Hoge and Petrillo found that, first, general cognitive capacity had either a modest impact or no impact at all in every denominational group; second, the impact of religious beliefs was consistently strong and in every group assent to creedal beliefs was related to more concrete religious thinking; third, Bible knowledge had an influence on Catholic youth only toward more abstract religious thinking; and, fourth, religious education tended to increase Bible knowledge but had very little impact on religious beliefs except among the Methodists, where it produced stronger assent to creedal beliefs. Goldman's thesis that a "lag" in religious thinking would lead to faith rejection was difficult to test, but Hoge and Petrillo concluded that "most evidence suggests that Goldman's theory is wrong; more abstract religious thinking among these high school students is associated with more, not less, religious rejection" (p. 153).

Studies That Have Adopted Goldman's Piagetian Framework

In addition to giving rise to replication studies and studies that have sought to test his conclusions, Goldman has had a much wider impact on subsequent research by establishing a Piagetian paradigm in the study of religious thinking, although, as McGrady comments, "much of post-Goldman research is disturbingly light-weight in Piagetian analysis" (1983, 129). Goldman's Piagetian framework has been adopted by a number of independent research studies (e.g., Greenacre 1971; Miles 1971; Richmond 1972; Beechick 1974; Gates 1976; Streeter 1981), and is reflected in the definitions of religious thinking employed, the methodology of studies, and the interpretation of results. Following Goldman, these studies have tended to operationalize religious thinking as "the application of different levels of logical thinking to religious material" (Francis 1979, 110), taking the Piagetian account of the nature and stages of logical thinking as normative. Religious thinking has been measured by the application of stage criteria to subjects' responses to Piagetian-styled dilemmas, modeled on Goldman's research design. The results of studies are then interpreted within the framework of Piagetian stage theory.

Many of these studies have been concerned with children's comprehension and interpretation of different kinds of religious narrative. Thus, Greenacre (1971) conducted an inquiry into the development of the understanding of religious allegory based on a Piagetian model of cognitive development. Arguing that "the interpretation of religious allegory involves the transference of the symbolic forms to the events or figures which they in fact represent" (p. 4), Greenacre hypothesized that the understanding of allegory would not be achieved before the onset of formal operations. However, the results showed that a quarter of the 8– and 9–year-old group of subjects achieved partial transfer, and thus Greenacre concluded that some children are able to articulate the comprehension of religious allegory before the age of 13. Beechick (1974) tested children's understanding of parables and discerned a three-stage progression of understanding related to Piaget's stages of logical thinking. In contrast to Greenacre's findings, Beechick's subjects typically did not achieve the third stage until age 11, in which the child is able to relate elements within the parable and generate meanings beyond the concrete. Gates (1976) and Streeter (1981) likewise traced stages of development in children's understanding of biblical and contemporary parables, though Streeter attempted to refine his study by comparing responses to different categories of biblical parables, and, like Murphy (1977, 1979), found significant differences between children's understanding of the different kinds of parable. Richmond (1972) analyzed pupils' understanding of prose passages adapted from the Bible and found evidence of a progressive development from ages 13 to 16, but few of his subjects reached the highest levels (for a critical discussion of the limitations of these studies of biblical parables, see Slee 1983).

Studies Reflecting a "Negative Influence"

Finally, it is important to note a number of studies currently emerging from the British research scene which, while acknowledging Goldman's major contribution to the field, deliberately seek to go beyond the scope of Goldman's enquiry and to examine features of religious thinking ignored by him, particularly aspects of religious language development (e.g., Murphy 1978; E. B. Turner 1978a, 1978b, 1980; McGrady 1987). Insofar as these studies deliberately move beyond a Piagetian paradigm, they are, strictly speaking, beyond the scope of this survey. Nevertheless, insofar as they suggest necessary correctives to the Piagetian-based account of religious thinking, then they need to be taken account of in such a review.

Building on earlier linguistic studies (e.g., Singer 1959; Deconchy 1965) and on a number of highly suggestive theoretical statements (e.g., Francis 1979; Smith 1981), these studies have attempted to bring a linguistic developmental perspective to bear on the analysis of religious thinking development. Murphy (1978, 1979) employed two kinds of test to study religious language comprehension and usage. The first tested the acquisition of certain pairs of opposites commonly employed in religious language by children between the ages of 6 and 9. The results showed partial acquisition by the sample, but by no means all of the pairs of words had been acquired.

The second test was used to examine the way in which children sorted and grouped religious words in relation to each other. Murphy found evidence of the clustering of words with a high degree of relatedness in all age groups, though ability did increase with age. He concluded:

> Even at 6 years of age the groups of words tested had sufficient meaning for the children to relate them to one another, and at 8 and 10 years of age there seemed to be a development in the features of meaning which were used to relate the words, as well as in the degree to which particular groups of words were related to each other. (1979, 165)

E. B. Turner (1978a, 1978b, 1980) has developed a standardized test of religious language comprehension consisting of a series of words commonly employed in religious discourse, with half of the words contextualized in biblical passages, and has administered this test to large samples of pupils, mostly in Ireland. The results confirmed an age-related development of understanding, and Turner found evidence of both confusions and misunderstandings, but also of developing insight. "The use of abstract terms increased with age, words like 'infinite,' 'immutable,' 'omnipotent' and 'ultimate' being used occasionally, with apparent understanding. There was also evidence of increasing ability to disregard superficial detail and to abstract that which had religious significance" (1980, 189). Turner concludes that, while his results confirm the "continued limitations of religious understanding in adolescence," they also give grounds for "a cautious optimism." A fair number of his subjects "display a surprising facility with the 'specific terms and expressions used by religion' and this facility is not wholly a function either of age or of general intellectual ability" (ibid.).

These linguistic studies represent an important new initiative in religious thinking research and suggest a rather more optimistic picture of religious thinking development than that which emanates from the Piagetian-based research literature. Existing studies are somewhat limited by an undue emphasis on individual word use and comprehension, but there are promising signs of recent development in this area of research (e.g., McGrady 1987), although it is too soon for the results of such research to be known (for a fuller discussion of linguistic approaches to religious thinking, see Francis 1979; M. E. Smith 1981; Dykstra 1986b; Heimbrock 1986a; McGrady 1987; Slee 1987).

Fowler and Oser

Ironically, it is only more recently, in the 1980s, as the monumental impact of Piaget himself shows some signs of waning in the wider world of cognitive psychology, that cognitive developmental research and theory in the fields of religious development has come to a profounder maturity itself in the works of James Fowler (1976a, 1978, 1980a, 1981, 1984a, 1987a) and Fritz Oser (1980, 1985; Oser and Gmünder 1984; Bucher and Oser 1987b). In Fowler's and Oser's work, we find the first fully systematic and comprehensive outworking of a stage theory of religious development extending across the entire life span, based on Piaget's genetic epistemology and comparable in stature to Kohlberg's moral development theory. Grounded in mature theological reflection and considerable empirical research, and claiming potential universality of reference, the theories of religious development advocated by Fowler and Oser represent a qualitatively new stage — though doubtless not the final one — in religious developmental research itself. (It is not the intention here to summarize Fowler's and Oser's theories, since the most recent refinements of their thought are available elsewhere in the collection.)

While Fowler's theory has attracted wide-ranging interest in the United States and beyond and has spawned a well-established secondary research literature (e.g., Mischey 1976; Shulik 1979; Chirban 1980; Parks 1980), it is only very recently that Oser's work is becoming known outside his native Switzerland and neighboring European countries. This state of affairs is reflected in the British scene, where Fowler's work has attracted some interest from researchers and religious educators but Oser's name is barely known.

Marion Smith has probably done more than anyone else to bring Fowler to the attention of British debate and to popularize the results of his work (M. E. Smith 1983, 1986a, 1986b, 1986c). Smith is broadly sympathetic, though not uncritically so, toward Fowler's work. In elaborating Fowler's theory, she relates it to his own personal faith journey, emphasizing the theological and pastoral commitments that undergird it and its provisional and unfinished status. At the same time, Smith locates the theory within the context of social scientific theories of development, though she remains perplexed, along with other writers, by the way in which Fowler's writings fail to conform to the customary categories of social scientific research and theory. Smith's verdict is cautiously affirmative, but it is clear that she would like more attention to be given to the empirical base of the theory and to the relationships between the various theoretical strands that underpin it. "It is unfortunate that he [Fowler] has written so many 'popular' versions: his account is still tentative and provisional, and not, as some may suppose, the end-product of an investigation in which the details have been confirmed after informed and thorough scrutiny" (1983, 225). Similarly, Webster (1984) finds Fowler's writings attractive but raises doubts about the experimental design and methodology of the research, the relationship between the theoretical aspects of Fowler's work, and the relationship between religious belief and faith as Fowler construes it. (M. E. Smith, however, challenges Webster's account and counters many of his charges [1986c].)

More fundamental doubts are expressed by Heywood (1986) concerning the Piagetian paradigm upon which Fowler's approach rests. Heywood argues that Piaget's genetic epistemology is fundamentally antithetical to some of Fowler's central concerns, especially his concern to widen the Piagetian focus on "the logic of rational certainty" to a more inclusive "logic of conviction," since, according to Heywood, Piaget's description of the process of development "rules out entirely the existence of an underlying 'logic of conviction'" (p. 76). This sets up a fundamental contradiction at the heart of Fowler's theory, since, "in order to broaden Piaget's theory into a theory of faith, Fowler must bypass its structuralist assumptions," while at the same time drawing on them to elaborate his own theory of stages (ibid.).

Although there has been some fruitful discussion of Fowler's theory in the United Kingdom, there is very little related empirical research to date. The only British studies located by this author are a study of religious and moral thinking by Kalam (1981) and a small-scale exploration into symbolic functioning by M. E. Smith and Miller (1984). Whether even Kalam's work properly counts as "British" is doubtful, since it is based on a sample of Christian, Hindu, and Muslim South Indians. Kalam used indianized versions of Kohlberg's moral dilemmas and an adaptation of Fowler's interview schedule and compared subjects' scores on each measure in order to examine the relationship between moral and religious thinking over the life span and to test Kohlberg's and Fowler's conflicting hypotheses about this relationship. (While Kohlberg suggests that moral development is both logically and chronologically prior to faith development, Fowler holds the reverse to be the case.) Kalam's findings are somewhat perplexing and too complex to be discussed here. His main finding, however, was that there were significant discrepancies between the stages of moral judgment achieved by half his subjects and their corresponding stages of faith development. Kalam concludes that the evidence supports neither Kohlberg's nor Fowler's hypothesis about the primacy of moral or faith developmental stages. Indeed, Kalam is skeptical about the whole idea of stages and sequence in moral and religious thinking, as the title of his thesis indicates: "The Myth of Stages and Sequence in Moral and Religious Development."

The study by Smith and Miller (1984) is a much smaller, but nonetheless important, pilot study of symbolic functioning in faith development; it examines the understanding of the ritual action of Christian confirmation held by a group of fourteen adults, comprising Anglican priests and theology undergraduates. The study does not attempt to test Fowler's theory concerning symbolic development in any formal sense so much as to probe an area of the theory that has received scant empirical attention. Some interesting interview data are presented and the authors cautiously postulate a threefold distinction between increasingly complex and integrated forms of symbolic thinking, which, it is suggested, may represent a developmental pattern in the symbolic realm of faith development. The results are seen as supportive of Fowler's theory, in a very broad sense, but as requiring fuller examination and testing.

Summary and Discussion of Research Findings

It is not easy to summarize the results of the research literature surveyed above, still less to assess the significance of the findings. In general terms, studies are agreed concerning basic features of religious thinking development, but there are significant discrepancies between diverse findings, and such discrepancies can only be resolved by detailed analysis of the individual studies concerned, which is clearly impossible in a review of this nature. The intention of the final part of this paper must be limited to a summary, in the broadest terms, of the major agreed findings of the cognitive developmental tradition, and the identification of a number of critical issues which are considered central to an evaluation of the achievement of the tradition.

Studies are broadly agreed that religious thinking is essentially developmental in nature, in the sense that it is dependent on the acquisition and development of basic cognitive capacities and that, in accordance with general principles of psychological development, it develops in an orderly, sequential, and predictable pattern or series of age-related changes. There is also a wide measure of consensus regarding the basic pattern of religious thinking development. In conformity with the Piagetian account of cognitive development, religious thinking is held to proceed from an intuitive, undifferentiated structure of thought to thinking that engages wholly within the boundaries of concrete realities, to a final emergence of abstract, reversible, and fully logical thinking capacities. The process is marked by an increasing drive toward autonomy, differentiation, integration, and universality of judgment and thought. The majority of studies envisage the process of development in terms of a series of qualitatively distinct, sequentially invariant, structurally defined stages, although some studies have not supported such a stage model. Early studies identify three main stages in childhood and adolescence, corresponding broadly to Piaget's preoperational, concrete operational, and formal operational stages. Fowler and Oser have extended both the range and scope of the stages in their respective six-stage theories extending across the life span.

While the cognitive developmental tradition focuses attention on the structuring power of cognition in shaping the development of religious judgment and faith perspective, studies have not totally ignored the operation of other factors in the developmental process. A number of studies stress the influence of secondary variables on religious thinking development, such as attitude toward religion, religious affiliation and teaching, linguistic facility, and so on. However, there is little agreement concerning the precise role played by these variables, nor is there much clarity concerning their relationship to cognitive development.

Whatever the precise details of the developmental process, it is widely held that the broad pattern of development detected by research imposes strict limitations on the capacity for religious understanding at any given period of development. Throughout the life span, growth in religious judgment and faith perspective is necessarily defined by the limits of the existing cognitive structures available to the individual. Ideas and concepts can only be grasped, patterns of thinking and perception can only become possible, when the requisite cognitive structures have been formed and there is a corresponding cognitive "readiness" to learn. This thesis has had far-reaching implications for educational and pastoral theory and practice and has led to radical revisions of traditional aims and approaches in these fields, and the development of alternative "developmental" programs of religious education, nurture, and pastoral ministry.

In the light of the authoritative claims made by the cognitive developmental tradition to offer a universal theory of religious development, and the profound impact of this theory on policy and praxis in a variety of contexts, the task of critical analysis and assessment of the tradition's claims is an urgent one. It is also a highly complex and multifaceted one, as ongoing critical debate testifies. In the welter of critical literature, however, a number of fundamental issues may be identified around which debate has centered and upon which the validity and significance of religious developmental stage theory ultimately rest.

First, the models of religious thinking, judgment, or faith which underpin the research studies and developmental theories have been subjected to considerable scrutiny. Critics have drawn attention to the selective nature and restrictive scope of definitions of religious thinking that are formulated largely in terms of Piagetian levels of logic applied to religious material and to a certain "theological imperialism" inherent in models that are formulated exclusively in biblical and Christian terms (e.g., Godin 1968; Langdon 1969; Francis 1979; Rowe 1981; Priestley 1981; Slee 1986a). It is argued that such models fail to take into account the interpretative, attitudinal, symbolic, linguistic, and narrative dimensions of religious thinking. Fowler's attempts to widen the narrowly logical focus of earlier studies to a more inclusive "logic of conviction" which takes into account the richer interplay between affective and cognitive factors is certainly to be welcomed, but critics have not been slow to find problems in this attempt (for a comprehensive survey of the critical literature on Fowler's theory, see Parks's chapter in this volume).

Second, the empirical basis of the stage theories proposed by the cognitive developmental tradition has been subjected to rigorous critique. Critics have drawn attention to recurrent methodological weaknesses in a good deal of the research (e.g., Murphy 1977b; Riccards 1978). Samples have often been small and highly selective, and methods of data collection and analysis employed have too often been subjective and idiosyncratic. Major weaknesses have been detected in both Goldman's and Peatling's research design (see Slee 1986a, 1986b; Greer 1983), and these weaknesses have been perpetuated in many subsequent studies. Considerable doubts and perplexities concerning the empirical basis of Fowler's theory continue to be expressed (e.g., Webster 1984; Heywood 1986). In particular, the empirical basis of the stages themselves requires most careful examination. In early studies, the construct of "stages" is used rather loosely and frequently lacks genuine empirical foundation or theoretical significance (see Murphy 1977b). Goldman's and Peatling's claims to establish stages of development rest on surprisingly thin empirical grounds (see Greer 1983; McGrady 1983). Certainly, in Fowler's and Oser's work the construct of stages takes on a much richer and more rigorous status and significance. Nevertheless, critical questions concerning the status of stages in their work, the criteria employed for scoring stages, the reliability of scoring procedures, and the correlation between stages proposed in their respective theories remain, at present, unresolved (for a critical discussion of these issues concerning the stage construct, see Power's chapter in this volume).

Finally, the Piagetian basis of religious developmental research and theory itself has been the focus of intense critical debate. The viability and applicability of such a paradigm in religious developmental research are clearly a foundational issue for the tradition and strike at the heart of its self-identity. Critics have drawn attention to the limitations as well as the insights provided by the Genevan paradigm and to the uncritical way in which Piaget's theory has been utilized by religious thinking research (e.g., Roy 1979; Rowe 1981; Moran 1983; Heywood 1986; Slee 1986a; Schweitzer). The Piagetian model of logical, abstract thought as the ideal of human development; the linear, sequential, and hierarchical model of stage development he advocates; and the presuppositions of the Genevan clinical interview method have each been seen as imposing severe limitations on religious developmental research. Surprisingly, there has been very little justification at all of the adoption of a Piagetian paradigm in research, and the Piagetian basis of many studies lacks coherence and adequate development.

Conclusion

The development of the cognitive developmental tradition itself within the psychology of religion is a fascinating story, and one that we have sketched out only in the broadest terms. The tradition has come a long way since its infancy in the late nineteenth century, not without many growing pains and some developmental regression along the way, but perhaps it is not entirely fanciful to detect a movement within the tradition toward an increasing complexity, flexibility, comprehensiveness, and integration of theory and research in recent work. What the next stage of development (stage six?) will look like is a matter for speculation, but it is the conviction of the present writer that progress toward that stage will be inhibited unless the tradition is prepared to engage actively with the body of critique that has grown up alongside it, to assimilate its insights, and to adapt and transform its own structures of thought and activity accordingly.

Part 4

Alternative Perspectives on Religious Development and Spiritual Growth

8

Alternative Developmental Images

GABRIEL MORAN

I WISH TO ADDRESS the issue of religious development in the most comprehensive way possible. I presume that I am invited to do this by the title given to me: "Alternative Developmental Images for the Individual Religious Story." The word "individual" in the title may have been intended as limiting the ground to be covered, but I interpret the title to mean that the individual should be placed at the center of the total context of religious development. It is the imagery of the context that most interests me.

I think that what I have to offer is not in direct conflict with either J. Fowler or F. Oser. I make no attempt to posit stages of religious or faith development. Nevertheless, I would hope that my presentation raises some questions about the descriptions of Fowler and Oser, particularly about the imagery that is assumed in discussions about development. I have four main points: (1) the history and present meaning of development, (2) the meaning of religious in the context of development, (3) the imagery of development, especially in the relation of human and nonhuman, and (4) some implications for education.

Development

Development itself is a fascinating and mysterious idea that is not often explored. Because it is one of those words that organizes the modern world, one cannot easily dislodge this idea and bring it consciously before the mind. Some day someone may be able to write a work entitled "The Development of Development." I do not think such a project is possible today, but we can try to unearth the way in which this word operates in daily conversation and in a multitude of academic disciplines.

I am interested in the *meaning* of development. Following Wittgenstein here, I am interested in how the term is used in the modern world. My interest is meaning and not definition. An individual can simply make a definition, that is, set limits to a word's meaning. But if one is going to discover a wider and deeper meaning of a term, one has to listen. The meaning of a term will probably be variegated. Except for artificially constructed jargon, no answer will be *the* answer to the question of meaning. But as Wittgenstein notes, we do correct children; that is, in patterns of speech, all answers are not equal. Some answers are more richly textured than others; some answers can simply be called wrong.

After much listening, I would like to offer the following description of development. Development means that there is direction but not a point of termination; there is improvement but never a finished state; there are ends within human activity but no end external to human activity. Like its close relatives, evolution and progress, development arose from a combination of three sources: modern scientific data, the need to believe that the power controlling human life is benign, and the assumption that Christianity is an anachronism beyond reform. Christians who are skeptical of development (evolution, progress) have good reason for being so. Development is in large part a religious term, and it can easily slip into being a competitor to or a substitute for Christianity.

Development is the modern world's alternative to providence, predestination, and heaven. At least, it is the alternative to what is assumed to be the self-seeking and narrow constraints of Christian piety. Modern people who dismiss the idea of heaven as childish still have to believe that their lives are going somewhere. Theories of development are a fervent belief, backed by scientific data, that human life will get better if we do our part by clearing away the obstacles to continued growth. The potential is there from the start; we have to "get it out of the envelope" and let it blossom.

Development is unavoidably a moral term; that is, developmental theories presume that the movement is from good to better, or at least from bad to less worse. The phrase "moral development" should therefore be a redundancy. Kohlberg's theory, I note in passing, is not one of moral development; it is a theory of the development of moral reasoning or a theory of reasoning about moral dilemmas. In addition to development implying moral meaning, I would offer a more debatable proposition, namely, that all theories of development are at least implicitly religious. The term "religious," which I explore in my second point, has less unanimity of meaning than does the word "moral."

The idea that development is a movement without end point may not be immediately evident, and in fact development is always threatened with closure. As traditional religions could have warned, something keeps popping up as the end point. The overall movement becomes obscured or taken for granted, and then one line of development gets equated with development itself. Piaget's endless dialectic of assimilation and accommodation gets lost in textbook accounts that are interested in the child's capacity to reason properly. Piaget, toward the end of *The Moral Judgment of the Child* (Piaget 1962), acknowledges that there is a "beyond justice" where his language cannot go. Kohlberg seems to disregard that warning, and he extends Piaget to an end point for moral reasoning. Religion, I will suggest, is needed in developmental theories for the purpose of deidolization.

In contemporary discussions, there are two groups who use the term development with an assurance born of the presumption that they invented the idea: economists and psychologists. Psychologists assume that economists have taken over *their* word and extended its meaning for the comparison of national economies. Economists consider psychologists as having come rather late on the scene.

If one had to choose between the importance of psychology and economics for discussing religious development, it is not clear to me that psychology should take precedence. Actually, that question does not have to be decided, because the economic and psychological uses are not so totally dichotomous as one might assume. The idea of development, I have suggested, is born of the eighteenth- and nineteenth-century modernization process: Life can be better right here on earth. Psychologists and economists are two of the prominent twentieth-century offspring who have appropriated this language, but bits and pieces of the language are in most everybody's vocabulary and imagination.

Everybody seems to be in favor of development. Is there a flaw, however, in the assumption that everybody can develop to his or her fullest potential, that every nation can become rich and powerful, that life can get better and better for everyone? Perhaps there is no logical contradiction in that vision, but history seems not to have gone that route. Before saying that efforts must be redoubled, those who think themselves the more developed have to examine the assumptions built into their idea of development.

The modern idea of development began as a protest against a closed world, against the assumption that there is a finite set of resources and goods which society has. For the individual, life had been closed, because an all-knowing God foresees the path that freedom must take to arrive at its proper end. Over a period of several centuries this picture changed. Genuine novelty was possible; the supply of goods could be increased; history was now open. One of the worst things you can say to a modern person is "You have a closed mind." But is the only alternative "an open mind"? Development as a protest against eternally fixed limits still has to address the question of limits. If development is a movement that has direction without an end point, how does one describe the direction?

In economic terms, the opening up of history translated into an increase of wealth. Economies develop as they increase their goods and services, as they provide a higher standard of living, as they free people from the limitations imposed by individual, family, and natural place. Eighteenth-century moralists believed that a divine plan, or at least human compassion, was needed lest individual selfishness take over the process of development. But the nineteenth-century utilitarians were confident that there would be enough goods for everyone. If national economies keep growing, then development means happiness for all. Although there have been voices of warning about the ecological danger of this image, we still live under the direction of this imagery: to develop means to rise higher and to grow bigger.

At the personal level, the image of growth worked its way into all our thinking about development. The two words, growth and development, are often used interchangeably. When "human development" was really a term for child development, the close association of the two words was more understandable. But growth as a way to describe the whole of human life is a questionable image. Growth in the organic world is healthy only when it is decelerative, that is, when it moves toward a stable interchange of organism and environment. The psychological may seem not to have this limitation, which is why the idea of development has been congenial to an area called cognitive. The mind can grow endlessly in its comprehension.

The Religious

During the last thirty years, at least in the United States, a remarkable new alliance has been forged between "growth psychology" and an area called "spirituality." The best-seller list is dotted with books that have a psychological version of religion or a psychology "open" to the spiritual. The U.S. book which may be the number one seller of this decade is *The Road Less Traveled*, by M. Scott Peck. It is a book whose message is "spiritual growth." The author criticizes people for whom "wealth or power have become . . . ends in themselves rather than means to a spiritual goal. The only true end of love is spiritual growth or human evolution." This author is confident that he has found the answer. Although I certainly am not in favor of "spiritual contraction," I think his end of spiritual growth is a dangerous illusion.

The emergence of this literature suggests that development cannot avoid a religious question. A popular U.S. book on adult development has been Gail Sheehy's *Passages*. The author's attitude to religion in that book is distinctly negative; religion inhibits people from growth and openness. Not surprisingly, however, Sheehy's follow-up book, *Pathfinders*, begins with a long discussion of "spiritual well-being." An increase of power, money, and material possession has not brought happiness. Where to turn? Above and beyond to spiritual growth. This new goal sometimes has a vague connection to the historic religious traditions; overall it takes a disparaging attitude, especially to the limitations of Judaism and Christianity.

In saying that development was from the beginning a religious idea, I am not proposing some very general definition of religion (symbol system, *Weltanschauung*) and then claiming that everybody is religious whether they want to be or not. I am proceeding along a different course. I assume that the word "religious" connotes a particular way of living, especially protest and resistance in the name of something so great as to be beyond our power to control by naming. Development is a protest for humanity against the closure of an end point, and to that extent development is a religious impulse. This impulse can generate either a dangerous religion or a helpful reform of existing religion.

The liberating or emancipatory principle of development is at least a stepchild if not a direct descendant of Jewish and Christian history. Contemporary theorists are often unaware that the protest against an end point is found throughout Jewish and Christian history, especially on the mystical side. Development can be a competitor to Christianity, or it can be a partner in dialogue. Within true dialogue, elements of one's own position may have to be qualified to hear the other's position. Christian educators, for example, cannot easily take over developmental theories and use them as a means to a Christian goal. Development is a protest against the claim that there is a goal, at least in the sense of point, state, or possession. In the other direction, I have criticized the absorption of Christianity into theories for which "spiritual growth" is the goal. Such a new religion is not only unhealthy for Christianity, it is also a dangerous and illusory form of religion. This meaning of development downgrades the ordinary, material world and promises salvation to an elite who have the advantages to be able to pursue such a goal.

One way to pose the question of traditional religion and the modern idea of development is to ask whether development and conversion are compatible? James Fowler asks this question, particularly in his book *Becoming Adult, Becoming Christian*. Perhaps responding to his critics on the right, Fowler asserts that the Christian vocation "requires not only development but also *conversion*. . . . Conversion, then, is not so much a negation of our human development as it is a transformation and fulfillment of it" (Fowler 1984a, 140–41). I certainly agree that conversion is not a "negation" of human development, but I am not clear how Fowler adds the two together.

The answer I propose to the relation of the modern idea of development and the religious idea of conversion is that not only are they compatible but that they need one another. Separated from each other both ideas are dangerous. Unless the idea of development contains within itself a conversionary movement, then development will self-destruct; it will bring in a limit point or it will exhaust itself in limitless growth. Development imagined as a straight line up and forward is insupportable in an individual life. Death is an obvious reminder of this fact even if death is not spoken about much in developmental theories. At the cosmic, or at least earthly level, development as conquest and growth has an appointment with disaster, the denial of reality by some current governments notwithstanding.

On its side, conversion needs to be conceived of as developmentally life-long. Otherwise, conversion tends to be a one-time entrance of God into human life. This vertical line running downward stops "human development" or relegates it to the bottom story of a two-story building. Buried in this imagery of conversion, imagery that conveys little of what the word's etymology suggests, is something still important for individuals and nations in our day to hear about power, failure, evil, and hope.

One way to put the question of religious development is to ask: Are the people who are the most developed (physically, psychologically, economically . . .) guaranteed to be the most religious? The conservative and liberal wings of the church would agree in answering no. From there, however, a big difference would appear. The Christian right would say that what is important is a change of heart, faith in Christ, salvation from God. The liberal wing might affirm the same phrases, but it would put its energies into preparing the ground for divine influence and into going as far as one can with human skill, knowledge, and effort. We have an age-old debate here, but the modern emphasis on development gives the question greater urgency and perhaps new clarity.

A recent book by Lucy Bregman, *Through the Landscape of Faith,* raises the question pointedly. She is critical of a reductionism which she illustrates with this passage from psychologist John McDargh "Our sense of ourselves as available for . . . 'loving self-donation' never proceeds from a deprivation or an inner emptiness, but rather from a taste of the satisfaction in sharing" (Bregman 1986, 93). Bregman associates this view, namely, that faith in God arises from early strength, with the work of Fowler; this emphasis, she says, is on *continuity* and is typical of Catholic tradition. In contrast, Bregman says that her own view is more "pessimistic," that it "focuses upon discontinuity between yearning and reality, between human incapacity and divine action, between childhood unfaith and Christ's identity as the source of all true faith. It depicts a flawed human order and a divine reversal of it" (Bregman 1986, 103).

Her contrast may be the standard one between Catholic and Protestant. (Interestingly, Fowler is criticized for being too Catholic.) Nonetheless, the imagery should be looked at carefully. For example, she offers as choice of models "horizontal," "vertical," and "spiral." I would agree with her that the third is the best of the three. I nonetheless am skeptical of how far a spiral can take us. A spiral movement does not resolve the question of continuity and discontinuity.

Where I do agree with Bregman is in her contention that we must be ready to give up our particular *constructions* of the past. "The death I die with Christ is a place where the schemata of my remembering are surrendered. . . . From this shadow existence, I must call it (the unconscious, hidden past) forth into life, if only to free it to die in its turn" (Bregman 1986, 96–97). This imagery casts suspicion on "constructions," any constructions. It allows that the poor, the lame, and the halt as well as the unschooled may be more religiously advanced than those who are trained in logic, science, and criticism. I hasten to add that allowance of such reality is not the same as saying that it always happens or usually happens. The point is not to abandon schooling in scientific thought. Rather, it is to ask how we can resist the strong tendency to turn Christian faith/religion into a superscience. The language of death/resurrection used above is, I think, one of the signs to consider.

Imagery

I come to the central question of my title: What are alternative images for development? I am glad that the word "image" was put in the plural, because I do not think that there is an alternative image (e.g., spiral) that is a solution. The plural term "images" at least offers me some ambiguity within which to move. The ultimate choice, I will propose, is not between image A and image B; it is between movement toward an imagined object and movement that has no imaginable object at the end. Of course, for freeing oneself from a single image, it may help to introduce a multiplicity of images. For example, contemporary feminists who object to praying always to a Father God have a valid point. In addressing God as mother, lover, or rock, we have not necessarily discovered better images, but they should remind us to relate all aspects of our life to God and not to identify God with any image, even the best.

Modern developmental and evolutionary theories took their inspiration from two different strands of Christianity that sometimes were blended together. One was the image of chain or ladder extending down from heaven. The other was a belief in the intelligibility of the material world, a belief that encouraged pushing ahead to discover solutions. A modern misreading of the chain of being saw the return to God as proceeding up the chain or ladder until God was found on the top rung. Sometimes Christianity did encourage such a climb above the material world, above the community of one's people, above one's own bodily self. As modern science took over the Christian trust in the intelligibility of the cosmos, it also absorbed the image of chain or ladder. Evolutionists tended to sling forward the chain, in part to avoid the question of moral superiority. Darwin actually avoided the word "evolution" and regularly reminded himself to avoid claiming a superiority for the latter part of the chain. Developmentalists in this century have been less bashful about the claim to go up, with the implicit or explicit claim that higher is better.

In trying to overcome the inadequacy of this ladder image, I suggest that there are three different approaches:

(1) *A Multiplying of Images.* Is development a horizontal line, a vertical line, or a spiral? My answer is: all three. Neither the first nor the second will ever be eliminated, even if the third is more adequate (or less inadequate). Sometimes life is experienced as a climb upward, sometimes as a push forward, sometimes as a cycling back or a spiraling down. None of these is simply wrong, but none of them taken alone will do.

(2) *Three-Dimensional Imagery.* In trying to get a more adequate imagery for human development, the important choice is between two and three dimensions. A choice between straight line and circle is not much of a choice; both are linear images. A choice between line and sphere provides richer possibilities. A sphere includes dozens of linear movements, but it is not reducible to any one nor to the sum of them. The image of spiral is perhaps an attempt to get a three-dimensional image; if so, that fact has to be insisted upon because the spiral slips back to being a linear figure with one complex movement.

(3) *The Multiplying of Senses.* Even the three-dimensional sphere is inadequate insofar as it is only a *visual* image. The phrase "visual image" may be a redundancy because the English "image" is heavily weighted toward the visual. If there is any imagined object above, below, in front of, behind, then the process of development is threatened with closure. The human being ought not to be subjugated to any object that is imaginable. Every idol must be smashed if the human being is to be free. Therefore, the most radical answer to the question of an alternative image is: no image at all.

Human beings cannot give up imagining even if we wished to do so, and I am not proposing that we should try. The question of "expression" of "representation" is always with us. The way to counter our tendency to submit to any (visual) image is to introduce complementary sensual experience. As a vertical line is not wrong—just dangerous when used alone—so (visual) images are not wrong, just in need of the auditory and tactile.

We all assume some image of "what reality is like." Perhaps the most common choice in modern times has been between organic and mechanical imagery. Is the world like a big tree with myself as a growing branch? Or is the world like a clock and I am a metal spring? Many people today are switching back to the organic model. Nonetheless, both images tend to function as objects that are a backdrop for understanding the human being. The idea of development is a protest against the restriction of all objects, a plea to "open" reality beyond the best of objects. Several different strands of twentieth-century thought represent attempts to grapple with this issue. Some of these strands are deeply rooted in Jewish-Christian history, others are at least compatible with that history.

Developmental and evolutionary theories imply a world not of isolated objects but of mutual relations. Everything is related to everything else to such an extent that there really aren't things so much as *relata*, poles within relations. The modern sciences, whether physical, biological, or historical, go in this direction. That strand should not have been news to Jewish and Christian religions; at least the idea should not be entirely foreign. The fundamentalist attack on evolution is ironic considering the organized and related flow of things from the creator in the first chapters of Genesis.

The human mind cannot place a picture before itself that "represents the interrelation of all in all." Some pictures are more adequate (less inadequate) than others. To even the best of pictures, the religious attitude is: that's not it. In fulfilling the vocation of protest, one of the main powers of religion is listening. The sense of hearing moves in a very different way from seeing. Seeing "objectifies" at a distance; hearing is oriented to silence, listening, response, cooperation; one moves closer to hear. How could Christians forget that the human being is a hearer of words? "In principio erat sermo," was Erasmus's translation of the first sentence of the Fourth Gospel—not an isolated word but a flow of speech. In the sixteenth century, Erasmus and Luther agreed on one thing, namely, the importance of the spoken word. They could not foresee the onrushing power of the printed text in shaping our idea of knowledge as "taking a look." But in the twentieth century, we are being forced to rediscover the sense of hearing. Human development, rather than a movement toward anything, is the movement of a conversation.

On the importance of images and metaphors for development, let me try one example of a current debate. I think this debate might throw some light on the stages of Fowler and Oser. The debate—which is intense in the United States and, I presume, in many countries today—concerns the environment. I refer not to a debate between industrialists and environmentalists but to a debate within the ecological movement itself. To outsiders, ecologists may all look alike (as Christians do to Jews or Westerners to Easterners). But there is one wing of the movement which stresses "animal rights" and tries to get other animals equality with human beings. What is attacked is the human claim to superiority that leads to the slaughter of other animals. There is another wing that is far more interested in questions of balance. Is it all right to hunt deer? The answer here is that the herd has to be thinned for the sake of the fauna. The human being has been a hunter for thousands of years; animals kill other animals; that's the way nature is (Regan 1983; Stone 1972). What unites these two parties is their opposition to "anthropocentrism," a belief in human superiority that is the result of Christianity.

The ecological movement can truly be called a religious movement; in fact, there is probably no stronger religious impulse in our time. In fighting the *hubris* of "man putting nature to the rack and demanding answers" (Bacon), ecology is genuinely religious. Development has to be both human and nonhuman; it is not enough to move between cognitive and ego or between individual and social. The human animals have to move with all their fellow travelers on earth and with the earth itself.

While I would grant that ecology has the right issue for our time, I think the argument is badly flawed. Most speeches on ecology that I hear are like church sermons delivered with the passion of the true believer who cannot understand why everyone else is not equally convinced. But, as I have indicated, there are bitter disagreements within the movement. I would suggest that the bitter dispute arises because of the one thing they agree upon, namely, that "anthropocentrism" is the enemy. The worst of all problems is one in which the name of the cure is given to the disease. The problem we have is that the isolated, rationalistic, oppressive man conceives himself to be at the *top* of the world (as vicar of God or substitute for God). It is absurd to call this picture anthropo-*centrism*. In fact, the alternative to the oppressive man on top is to place men and women at the center, where they can engage in conversation with each other and listen to all the nonhumans. I might note in passing here that I am amazed at the willingness of Christian writers to accept the metaphor of "making meaning." The alternative to a passive acceptance of meaning from on high is not necessarily the "making" of meaning. If men and women are at the center of creation, the alternative is listening, responding, and cooperating in meaning.

In a famous essay twenty years ago, Lynn White wrote that Christianity is in large part responsible for our ecological problems and that the answer will also be in large part found there. Few in ecology disagree with the first half of White's thesis, just as few follow him in the second part. Instead, the solution is sought in the modern ideal of "egalitarianism," the ideology that there is no superiority even when it comes to species. Such a principle seems to me to fly in the face of reality. I doubt that the principle can be seriously and consistently applied. What is missing is the paradox in Judaism and Christianity where strength arises from weakness. The human beings are called to be superior through care, receptivity, and love; the humans have no right to lord it over others because we are all united in kinship; the humans must be ready to listen for the truth wherever it may be found. Only with that kind of anthropocentrism is there hope for the earth and all of its inhabitants.

I think that in any developmental theory a relation between human and nonhuman is there from the start. Usually, however, the nature of this relation becomes apparent only at the farther reaches of the developmental theory. If the human and nonhuman develop together (with negotiated settlement of conflicts as part of the story), then the latter stages of development will show a rich unity of differences. If the language of the theory is not relational (between sexes and between species), then the last step of the theory may lead to a disappearance of the person. For example, in Kohlberg's theory, the individual (male) rises higher and higher to a sixth stage, but when Kohlberg speculates on a seventh stage, the individual totally disappears. What was going up the ladder was not a person related to personal and nonpersonal lives, but a separated mind which, having achieved the principle of equality, is now dispensable (Kohlberg 1981a).

I would not wish to make a judgment on Oser or Fowler, but I think it is worth discussing whether the language that each of them chooses can carry the weight of their projects. Specifically, what of the latter stages in each theory? Are Fowler's last two stages perhaps two parts of a whole, so that an individual must go deeper into the center of paradox rather than go beyond it? Does the last stage that Oser describes have enough of a sense of paradox? What is the relation of personal and nonpersonal (not just individual and social) in each scheme. I am not asking what is the "normative end point." I am asking what kind of language is needed to avoid any normative end point. The direction of development, I am asserting, is toward greater and greater communion between human and nonhuman. The least inadequate image of development is a spherical movement of men, women, children, and nonhumans. Personal development is a permanent contribution to the richness of the unity, and in Christian terms the Christ figure is the center of all.

Educational Implications

I can suggest here only a few implications to be worked out educationally. Most important, however, is that this idea of development helps to clarify the meaning of education itself. In the United States we put enormous trust in the schooling of the young; then periodically we have a rebellion against our misplaced hopes. The cry goes up: why do we need schools at all; education is life. Developmental theory which has a definite direction but not an end point offers a way out of this fruitless debate. Is education a preparation for life, or is education life itself? It is neither. Education is the reshaping of life's forms with end (meaning, design) and without end (termination, conclusion). It would take many pages to lay out a position on what are the main forms of life (e.g., family, work) and how to reshape them. But at least the process can be seen to be very directive (toward ends) while always in response to what is given (it is reshaping not shaping). Obviously, the process is lifelong; the phrase "lifelong education" should be redundant. Within that process, the schooling of the young is indispensable and more important than ever.

Helping the child to think, to analyze, to abstract, to deduce, etc. is an important part of psychological, moral, or religious development. There comes a time, wrote C. S. Lewis, when the child who has delighted in Homer's stories must settle down to learning Greek grammar. But neither the child nor adult can lose sight of that larger context which the grammar book serves.

For development, there are "privileged cases" educationally. Human activities that engage the person in serious effort but have no final point of termination are likely to contribute to a (religious) development; thus, for example, the importance of play in human life. Piaget tends to disparage play beyond a young age, but play is important throughout adult life. In games and sports one tests the limits of one's abilities in relation to the surrounding environment; one learns about life and death. The individual players come and go while the game is without end. No matter how great the sports hero, he or she eventually discovers the fragile finitude of knees, arms, and lungs. But when individuals retire from center stage, they need not retire from playing. Everyone can have a part, including that of intelligent spectator, which is an indispensable part of most sports. The appreciative fan draws out the best in the players who are at center stage.

In trying to measure a child's development in thinking, the context of play should not be neglected. Piaget was attentive to play in children's lives but may have neglected elements of play in his interviews. Margaret Donaldson, for example, got different answers from children when the Piagetian questions were asked by a panda instead of a person or when the questions placed the child into a child's drama (Donaldson 1978). Robin Maas's criticism of Ronald Goldman's questions is similarly revealing. The children may have understood the biblical text better than did Goldman because they had a sense of story and composition (Maas 1986).

Given what I have said about the movement of development, I would not be surprised if very young children had profound religious understanding. I team-teach a course on death with a woman whose work is to counsel dying children or children whose parents have just died. She recently completed her dissertation based on interviews with 3-to-5-year-old children. The picture she draws is very different from the best known study of children's developmental thinking on death. In Maria Nagy's study, the children are assumed to develop in a straight line regarding their thinking on death. Her rationalistic assumptions blind her to the possibility that young children may be saying something about death that adults should listen to (Nagy 1948). I am not being romantic about childhood, just emphasizing that adults have to rediscover some of the mystery, play, and vulnerability that come easily with childhood.

Implied in that movement of recovery is an intermediary stage in which children or young people become less religious (although I grant the logic of Oser saying that such development can be "progress" in a theory of religious judgment). They grasp for solutions to problems, which is not a bad thing. They need encouragement, discipline, and instruction to help them in the search. At the age of young adulthood one may not and perhaps should not accept the refrain of Beckett's *Endgame:* "You're on earth and there's no cure for that."

The dreams of youth are often too narrow, but older adults do not help by just saying that. Perhaps the most that the older generation can do is to keep alive alternative interpretations. That is, no one gives up their ideology by having it argued out of their grasp. By ideology I mean a set of ideas that are opposed to development because they provide a final explanation and closure. People let go of their ideological grasp when they come to realize that their system explains much but not all. There may be truth in alternative explanations that they have passionately denounced.

My main educational plea is for intergenerational conversation of every kind. Parents have something to teach their children and children have things to teach their parents. Eighty-year-olds can teach the art of dying to 6-year-olds; the 6-year-old may have something to teach in return. The death of a domestic animal can be a painful moment of development in the life of a child. The genuine sense of loss in the child's life deserves a better response than: "Forget it, we'll get you another puppy tomorrow." The total environment of the child—physical, living, personal—provides the communion in which his or her religious life develops. Children can transcend terrible experiences, although one must emphasize it is the response to suffering, not suffering, that contributes to progress. What makes such response possible is beyond any individual's grasp, but that is no excuse for our not doing all we can to provide positive surroundings.

The main religious implication for those of us who are older is twofold: no matter how underdeveloped one may be, there is always time; no matter how developed you think you are, failure is still possible. If one imagines development as a straight line up or forward, then ground gained is an individual and permanent conquest. It seems to me that Christianity and every other major religion oppose this assumption. One's life as a whole is at issue throughout all of one's life. That could be terrifying because no ground is securely possessed. However, not being in control of everything, we don't have to bear the burden of constructing the whole world. We just have to sit ourselves at the center of creation, listen attentively, and then respond the best we can. When we come to die, we do not have to change our position radically, except perhaps to lie down rather than sit. Many theories of psychological development are like an elevator to the roof of a high-rise building; they keep secret the fact of being pushed off the roof when you get to the top. A theory of religious development is a circling about the unreachable center of our own lives and the lives of all creatures. What we call the end of life is immersion into some new form of being which is beyond our imagination but not beyond our hope.

9

Oser and Gmünder's Stage 3 of Religious Development and Its Social Context: A Vicious Circle

RAINER DÖBERT

MODELS OF RELIGIOUS DEVELOPMENT must be taken as contributions to the structuralist theorizing in the Piaget tradition. They aim at identifying structure, that is, systems of internalized actions or cognitive operations. In spite of this intention this chapter's line of argumentation must focus on functions and content heavily. The reasons for the choice of this strategy have to do with the fact that it is very difficult (if not impossible) to correlate the level of ontogenetic personal development and that of the societal context without recourse to functions and contents. One must, so to speak, go via contents, that is, via ready-made patterns of meaning which have to be "deciphered" by the individuals, and via need-dispositions (functions) to which meaning answers, in order to set up the connection with structural stages which is to be looked for. This is because one of the central tenets of the Piagetian paradigm holds that structures have to be built up by the individuals in a stepwise sequence and cannot simply be absorbed. In the beginning of a learning cycle a given tradition is just content, the internal structure of which has to be decoded if the respective patterns of meaning are to be taken as acquired.

If contents and functions can be taken for granted ontogenetic development and the social context can in principle be connected in such a way that individuals are confronted with certain action problems (functions) with which they cope religiously as long as the religious tradition is transmitted to them successfully and a-religious patterns of action and interpretation do not monopolize the consciousness of subjects. In this line of reasoning, the social context is taken as an amalgam of stimulating and inhibiting conditions of individual development, whose composition is to be clarified empirically.

In the course of this clarification one will certainly have to take into account the familiar question of tendencies toward secularization. In the structural development models these represent the independent variables, which negatively affect the religious development of the individual, conceived of as the dependent variable. Opposed to this unilinear model, it is proposed here that *the social conditions of development and the structures of one stage of religious development are intertwined in such a way that a vicious circle results: the thought patterns of the individual do not only reactively, but actively contribute to a process by which the relevance of religion for daily life is reduced to a minimum.* This happens on stage 3 of Oser and Gmünder's stage model. Its structures are such that opportunities and motives for religious growth are rare. This tendency is enhanced by social-structural factors and trends of societal value change. This gloomy picture results necessarily when one focuses exclusively on the structures of religious consciousness. It becomes brighter only when one takes also the functions of religiosity into account.

To support these hypotheses I shall introduce, first, some building blocks of structural theories in the hope that the reader will gain some feeling for their architecture and for the present state of the art. In the next step, Oser and Gmünder's stage model of religious development will be briefly depicted and, finally, a rearrangement of the theory will be offered in such a way that individual development can be related to the global social context.

Basic Theoretical Presuppositions and State of Knowledge in the Domain of Social-cognitive Development

Piaget had constructed a relatively rigorous model of cognitive development which, because of its effectiveness, was transposed to more and more variables (social cognition and role taking, moral development, ego development and religious development). Experiences gained in reconstructing the development of moral consciousness (Döbert 1986, 1987) suggest that theorizing becomes more and more misleading when it is not permanently controlled by the architecture of Piaget's theory. Function, experiences, elements, and operations are the building blocks which have to be put together. Knowing serves the function of constituting a representation of the world which allows us to cope with the environment through coordinated, reversible actions. The "pressure" for forming and maintaining this function is constant throughout the whole developmental sequence: this is what has to be accomplished all the time! In coping with our environment we gather experiences with the objects, that is, with the relatively constant elements of this environment. To coordinate these experiences we may be forced to construct new representations of objects or object-constancies of a higher order. In constructing these constancies/equilibria we use operations (structures) which enable us to compensate for transformations or to dismiss change as irrelevant. These structures operate "behind" the object-constancies and cannot be "read" from these directly. They represent Piaget's genuine discovery: the field of the cognitive (as opposed to Freud's affective) unconscious.

This cognitive unconscious has at least partly been decoded in the field of physical knowing. When we extend this analysis to deal with the study of social cognition, moral consciousness, ego-development and religion, however, we deal overwhelmingly with surface phenomena, not structure. I state this without any critical intent. Scientific as well as all other learning processes have to begin with the obvious and manifest—this is just the normal course of events.

To substantiate this diagnosis with respect to the present state of our theorizing, it may suffice to look briefly at Kohlberg's most recent attempt to specify the operational deep structure of moral thought (Kohlberg 1986). Kohlberg claimed that moral development—contrary to ego development or religious development, for instance—is based on the development of fully reversible, "hard" structures (Kohlberg 1981a and 1984). In view of such a claim, it becomes inevitable that one offer a reconstruction on the level of systems of operations proper. The operations proposed by Kohlberg are the following: sympathy, ideal role-taking, and universalization. I must confess that I am unable to recognize any analogues to the underlying, internalized operations focused on by Piaget in any of these processes. Sympathy is just another word for moral motivation. Role-taking is just the social counterpart to perception in the physical domain. Certainly, in any moral conflict, the problem must be perceived adequately, but the perception of the conflict is not an integral component of its solution—as are operations! Universalization may seem to be an acceptable candidate for the status of a genuine operation—at the first glance. But this supposition does not stand under closer inspection. A true or adequate moral judgment admittedly is universalizable. Nevertheless, it is just the result of our moral considerations, which may be structured by operations. The result of thought belongs to the level of surface phenomena, not to the level of deep-structural generation. The same holds for attributes of results like universality. If we want to identify operations, we must analyze the processes through which we get at universalizable statements, not simply look at these statements themselves!

In view of the fact that the level of generative principles has not been grasped in our theorizing, the question arises, what do theorists like Kohlberg focus for us in the study of development? The answer to this question seems to be: surface phenomena. Among these surface phenomena are series of stage specific objects, functional milestones, and functional losses, which will be dealt with in some detail in the following sections. These constructs are essential for understanding the mean state of religious consciousness, and they make it possible to bridge the gap between theorizing on the micro- and macro-level.

Object-constancy ranges among the earliest cognitive achievements of the child: an object vanishes from the visual field of the child, but is not annihilated by this "transformation." It can be brought back and has thus gained constancy with respect to a spatial transposition. The construction of object-constancy is not a unique process restricted to the earliest phases of development. Instead, object-constancies have to be constructed again and again in order to counteract new classes of "transformations" and gain equilibrium on higher levels. Flavell (1963) seems to have been among the first authors who have noticed that the construction of stage-specific objects may have been neglected a bit in the Piaget tradition because of Piaget's focus on groupings.

It will be useful to give some examples of series of stage-specific objects. To begin in the domain of moral development, let us take an act of sharing. A child shares some candies with another, because it wants to get something from the latter. The constant object in this case is the act of sharing, which will be produced and reproduced as long as the given constellation of interests prevails. Shifts of interest will be counteracted by the intervention of a new type of object, namely, the social norm of sharing. Sharing is stabilized. Norms in turn may be stabilized by universal values, an even more constant type of object. To illustrate the working of values, let us analyze briefly a typical series of decisions in an interview on moral development. One of Kohlberg's subjects (Joan in Kohlberg 1986) would, for instance, steal the drugs to save a human life in the Heinz dilemma. In the euthanasia dilemma she pleads for the right of the individual to end one's own life. Thus the constancy of the norm "Human life has to be preserved!" seems to fall apart. But the value of human dignity provides a higher level constancy, which allows Joan to "have" the respective norm (in Kegan's [1982] sense of reflectively and consciously owning a norm) and construct a legitimate exception: When a life in dignity cannot any longer be led, the individual should have the right to decide upon her/his own fate. "Life in dignity" is the new constant object that is upheld.

In a similar way, sequences of stage-specific motives and motivational constellations (impulses, goals of different ranges, character traits, etc. [Loevinger 1976]) and of other elements of the action space can be deciphered. This holds also, I would maintain, for conceptions of God. When a magical deity does not function, it may be nonexistent—at least weak and therefore irrelevant. A personified god may simply be in a bad mood and one may stick to him despite his temporary nonfunctionality. Finally, a transcendent god, whose will is unknowable, may even be held to do the best for me when my misery reaches its climax. This is true "ultrastability"! In all these cases we deal with series of stage-specific objects and not with operations. At the moment we do not know exactly on which infralogical operations (Piaget 1947) these objects are based. In our stage descriptions they function as the elements which are to be connected in our reasoning, and therefore as content, not structures. As elements, abstracted from their infralogical structure, they are the content of the developmental stages, not the underlying operations which link and order such elements.

It is also important to notice that the emergence of new objects may go hand in hand with the emergence of new functions or action problems. In cognitive development as analyzed by Piaget, this factor seems to be of less importance. But already in Loevinger's scheme of ego development it becomes prominent. Her model entails a dimension of "conscious preoccupations" which incorporate a variety of different functions. The self-protective ego is dominated by wishes (elements) and wants to control its environment in the relevant aspects (function). The conformist ego is oriented to external social norms (elements) and "conforms" in order to be socially accepted (function). When the integrated ego is confronted with its manifold and conflicting inner states and needs (elements), the problem may arise whether this heterogeneous complex of orientations can still be viewed as representing one and the same identity (function). Intuitively it should be obvious that in all these cases the emergence of new functions is directly tied to the emergence of the new object constancies—a fact that relativizes the current opposition between structural and functional paradigms considerably.

There are, it seems to me, good reasons to believe that we will find a similar state of affairs in religious development. "Redemption," for instance, cannot become the goal (function) of religious action unless the concept of a transcendent God has been constructed. The tenet that religion pertains to the constitution of meaning in life does not make sense unless it can be presupposed that individuals focus on their life as a whole, that is, construct it as a single object. Thus in this field of religion, the same type of pairing objects with functional milestones seems to occur.

Loevinger has thematized these functional milestones under the topic of "conscious preoccupations." This implies that we are not dealing with latent functions, but with manifest ones. Functional thought is, as I tried to show elsewhere (Döbert 1984), no peculiarity of science, but penetrates deeply into naïve religious consciousness. G. Nunner-Winkler and the author have asked 113 female and male adolescents in the age range from 14 to 21 years, among others, the following question "Religious people sometimes say that they find in religion something that they cannot find elsewhere. Do you have any idea what they may have in mind?" Even most of the a-religious subjects are able to specify some function—if only in the vaguest form of insisting on the functionality of religion as such "Religion is somehow necessary for the human life." More substantial answers deal with all sorts of contingency in the life cycle, ranging from concrete frustrations, death, backing of conventional morality to more diffuse psychological imbalances, commitment to overarching life goals, and the problem of meaning in life. Concrete help in situations of emergency is typical for the younger, the constitution of meaning in life for the older subjects. Evidences like these support the suppositions that there are functional milestones and that these are "conscious." This circumstance will facilitate the task of tying together ontogenetic development and social context, because in one respect the social system can be viewed as a huge mechanism of contingency reduction.

Finally, the emergence of new functions has a counterpart in the loss of old functions. The maintenance of identity, for instance, may require that one oppose one's social surrounding; that is, it can endanger social acceptability. At the least, development involves a certain tension. In the case of religious development this tension seems to come to a head in functional losses. The emergence of new conceptions of God may imply that certain functions cannot be fulfilled any longer. Max Weber has already emphasized that popular belief is very often dominated by outmoded forms of religiosity because the latter are better adapted to the imperatives of daily life. A magical deity can be "forced" to make rain. Once God has been "refined" to a transcendental condition of human freedom, it is impossible to expect the "ultimate" to send help against the drought. The new conception of God has implications for coping with the contingencies of the weather: a functional loss has occurred!

Summarizing, we should perhaps keep in mind that content in the form of constant objects (elements), functional milestones, and functional losses seems to play a significant role within the stage models of religious development. They are the tangible indicators of structural development, the operational deep structure of which we do not reach at our present stage of theoretical inquiry. It has to be emphasized that the topic of functional losses seems to be especially prominent in religious development and poses theoretically interesting problems. In the standard version of structural theories we presuppose that development takes place under the pressure of a constant function which is being fulfilled more and more adequately as development progresses. This is one of the reasons why development is motivated (competence motivation). This raises an important set of questions. Which developmental courses have to be expected when developmental progress is accompanied by functional losses? Is progress to be expected at all; are regressions not equally probable? One may suspect that a given state of religious consciousness can never be explained in terms of structural level alone, but must always encompass also some sort of net balance of functional milestones and functional losses. With this hypothesis we may end our theoretical considerations. In the next step we will try to find out the form in which Oser and Gmünder's stage model of religious development presents itself when we look at it through the glasses of the "functional structuralism" proposed above.

Functional References in Oser and Gmünder's
Stage Model of Religious Development

We have argued that the theory of moral development has—despite the combined and longlasting efforts of so many researchers—failed up to now to penetrate to the deep structures of operational thought. If this is not accepted, it is not surprising that the much younger theory of religious development should also focus on "development" via surface indicators like constant objects, functional milestones, and functional losses. In the following we will have to test whether this suggestion holds. To do that, a short summary of Oser and Gmünder's model is required.

As a starting point I will take that variant of their theory in which the strongest structuralist claims are put forward: a "religious mother-structure" is their topic (Oser and Gmünder 1984, 61ff.). This mother-structure is compared with the topological, algebraic, and ordering structures as depicted by Piaget (who follows Bourbaki). Oser and Gmünder explicitly refute the hypothesis that there is "only one cognitive basic structure, namely logic." Instead they want to demonstrate that there is an autonomous religious region, which defies all attempts at reduction to "logical, ontological, moral, social or cultural forms and particles" (Oser and Gmünder 1984, 62).

The religious mother-structure is conceived of as an operational structured whole in which the elements of "meaning constitution, hope, transcendence, freedom, timelessness," of trust, control, and of the "Holy" are interconnected (see Oser and Gmünder 1984, 66). It is noteworthy that the term "meaning constitution" is given a very strong reading: In it "the ultimate borders of thought" (Friedrich Schelling 1985), "absolute justification and meaning construction," and the "question of unity" are all at stake.

These elements of the religious realm are coordinated on each stage by "common attributes," which can be abstracted from the utterances of the interviewees. They are formal and represent thus the truly structural components of their model. Examples of these common attributes are orientation to absolute authority, conformity with rules, gratification–punishment thinking, moral reciprocity, *deus ex machina,* autonomy of god and human beings (Oser and Gmünder 1984, 76 ff.). It seems to me that the attributes refer to basic conceptions of God and human beings and to specific relationships between them. Their affinity with Loevinger's milestones and with the object-constancies depicted above seems difficult to be overlooked. Accordingly, they would represent—and now I shift to the terminology developed in the introduction—the genuine elements of the theory. Since new object-constancies and invariants of relationships are constructed on each developmental stage, these elements do indicate development. But they do not penetrate to the operational deep structures of thought. Claims of analogies with the Bourbaki structures are therefore a bit farfetched.

But how do we deal with those components, which Oser and Gmünder themselves call "elements"? I think that they incorporate overwhelmingly the functions for which we are searching. They pertain to what the coordination of elements has to accomplish, not to the elements themselves. Freedom of human beings has to be guaranteed in spite of God's almightiness; meaning and hope have to be generated; trust must be built up; control over the environment has to be gained—each time we are dealing with an action problem or "function" to be solved or fulfilled. Because Oser and Gmünder conceive of these functions as "elements" characteristic of the religious realm as such, they unite all these functions on each developmental stage under an overarching principle (common attribute, e.g., *deus ex machina*) in such a way that more and more stable equilibria result. This strategy is completely in line with the usual theorem, that functions remain constant, structures change. But if the functions listed by them should be seen to contain functional milestones, one cannot fail to miss certain important developmental steps.

To support this suggestion, let me shortly try to show that the problem of meaning constitution should be conceived of as a functional milestone. In the study previously mentioned, G. Nunner-Winkler and I asked our subjects whether they felt their life to be meaningful. Subject 106 gave the following answer to this question "All is fortuitous, but my life has meaning, nevertheless. The meaning arises from detecting and experiencing many beautiful things and from circumventing the evil." He is not a religious person but suspects that religion offers to other people some sort of support), and grants that he from time to time needs support, too. Where does he find it? Let me quote again "Yes, certainly I need this also. Well, support is conferred to my life, for instance, by a statement of account which shows a little bit on the credit side—this gives me a lot of support, because now I know that I can afford to do some things without damaging myself." Or let us take the utterances of subject 110. In his understanding, religion indeed deals with the meaning of life and this meaning is generated by commitment to a goal. Asked to specify his goal, he states, "Well, the goal in my life is that I feel everything to be right, and as a proletarian one would say: a lot of sexuality and drunkenness, I mean . . . at least you can't have these things in the hereafter." Of course, one can call all this "constitution of meaning," but certainly this type of meaning has little to do with "final justification," reference to the "totality of being," or "the ultimate borders of thought" as presupposed in Oser and Gmünder's concept of meaning generation. What

Oser and Gmünder have in mind is probably a functional milestone characteristic of the highest stage of religious development, and it is by this very fact much more interesting for a developmental theory than a stage-neutral dimension could ever be.

Whether Oser and Gmünder's stage model encompasses further functional milestones (God as protector of the moral order; see below) will, for reasons of space, be left open. "Functional losses" are our topic now. There are, it seems to me, clear-cut indicators for this phenomenon in their theory. We had supposed that the emergence of new conceptions of God may preclude certain types of interaction between believers and the Ultimate. Once the gap between immanence and transcendence has been opened up, it is extremely difficult — if not impossible — to expect help and support from God in situations of concrete emergency arising in daily life. In the same way, the "ultimate" loses the capacity and therefore the function of maintaining the social order by punishing deviant behavior. To illustrate, let me quote from Oser and Gmünder's "anchor example" of stage 3, on which immanence and transcendence are completely separated:

> When you postulate such a higher power ... then the first thing which comes to my mind is that there are no logical connections left in the sense — "You broke this rule, and therefore you get punished." On the level of the Ultimate, no evaluations take place. There are no more distinctions between good and evil. God does not punish or evaluate. (Oser and Gmünder 1984, 95)

Other evidence from Oser and Gmünder seems to hint in the same direction. It is a well-known claim that religiosity becomes more important toward the end of the life cycle (Bargel 1979). Now, the basic assumptions of structural theories imply that an intensified preoccupation with religion would instigate religious development. The opposite seems to be true: Oser and Gmünder's data show that a regression to stage 2 of religious thought is the more probable outcome. Naturally, they have some difficulty with this result and try to interpret it in terms of an "old-age-socialization effect" viewed as a variant of "learned helplessness" (Oser and Gmünder 1984, 197). The concept of "functional losses" suggests a more parsimonious explanation. God, interpreted as a "transcendental condition of my freedom," is of little help when one is confronted with death. The image of God as the "old man with the white beard" is in this respect much more functional, and that is why one regresses to the respective developmental stage. Evidences concerning fundamentalist patterns of religiosity (hell, devil, purgatory) can be interpreted analogously. They belong to the lower developmental stages and are not very prevalent — except the *belief in life after death* (Laeyenddecker-Thung 1984, 68). It can be suspected that in this case "functional pressure" seeks an outlet: one wants to hope! Sometimes this sort of compensation of functional losses becomes very tangible in the interviews. Subject 11, for instance, replied to the question, what might happen after death: "Hmmm, I hope that otherwise, that there is also a life. I mean not only 'Now dead and over!' One hears so much from people who came back [from death], but who knows whether it is 100 percent true. . . . [Interviewer: And what sort of life will that be? Similar to our life here?] Possibly, but certainly not exactly like our life here, but somehow it will continue in any case." What has transformed the initial hope of the subject into his/her final certainty if not need, function?

Summarizing, one may perhaps come to the following conclusions: Oser and Gmünder's "common attributes" are genuine elements, that is, object-constancies and invariants of relationships (*deus ex machina*, moral reciprocity). Five of the seven polar dimensions that they conceive of as "elements" turn out as functions (trust, identity), and at least some of these functions must be taken as functional milestones. Following Oser and Gmünder (who in this respect follow Luhmann 1977), we can bundle up these subfunctions and functional milestones under the superfunction of "coping with contingency." They refer to variants of contingency, some of which become visible only when development progresses. Only the super-function of coping with contingency remains constant over the whole developmental sequence—and we need one constant function. We have also seen that religious development seems not to progress without functional losses. Therefore some caution seems to be in order in applying to religious development the general structuralist theorem concerning the constant function under whose pressure development takes place. It might turn out that the net balance of subfunctions and functional losses may equally well favor regression as progression.

Religious Development and Ego Development

There seems to be no relevant psychological theory that would not conceptualize coping processes as a core function (in the sense of continuous activity) of the ego. When it has to be supposed that religion is concerned with coping with contingency, the conclusion suggests itself that religious development is part of ego development and requires as such no separate developmental logic. Fowler's theory (Fowler 1987a) is—not exclusively, but to a larger degree than that of Oser and Gmünder—based on this theoretical option. Indeed, many of the trends of ego development are also to be found in religious development (autonomy, external-internal states of subjects). Nevertheless, there are also good reasons to assume that the relationship between religious and ego development is characterized by a principal tension. This tension manifests itself perhaps better in Oser and Gmünder's theory than in Fowler's. One can approach the problem by a closer inspection of those two "elements" in Oser and Gmünder's theory which cannot be reduced to functions.

I refer to the two polarities of immanence/transcendence and sacred/profane, which we will, simplifying, lump together in the concept of "ultimate reality." This brings us to the substantial definition of religion, which has always been oriented to the traditional stock of knowledge (God as topic of religion). Among sociologists this substantial approach has often been criticized as "untheoretical" and been opposed to the putatively more efficient purely functional approach of, for example, Luckmann (1967). But it seems far from fortuitous that a prototypical functionalist like Luhmann (1977) found it necessary to combine "substance" and "function." The reasons for the superiority of such a combinatory approach have, on the one hand, to do with the fact that profane, substitute religions seem to offer no fully adequate functional equivalences for genuine religion. On the other hand, the "naïve" religious consciousness seems to operate with a well-entrenched distinction between "sacred" and "profane." This distinction has to be reflected on the theoretical level, if we do not want to mix up the heterogeneous (Kaufmann 1984; Döbert 1984).

This substantial minimum definition (there is no reference to the problem of meaning of life) must and can justify Oser and Gmünder's contention that religious development cannot be reduced to cognitive, social, moral, or ego development. Forms of interaction depend, among other things, on the characteristics of the interacting parties, and "ultimate reality" is a party with very special attributes. However abstracted in the course of religious evolution, the "ultimate" remained always a higher power which is beyond human control. Even when conceptualized as an entity that manifests itself only within human communication, it can never be completely identified with the latter. Intersubjectivity merely testifies for the "ultimate" and its "calling" (Fowler). The idea of a "beyond" which delimits human freedom has never been abandoned completely in these late forms of religious belief. If this holds, one conclusion seems to be inevitable: There is a natural tension between religious and ego development. Ego development aims, among other things, toward increasing autonomy, but the idea of a "higher power" makes it more difficult to gain full autonomy. This complication justifies the construction of an independent logic of religious development—even in view of the circumstances that religious development may be part of ego development and that human autonomy may in the final instance also assert itself in religious development.

It seems to be possible, further, to derive under these premises some substantial hypotheses concerning the relationship between religious development and other realms of ego development. To give one example: One would always expect that the achievement of full autonomy in the religious sphere lags behind the respective achievement in profane spheres of the ego. Gut (in Oser and Gmünder 1984, chap. 6) presents evidence that supports this supposition. The superiority of the ultimate offers a parsimonious explanation of these data. On the other hand, this sort of *decalage* is not equally probable on all developmental stages. As long as the child conceptualizes God as some sort of "super-father" — not qualitatively different from the real father — religious and moral development should proceed in tune: it does not make a difference to obey the two sorts of "father." In a recent study Oser and Reich present data that support this differential hypothesis (Oser and Reich 1987a).

Summarizing, one may perhaps conclude that Oser and Gmünder touch on a specifically religious action problem, because they start from the substance of religion instead of constructing directly in terms of ego development: human freedom must be reconciled with the idea of an ultimate principle beyond human manipulation. This problem — and not that of meaning construction — is posed in some form to the person undergoing religious socialization from the very beginning; it has to be tackled again and again. In this respect it is to be expected that the course of religious development can be depicted as an aggravated dialectic of human autonomy and God's "almightiness." In the following section it will be shown that as this dialectic unfolds a constellation will result, which can be taken as a structurally generated developmental impasse.

Oser and Gmünder's Stage 3 as Developmental Impasse

Oser and Gmünder call their third stage of development "deistic." Subjects on this stage operate with a "two-kingdom doctrine." They attribute "great responsibility of planning and decision-making to themselves" and "separate the ultimate . . . completely . . . from their own sphere of action" (Oser and Gmünder 1984, 94). Atheism represents one extreme variant of this stage.

This danger of atheism has triggered doubts with respect to the status of this stage several times. Oser himself (this volume) also recognizes a certain anomaly of this stage and points out that development stagnates on it sometimes. But "sometimes" seems to be a very optimistic formulation of the facts. Not "sometimes," but in most cases, development seems to become fixated at this point. Stage 3 is in Oser's own data the prevalent one, and opinion polls support this fact again and again. The trend goes toward some sort of "minimal religion," which presupposes a higher power or some final principle of order that is only vaguely known. It has to cover residual or "rest risk" (Restrisiko; Kaufmann 1984, 184), but it is not an integral component of meaning construction in daily life. "Life has meaning only insofar as the person herself/himself confers meaning to it" is one of those everyday truisms that enjoys the widest degree of acceptance (see Seyfarth 1984, 30)!

It could, of course, be argued that stage 3 thought does not represent a genuine stage of religious development, but has to be taken as a mere reflex of a secularized culture acquired via content learning. Against this argument, it has to be pointed out that we find a similar step in the societal evolution of religious symbol systems, as can be learned already from Weber's sociology of religion. "The old religion is according to Gehlen oriented to transcendence in this world. At the moment, when a transcendent god emerges historically, exactly this form of societal religion . . . becomes dubious. The worm is in the apple since we believe in a transcendent god, and not only from Kant's time on" (Kaufmann 1984, 178). To which problem does this learning step on the sociocultural level react if not to the same problem which dominates also the development of the individual: one's own freedom must be able to coexist with the concept of the "ultimate."

A logically possible, a probable, and even the standard solution of the problem consists in a clear-cut differentiation and demarcation of the regions of the "sacred" and the "profane." It is simply a normal developmental strategy, when this solution is chosen. Therefore one recognizes without astonishment in Fowler's stage 4 components, which correspond to Oser and Gmünder's stage 3, although Fowler focuses his theory not as strongly as Oser and Gmünder on the respective problem. For all these reasons I support Oser's answer to his critics fully: There must be something like stage 3 in the developmental sequence!

This stage is the "worm in the apple" of religious consciousness. When the subjects themselves live within one of the differentiated regions, this will tend to become "figure," the other "ground." The individual is responsible for her/his fate in this world and the latter is open to our manipulations. Therefore, the profane capacities of the ego can and must flourish. The opposite holds for the religious ego: motives and opportunities to think about the sacred become rare, since its practical relevance is diminished. Because it is "transcendent" and "Wholly Other" (ganz anders), its conception is simplified and destructured: there is "something"—nobody can know what! Compared with the richly structured pantheons of polytheistic religion, even compared with the "old man with the white beard," this "something" comes close to nothing! Looking at this cognitively impoverished "entity" exclusively from the angle of cognitive structures and competence motivation, one conclusion becomes apparently inevitable: religious development has reached with stage 3 a developmental impasse. The benefits of development go by and large to the profane ego; the religious ego has hardly any motive to grow.

One may object that differentiation is in all developmental models balanced by integrative tendencies. And, in fact, Oser and Gmünder's stage 4 brings the expected integration. But only a few people in modernity seem to feel the need to "integrate" the sacred and the profane: stage 4 responses are rare—not to speak of stages 5 and 6! Thus the question arises, Why does the imperative of integration leave such a weak impact! To find an answer, some general remarks on the theorem of differentiation/integration are required. This theorem catches—as already Max Weber has emphasized—only the results of, not the dynamic forces behind, development. When incompatible orientations co-occur in one situation, differentiation takes place. When a rigid insistence on given forms of differentiation generates negative consequences for the differentiated action patterns, integration takes place. To give an example: Family and economy are differentiated and the economy is structured according to the principle of profit maximization; to accomplish this, the duration of the workday is extended excessively, with the result that the reproduction of the labor force is hampered. At this point, integrative processes become imperative and the duration of the working hours is reduced. An analogous sequence of events and exchanges between sacred and profane would have to be specified, if we want to grant to the integration theorem any force with respect to religious development. In view of the circumstance that only minorities have religious experiences it is difficult to see how the required argument could be constructed. For this reason I conclude that the religious differentiation of stage 3 tends to be self-maintaining and stable. This stability is, as will be seen in the next section, enhanced by recent trends of social change.

The Interchange between Stage 3 and the Social Context: A Vicious Circle

In this final section I would like to show that the pattern of thought of stage 3 is amplified by recent trends of social change, trends that in turn are, so to speak, welcomed by stage 3 with enthusiasm, because they show an "elective affinity" (*Wahlverwandt*). The result is a vicious circle which is difficult to transgress and which guarantees the reproduction of minimal residual religiosity (*Restreligiosität*). The relevant trends of social change will be grouped roughly according to "functional relevance" and "socialization/inculcation" —this because under the premise that religious experiences are on the whole rare, religiosity can be kept alive only by socialization and functional necessity. Social change has therefore to be tested to find out whether it affects one of these two dimensions.

Change with Functional Relevance

Briefly and without claims to completeness, it may be contended that the invention of insurance in the eighteenth century, the establishment of the systems of social security (welfare state) and the considerable prolongation of the life span have had the effect that contingencies are much more infrequent or have to be coped with at a much later time within the individual life cycle nowadays. Those contingencies, which still intrude into the routines of our daily life, are dealt with by profane agencies (medical specialists, therapists), and that is exactly what the stage 3 theory postulates. The monopoly that religion still has in coping with death testifies only for Kaufmann's "remaining risk" religion. Whether the new global contingencies (environment, nuclear war) — typically also the focus of religious movements — will raise the level of religious engagement in the long run is an open question. One may begin with a new awe for nature to find out too soon that everything depends on new technologies.

In addition to the "external contingencies" dealt with above, there are also "symbolic contingencies" that are handled religiously. Transition rituals in the life cycle, the dramatization of collective identities on the national (civil religion) or familial level (Christmas) all profit from the sacred "substance" of religion. But these activities are "periodic" by their very nature, and they can gain from religion exactly inasmuch as they remain periodic. The sacred is the "extra-everyday life" (*außeralltäglich*). Thus, this sphere does not exert a significant pressure to think about religion, and the overall balance of functionality remains negative.

Socialization/Indoctrination

The introduction into a region of meaning, which, on the whole, is cut off from its own channel of experience, has unavoidably to be built on explicit teaching and direct socialization. Empirical research has supported this suggestion again and again. Without religious socialization in the family, no religiosity! (Schweitzer 1987a). But social change seems increasingly to undermine the effectiveness of religious socialization.

First, it has to be noted that the process of "de-traditionalization" (*Ent-traditionalisierung*) seems to have speeded up and to have reached the last resorts of "givenness": We begin to choose our very physical nature! (Seyfarth 1984; van den Daele 1985; Döbert and Nunner-Winkler 1984). This is not the climate in which religious socialization can flourish, because at least in its initial phases it depends on a minimum of "dogmatism" and authority.

Second, the integrated subcultural milieus have been dissolved step by step (Beck 1983). Multiple forms of mobility (occupation, education, dwelling, leisure) counteract the repetitiveness and stability necessary for subcultures to crystallize. Many traditional dwelling quarters have been destroyed, and the former inhabitants moved to new accommodations in the satellite cities. In these, the anomy of loosely knit and freely chosen networks of interaction prevails. Where will we find the traditional catholic milieu, in which one had to go to church because all went to church? Schmidtchen was still able to identify clusters of religious-traditional attitudes. More recent studies seem to indicate that the clusters become looser, more fragmented (Laeyenddecker-Thung 1984). Social pressure and conformity can no longer back religious belief—and should not, says the stage 3 thinker.

Further, roughly since 1964 a process of value change (Inglehart 1977; Meulemann 1984; qualifying Mokrosch 1987) can be detected which amounts, among other things, to a sort of "second secularization" (Meulemann 1984, 102–3). This "silent revolution" has been widely discussed, and therefore some catchwords may suffice: egalitarian participation, autonomy, and self-determination, self-actualization. All these values undermine the unquestioned authority of traditional institutions—naturally also of the churches, which have to rely on authority in order to launch religious thought. Moral education has always been a central preoccupation of the churches. The majority of the population believes nowadays, however, that one does not need churchly advice in moral affairs (Schmidtchen 1979)! Additionally, autonomy is conceived of not only as a right but also as a duty. Even in "limiting situations" (*Grenzsituationen*), which instigate thoughts about suicide, it is a matter of course for most adolescents that the profane coping resources of the ego have to be mobilized (Döbert and Nunner-Winkler 1984). The discussion of suicide does not trigger religious ideas among adolescents.

The change of values has also affected educational goals: orderliness and conformity have been replaced by autonomy and self-determination (Meulemann 1984). In this case, not only a world of ideas changes but also educational practice (Schmidtchen 1979; Nipkow 1987a). Schweitzer has reviewed the relevant literature and concludes that parents begin to grant to their children religious autonomy early: children are sent to church as long as they agree (Schweitzer 1987, 182). Evidently, it would be a waste of time to review the respective research on adolescence!

Finally it is to be suspected that modern theology can easily be misunderstood by the stage 3 thinker in such a way that their own pattern of thought is confirmed. Theologies of liberation, hope, God, as "transcendental condition of the essence of humanity"—all this may very well be designed to integrate the "sacred" and the "profane." But little effort is needed to reinterpret and distort it in a way that the stage 3 dichotomy is reproduced.

To summarize: In order to dissolve the tension between human autonomy and God's superiority, stage 3 thought differentiates strictly between "sacred" and "profane." In this differentiation the profane becomes "figure," the sacred, "ground." It is difficult to see why this dichotomy should be reworked, because (a) contingencies have vanished, and remaining contingencies are dealt with by secular agencies; (b) because symbolic contingencies are of a periodic nature; (c) because pressure to conform religiously has lessened; (d) because value change has undermined the authority of religious institutions, has (e) weakened the religious socialization in the family, and (f) favored exactly those values which have an "elective affinity" to the pattern of thought of stage 3. In this constellation, inner readiness and social context reinforce each other such that a developmental impasse may be the most probable result.

At this point, the argument of this chapter has reached its goal. On the whole a rather gloomy picture seems to emerge entirely against the intention of the author. Therefore a little addendum may be appropriate. To begin with, let us listen again to some statements of subject 111 quoted the first time above. To the question what God means for him, he responds:

> Well, I used to say if nobody can prove that God exists, then I don't believe that. Let's say, every human being prays sometimes, when she/he feels miserable or so. But let's state it that way: I have no relationship at all to God. [Interviewer: You don't believe that God exists?] No, I don't believe it—one has to have a strong belief for things like that, and I don't have it. [Interviewer: But in spite of this, sometimes you pray?] Sometimes, yes, but I mean, what does it mean to "pray"! When one is a bit in a state of need or so, one says sometimes "Dear God, help me," or so. But true prayer, I do not practice that. I say one can pray wherever one is, nothing depends on the church.

These utterances are probably an atheistically toned version of stage 3. The "dear God" invoked in states of need, on the other hand, probably belongs to an earlier developmental stage, a fact that speaks again for the conception of "functional losses" developed above: only the God of our childhood can "reduce" all contingencies. But more important for the present context is the circumstance that the subject recurs at all to religious patterns of meaning and invalidates his atheism at least temporarily. From the supposition it arises that the loss of religious "substance" per se, irrespective of developmental stage, may—just as some stage transition—be connected with a functional loss that can be compensated only by religious "substance." To put it a bit differently: The "holy" is a very special "substance," for which no fully adequate equivalents exist. In this respect every purely functional definition of religion—whether based on "contingency reduction" or "commitment" (*Bindung*)—is in error. Therefore the process of secularization, conceived as a dissolution of the "holy," probably cannot simply be prolonged indefinitely. There could exist a functionally determined limit, which may already have been reached.

As a qualification of this argument, it should also be emphasized that the considerations of this article pertain primarily to the "once-born." But it seems to be rather certain that modern societies generate also a significant proportion of "twice-borns." Among the latter a longing for the "Wholly Other" may be vital and their religious development will certainly not stagnate on stage 3. But to address this issue this would require going far beyond the limits of the present chapter.

10

Against the Religious Headbirths: A Psychoanalytic Critique

Gott ist der Gott meiner Mutter, er ist der Gott meines Herzens, er ist der Gott ihres Herzens; ich kenne keinen anderen Gott, der Gott meines Hirns ist ein Hirngespinst. (Pestalozzi)*

I WOULD LIKE to introduce my psychoanalytic reflections on the development of religious ideas in children with some "classical" episodes of the psychoanalytic and pedagogical literature.

The five-year-old "little Hans," about whom Freud wrote a well-known study, had developed a phobic fear of horses. In a striking and obviously convincing way, Freud explained this fear to him as a fear of his own father. On the way home from this consultation, Hans said to his father: "Does the Professor talk to God, that he is able to know everything in advance?" (Freud VII, p. 278). Freud admits that he was extraordinarily "proud of this acknowledgement out of the mouth of a child"—I think he had a right to be!

In his study about "little Anna," the equivalent of Freud's "little Hans," C. G. Jung tells us something about a spontaneous religious experience of this five-year-old child. Anna asks her grandmother why she had such weary eyes.

> Grandmother ". . . I'm getting older and some day I'm going to die."
> Anna "But what then?"
> Grandmother "Then I will be an angel."
> Anna "And after that, will you be a little child again?" (Jung 17, p. 20.)

Asked about dying, the grandmother gives a conventionally religious answer; Anna counters it with a spontaneous religious fantasy—a fantasy about fading

---

*God is the God of my mother, He is the God of my heart, He is the God of our hearts; I know no other God. The God of my brain is a fanciful idea.

away and being born again, a fantasy about rebirth and transmigration of the soul. We can call this idea of Anna a "religious" one because it interprets life within a comprehensive frame of meaning, even though it is not in line with the Christian confession of faith.

I take these episodes as examples of a "religious judgment." The content of this judgment in the case of "little Hans" is: What "the Professor" told me was so convincing, so striking, so overwhelming—it is impossible that a human being can know and say this all by himself—this has to come from God.

What does it mean when a man, when a child perceives, feels, judges like that: Here, in this event, God was involved. This is what I want to discuss.

First I would like to emphasize (and with this I am taking a methodological counterposition to the representatives of a cognitivistically oriented psychology of religious development (Oser and Gmünder 1984), that such "religious judgments" do happen only as spontaneous events. They can neither be evoked by methodical questioning nor can they be initiated by the efforts of religious education; they "just happen." I will show later on how this character of spontaneity is rooted in the nature of those "religious judgments" and why the interviewer—who operates with psychological techniques of questioning—gets nothing but empty phrases and linguistic artifacts in his notebook or on tape.

For a second reason this emphasis on spontaneous religious judgments is important: It is the only way to avoid the pitfalls of religious socialization (which often means religious training). Children are, besides other things, little parrots who repeat without much thinking what adults have said to them. A two-year-old child who grew up in a pious family, while visiting another house, pointed to some picture on the wall with the comment, "It's Jesus." It took the astonished hosts some time to realize, that in the child's home one could hardly go wrong in guessing that Jesus was in a picture hanging on the wall.

Freud's "little Hans" came from a psychoanalytically enlightened and thus probably nonreligious milieu. "His parents . . . agreed not to use more force in the education of their first child than was absolutely necessary to develop good manners" (Freud VII, p. 244). This educational background gives more weight to little Hans's "religious statement." Literally, the same words out of the mouth of a "religiously well-socialized" child would not have had the same meaning.

Similar spontaneity in the "religious judgment" and comparable nonreligious social background we find in the "hypothetical" experience of God that happens to a young man in Makarenko's "Pedagogical Poem."

Karabanow had been sent to town to fetch five thousand rubles for the colony—an incredible amount of money. At the climax of his emotional conflict between his former delinquent self and his new loyalty to the colony, suddenly a "religious" thought comes over him while riding alone through the dark forest "I rode and thought: 'If there only were a God, if God would send someone to attack me here in the woods . . .'" (Makarenko 1959, 212). Also in another sense those "religious judgments" of little Hans and Kara-banow are spontaneous events: they were neither sought for nor provoked by the author, neither by Freud nor by Makarenko. Both mention those religious statements in passing but don't emphasize them. The classification of these statements as "religious judgments" is not theirs, but mine.

I think Fowler as well as Oser wants to find religious answers. To me, it seems that psychology of religion is pursued here not only as a descriptive and interpretative branch, but with a theological and educational perspective. Whoever describes the stages of religious judgment from the perspective of religious education, necessarily thinks in categories of "normative transformation." This means that the "higher stage" of religious consciousness is taken as an "aim of education" without further reflection (Oser 1981, 346). This kind of psychology of religion is based on fundamental theological assumptions. Thus it functions as a hidden justification of religion.

Thereby the problem is not that Fowler and Oser explicitly profess a religious statement and a theological position. This would not be a secret but an open professed religious position and in this form to be respected. The secret theology rests somewhere else; it comes along in the garment of empiricism.

This you can find already in, first, father Piaget, and then it is applied more or less analogically in Kohlberg, Oser, and Fowler. Piaget, for example, conceptualizes the development of moral judgment as the final state of the adult: "The child receives the moral rules, on which it learns to pay attention, mostly from adults, i.e., in a perfect form . . ." (Piaget 1954, 7). The preceding stages get their structural position from the view of the imagined final position. In case of determining the final position in another way, the stages and steps would have to be different.

Already Piaget's decision to quote a game (with rules!) as a model for moral development underlies a moral-philosophic preliminary decision. Morality seems to be something like observing any rules—a secret moral-philosophic preliminary decision.

In contrast to this I will try to maintain a "scientific neutrality"—a claim that hopefully will not be misunderstood—while dealing with the empirical occurrence, nature, and validity of religious judgments (compare Oser 1981, 347). I am seeking a way to those spontaneous religious judgments I have discussed, yet I want to preserve a personal and methodological distance. If someone states "God exists" or "in this event I can recognize God's hand," then I want neither to applaud the religious judgments nor in the manner of classical psychoanalysis to suspect it of having a close-to-neurotic illusional and infantile character. I want to restrict myself to the role of the psychologist and investigate what it means if someone comes to draw a religious conclusion and on what psychological conditions such a conclusion would be based.

Logical, Aesthetic, Moral, Religious "Judgment"

Perhaps it is a kind of mania to call every product of our mind a "judgment." There are *logical* judgments, connections of facts — and there are, as Piaget showed us, typical structures and stages of such connections in the child's development (Piaget 1954). There are *aesthetic* judgments: "The analysis of judgments of taste has to show what is necessary to call an object beautiful" (Kant 1922, 271). Hardly anybody has shown real interest in the development of this kind of judgment in children. Further on there are *moral* judgments: "The moral judgment refers to the moral meaning of actions which is expressed in terms of rules, laws and statements about justice" (Oser 1981, 38). The stages of the development of moral judgment in children have been explored extensively by Piaget (1954), Kohlberg (1974), and Oser (1981).

The new postulate now claims that there exists a "religious" judgment which functions in the same way as the moral one. It is described as an "expression of that part of the system of rules and patterns (??) of a person," which in certain situations examines the relationship between the individual and the transcendent (Oser and Gmünder 1984, 28). I must admit that at this time I don't have a clear image of this "system of rules" or its resting "capabilities."

If religion is an "almost independent dimension of cognitive structure" (Oser 1981, 34), then "religious judgment" constructed in analogy of "moral judgment" is almost a contradiction in itself. If we finally accept this confusing term, we might at least demand that "religious judgment" has to be understood as an emotional judgment and not as an intellectual judgment. This means that it has to be constructed in analogy with the aesthetic judgment and not with the moral judgment.

Aesthetic judgment is qualified by the following: "To distinguish whether something is beautiful or not, we do not concentrate our intellect on the object of our perception, but we do concentrate our imagination (perhaps connected with the intellect) on the subject and its perceptions of pleasure or dislike . . ." (Kant 1922, 271). Taste, if we follow the formulation of a contemporary philosopher's interpretation of Kant, is "a kind of cognition by feeling" (Cohen 1977, 204).

I would like to claim the same for the so-called religious judgment. And with this I am following the tradition of phenomenology of religion from

Schleiermacher (who called religion the feeling of absolute dependence) to Rudolf Otto. We do not have to deal with a cognitive operation that could be explained logically but with a perception of our "interior sense," our imagination, a very subjective thing "a kind of cognition by feeling." To me this seems to be the only possible definition from the point of view of the phenomenology and psychology of religion.

At least this definition fits the two examples of Freud's "little Hans" and Makarenko's Karabanow better than any other cognitive interpretation. In both cases it is the feeling that the human intellect is overwhelmed by something more total and comprehensive; this allows the idea of God to appear and the contradictions to disappear.

The "religious judgment," properly understood, is nothing other than a feeling of grace or beauty: the *feeling* that arises in the face of the "starry sky above me and the moral law within me," that there must be something that keeps all this together. Religion is the possibility to think of something like that—an act of imagination.

The church-bound theologians and the psychologists of religion, who are more hidden theologians than real psychologists, will not accept this definition. They naturally want to keep the triad of logical, moral, and religious judgment as close together as possible in order that the three will mutually support one another in the sense of a positive theological dogmatism. Religion shall be reasonable and moral; the gap between belief and knowledge shall be kept as small as possible—in a word: Psychology of religion shall serve as a confirmation of religion.

But if "religious judgment" should turn out to be a perception within the sphere of emotion and imagination, then scientific competence for the psychology of religious development is taken away from the cognitive psychology and given back to psychoanalysis. Freud was right when he called religion an illusion (Freud XIV, p. 356)—that means a product of imagination. The negative connotation of the term "illusion" is only due to the fact that Freud himself was a rationalist and did not accept the specific truth and value of judgments that derived from the power of imagination—whether or not they corresponded with intellectual judgment.

Is such a comprehension of religion "irrational"? It is as one takes it. Viewed as a basis for "religious judgment" it will be taken as an emotional grounding, not a grounding of reason; to this extent the grounding is irrational—just as is the grounding of an aesthetic judgment. But just as a philosophical aesthetic is possible as rational discourse about fundamentally "irrational" phenomenon, theology also is possible as reasonable speech about a "nonrational" phenomenon. However, theology should not pose the treated phenomenon itself as rational, but rather as capable of being made rational—and the same pertains to the domain of aesthetics.

Summary of a Psychoanalytic Developmental Psychology of "Religious Judgment": Oedipus, Archaic Mother, Oceanic Feeling

If religious judgment is an emotional judgment, then the "grammar of assent" (Newman 1870/1985) will be declined or conjugated with other paradigms than the cognitivists believe. This means that the elements of this grammar are not called "reversibility" or "orientation away from the center" (Oser and Gmünder 1984, 85 ff., 110ff.) but "oceanic feeling," "father- and mother-imago," etc.

Freud wanted to limit the deduction of religious ideas to the Oedipus complex, the basic human complex. However, he is first of all concerned with the religion of the common person: "the system of life and promises" and the "providence" one believes to be ruling one's life. "The common man can only visualize his providence in the person of a great idealized father" (Freud XIV, p. 431). In the short discourse on "a religious experience," the derivation of religious judgments is made concrete from the infantile sources related to the father: the prospective physician who is mentioned there felt indignation against God while looking at a naked female body in the dissection theater (compare Freud XIV, p. 395).

From a psychoanalytic point of view, objections have also been raised to the supposition that the Oedipus complex is the *only* source of religious feeling. Freud himself anticipated their justification when conceding that he had only wanted to criticize the religion of the common person by the statement quoted above (i.e., the denominational—the religion practiced in the popular church), but had not wanted to deal extensively with "the deepest sources of religious feeling" (Freud XIV, p. 431).

Because the religious imagination of children goes back to the third and fourth year of one's life, the classical Oedipal phase, one would have to postulate a pre-Oedipal source of religious ideas apart from the Oedipal one—not only the real and personal father, but also the archaic mother belongs to the ancestral line of concepts of God.

An unsuspected "predecessor" of Freud has illustrated this point best:

> How does the idea of God spring from my soul? Why do I believe in a God, why do I throw myself into his arms and feel happy, when I love him, when I trust him, when I thank him, when I follow him?
>
> This I soon see: the feelings of love, trust, gratitude, and the skill of obedience must be developed within me before I can apply them to God. . . .
>
> So I ask myself: How do I come to the point where I can love human beings, to trust people, to thank people, to obey people? How do the feelings come into my nature, on which philanthropy, gratitude and trust are mainly based towards man, and the skill that forms human obedience?—

and I realize *that they mainly proceed from the relation between the under-aged child and its mother.* (Pestalozzi 1932, 341).

Finally, if one wants to advance to the deep sources of religious feeling from the denominational and conventional "religion of the common person," the deepest and most original emotional attitude, which originates from the primary narcissism with which I want to deal in more detail, would take effect.

Freud's "Oceanic Feeling" and the Sources of Religion

Freud develops his reflections from a statement that Romain Rolland made to him personally:

> The real source of religiosity, he said, was a "special feeling" of eternity, a sensation as if something were unlimited, boundless, a feeling of "indis-soluble solidarity, or rather unity with the whole of the outside world." (Freud XIV, 422)

Freud doubts that in this case it is a question of fundamental "religious" feeling, which gives one knowledge about one's connection with the world around one from the beginning. From a psychoanalytic point of view a weakening of the boundaries of the Ego underlies this feeling, as one can find them in pathological conditions and in the early phases of human develop-ment "Originally the Ego contains everything; later it separates an outside world from itself" (Freud XIV, 425). This primary sense of the Ego is con-trasted to the "closer and more strictly-bounded sense of the Ego of matur-ity." It forms a sort of counterpart; both senses of the Ego exist side by side.

Freud acknowledges the fact of a feeling of solidarity with everything. He interprets it as an expression of an early stage of a sense of Ego—which can-not yet distinguish between Ego and world. But he thinks that this sense only subsequently is connected with religion. For Freud, the first and direct source of religious needs is the sense of infantile helplessness and the yearning for the father that it awakens.

Freud himself has already suggested that the "oceanic feeling" was con-nected with narcissism (compare Freud XIV, 430). This line of thought has been followed extensively in modern psychoanalysis. A contrast given by Grunberger (1987) can be used as the most recent example. He contrasted the Oedipal man with the narcissistic one: The narcissistic man is the paragon of all infantilisms and anachronisms; his manner of experience is rooted in a prenatal coenesthesia; it is characterized by the "sense of euphoric elevation," of completeness and perfection, timelessness, domi-nating fantasy, and the like. The Oedipal man, on the other hand, is the paragon of maturity—the Oedipal principle is the "fatherly" one. It adapts itself to "reality and causality" (Grunberger 1987, 8); it is constituted by "remembrance." The "oceanic feeling" described by Freud would doubtless belong to the experience of the "narcissistic type," but the narcissistic experience is being depreciated more and more in modern psychoanalysis. In contrast to Kohut's (1973, 1979) positive evaluation of narcissism, Grunberger particularly does not tire of maliciously mocking "narcissistic man" and his illusions. The modern trend in psychoanalysis is not favorable to a fair appreciation of "oceanic feeling."

Freud made a very personal confession concerning the "oceanic feeling." He said that he could not discover it in himself (Freud XIV, 422). He even said that he had difficulties in dealing "with this hardly understandable term" (p. 430). I will try to do something similar: From my own experience I do know the feeling of unity with the world only as a rare event—an event that can be found in sexual fulfillment as well as in a sailing trip on the Mediterranean (the North Sea is too cold for oceanic feelings) or in a spectacular mountain view in the Alps. These examples show that the "oceanic feeling" has a very physical character in my case. This fact makes me inclined to follow Freud's assumption that the connection of the "oceanic feeling" with religion is not an original one, but one that was only connected with it at some later stage.

I am more familiar with the opposite of this feeling of unity with the world: the feeling of alienation. The reasons can be very simple (but again they are rather physical!). While I am writing this down looking at the snow-covered Alps, no vestige of "oceanic feeling" is left. I am suffering from the flu and struggle with my runny nose. Those "nihilistic attacks," which Fowler counters with "faith," are combined with a feeling of all-embracing menace, reaching from Chernobyl to AIDS, and they have to do with the decay of personal relationship as well as with the unsuccessfulness of intellectual efforts. In this mood of a bird, fallen out of the "nest of the world," I could say with Pestalozzi "He did not fit in any corner of it. . . ." But if either of the two, the feeling of unity with the world or the feeling of alienation from it, has something to do with religion—I can hardly believe it.

The Religion of the Children and the Development of the "Basic Self"

It would have made no sense to me in this contribution simply to represent Freud's attitude toward the development of religious ideas once more. I believe, however, that I have something to contribute to this topic based on a theory of my own.

I will use one of Oser's dilemma stories to explain what I mean: the story of a young physician during an airplane crash—the "Paul dilemma" (Oser and Gmünder 1984, 130f.).

> Paul, a young physician, has recently passed his board exams. He has asked his girlfriend to marry him. Before the wedding, he goes on a trip to England paid for by his parents as a reward for having successfully completed his education. Paul embarks on his journey. Shortly after take-off, the plane's captain announces that one engine is malfunctioning and that the other one is working unreliably. The plane is losing altitude. Emergency procedures are initiated immediately: oxygen masks and swim vests are being handed out. At first, the passengers are crying and yelling. Then, there is deadly silence. The plane races toward the ground at an unbelievable speed. Paul's entire life flashes past his eyes. He knows, it's all over. In this situation, he remembers God and begins to pray. He promises that, if he was somehow saved, he would invest his life in helping people in the Third World. He would also renounce the marriage to his girlfriend, should she refuse to accompany him. He promises to forgo a high income and social status. The plane crashes in a field—yet, through a miracle, Paul survives! Upon his return home, he is offered an excellent position at a private clinic. Because of his qualifications, he has been selected from among 90 applicants. However, Paul recalls the promise he made to God. Now, he does not know what to do.

One may consider the story as fictitious and artificial (Schweitzer 1985, 322). Nonetheless, what is the central issue of the dilemma, despite its artificiality? Confronted with an unusual situation and unable to help oneself, one falls back upon "God," finding some kind of help. After returning to everyday life, the same dilemma arises: Is this agreement, made under special circumstances between his "basic-self" and "God," to remain binding on the everyday Ego?

We know this dilemma from a number of fairy tales. Under special circumstances a man is at a loss regarding what to do and promises, if helped, to turn over his child to the devil or to the wild lion. Some time later, after ten years have passed, the devil or the lion will come for the child. The man receives help, everyday life has returned, he barely remembers his promise—and one day the grey little man knocks on his door.

Last spring I had a similar experience when the Chernobyl reactor burned down and nobody knew what it all would come to. At that time I prayed to God and promised to make a small pilgrimage to the Würzburger Käppele if we survived this unharmed.

Up to now the reactor and fallout have not yet caused much harm. Therefore, it became necessary for me to fulfill my promise—despite the fact that, as my "everyday-Ego," I am not religious and do not believe in God. Thus I had to face the same dilemma as the physician in Oser's testing story: Whether to stand by something that I had experienced as wise under special circumstances, and being thereby forced to do something unfamiliar to my everyday-Ego. Consequently, on a beautiful sunny day in autumn I went to the Käppele, where I felt somewhat comical among those groups of real pilgrims; nevertheless I was satisfied that I had done it.

As a further development of the thoughts of Freud and Jung, I have developed the concept of a "split-ego" (Bittner 1974, 1977, 1988). As a result of the basic suppression during the age of one to two years, the thinking and willing ego has separated itself from the more sociable part of personality and declared it a foreign country in a psychical sense, effectively declaring it an "Id" or a collective unconscious. Due to this split, a double-ego (Dessoir 1890) developed: the relation between the basic-self and the conscious everyday-ego is normally of the same kind as the relation between the two hands when the right hand does not know what the left hand is doing. The basic-self on the other hand has a different access to the world, a different perception of reality and the world. The domain of the everyday-ego is the appropriate behavior in the social world. The domain of the basic-self, on the other hand, is the common feeling based on the body (what René Spitz called coenësthetic perception). It includes sexuality (in the comprehensive sense used by Freud), the world of the imagination, the field of parapsychological phenomena, the complex of artistic creation and reception (the aesthetic sensitivity; see above) and, especially, what concerns us here: the religious experience.

The human ego is bipolar (Grunberger 1987). It is a double structure that consists of a basic, "vegetative" part and a reality-oriented "cortical" part (see Bittner 1977, 1988). The "cortical" ego functions in terms of logic, causality, and utility. The basic-ego does not know of any boundary between itself and the outer world; it seeks harmony, meaning, happiness, eternity. Grunberger calls these two partial structures Oedipal human and narcissistic man (see Grunberger 1987, 6).

If we accept this fundamental bipolarity as part of the human nature, the religious experiences must be attributed to the basic, "vegetative" or narcissistic part of the ego. The spheres of basic-ego and reality-oriented-ego overlap in various ways. But if we do not pay attention to the fundamental difference between our logical and our archaic, instinctive means of orientation in the world, if we simply interpret our human search for meaning as a complex cognitive-affective process (Fowler 1981), we risk the theological indoctrination of the psychology of religion: The search for meaning then is looked upon as something meaningful and reasonable without further questioning. The idea that the search for meaning itself *could* (!) be an anachronism deriving from our archaic heritage is forbidden for the psychologist of religion who follows this theological doctrine.

With my thesis that religion is a mode of expression of the basic-ego, I differentiated myself from my psychoanalytic informants Freud and Grunberger (the latter representative of the newer psychoanalytic theory of narcissism): If Freud designates religion an illusion, he speaks against the sense of the search for meaning as categorically as Fowler presupposes it.

Conclusion: Further Examples

It was almost twenty years ago that I held my first, and up to now, only, class about the religious development of children. I asked the students then to write down a religious experience of a child, either from their own remembrance or from the observation of children.

We gathered a lot of material that I would classify as the results of religious *socialization:* a three-year-old girl kneeling devoutly on the floor and praying with folded hands just in the way she had seen adults doing it; a six-year-old boy who went to the cellar to steal some food and then remembered that God would see him even there; a four-year-old boy who looked at his hands while playing in the mud and said, "Luckily there is soap and water—otherwise we would have to pray with dirty hands."

It is exactly this kind of well-trained, acquired religion which makes the topic of "the child's religion" so boring for the nonconfessional observer. If there were not all those things that we tell children about "Our Heavenly Father," I think the yield of "religious experiences" in children would at once go down almost to zero. Only very few children are capable of a spontaneous experience that emerges from the depths of the unconscious imagination.

But there are seeds, presentiments, beginnings that develop relatively independent from Sunday school and religious instruction. "The religion of my childhood was mostly a religion of fear," writes A. Messer (quoted by Spranger 1960, 254). Fear surely is a legitimate source of a true, if rather "egocentric," religious feeling.

A student tells from his remembrance: "Around the age of six, I suddenly got the feeling that there was no need for fear, because God does exist." In another interesting statement from my material, even the insipid fairy tale of the guardian angel features as the basis for an original "religious fantasy."

> Of my earliest religious experiences I have a very clear remembrance: The guardian angel stands beside my bed in the evening, but he is invisible. If I take a hammer and nails and drive a nail right there into the air, the nail would stay there. But as it is not allowed to do that, the riddle remains unsolved.
>
> Is that not—in the conventional mask of the guardian angel tale—an experience of being touched by the reality of a Wholly Other existence in which, at the last, the courage fails to grasp, to pin down, in the sense of the biblical "I will not let you go, before you give me your blessing"?

And finally the story of a ten-year-old girl, who is overwhelmed by a feeling, coming from the depth of her person.

Around the age of ten I went for a walk with two friends. Just before reaching the forest, the two boys start fighting fiercely because of a previous quarrel. I stand by shocked and silent. My first reaction is astonishment.

Suddenly I feel compassion for the one who gets beaten because I always liked him more. In the same moment the commandment "Thou shall not kill" comes to my mind. I get very excited and that forces me to separate the brawlers by imploring entreaty. The force of this commandment grew so strong within me it was as if God himself stood by my side and had put those imploring words into my mouth. When they finally had released each other, I got such a strong grateful feeling, as if I had been responsible for what they were doing.

My excitement lasted for a long time and I was full of doubts. Should he have been allowed to strike back?

This was not my very first religious experience, but the first one I experienced with full consciousness. It was triggered and conditioned by a person that was very dear to me. I was touched in my most personal sphere. It was the same with the other, earlier religious experiences and that is the only thing I can remember about them.

Finally, I do not want to set the original religious imagination and excitement, which freely emerged from the depth of the unconscious, over against religious socialization. I know quite well that religious imagination needs corresponding cultural offerings to prosper. It appears to me that teachers of religion are merely in the first line of artists of socialization, but are not awakeners and midwives for religious experiences that emerge from the depths of human souls.

And my intention was to speak in favor of these original religious experiences.

11

Religious Development and the Ritual Dimension

HANS-GÜNTHER HEIMBROCK

I

A RECENT STUDY by Jan M. van der Lans (1984) suggested the employment of structural-developmental theories in order to obtain new insights into the connection between religious development and participation in, as well as comprehension of, rituals. To this end, the theory of Oser and Gmünder seems a likely candidate, since it discusses issues related to ritual from a developmental perspective (Oser and Gmünder 1984; Engl. forthcoming).

In the twentieth century, theories and research methods in the fields of psychology of religion and religious education have been oriented predominantly toward modern secular society (see Hull 1985; Paloutzian 1983). In this context, religion has generally been treated as a phenomenon to be studied with empirical methods supplied by other disciplines.

The theoretical approach to religious development elaborated by the Swiss researcher Fritz Oser and his team, too, is deeply indebted to the principles and values of the modern secular world. They place a special emphasis on the assumption that theories of religious development have to accept modern structures of plausibility, for example, a world view that is grounded in the principles of the Enlightenment (Oser and Gmünder 1984, 81).

In various publications, Oser and his research team claim that they view their stage theory of religious judgment as more focused and more precise than related, though wider-ranging, theories, such as James Fowler's faith development theory (Fowler 1981). The accuracy of this claim is evident, for instance, in the qualitatively and quantitatively much more restricted use of the concept of ritual by Oser and Gmünder compared to Fowler.

Fowler, in his elaboration of the faith stage aspect "symbolic functioning," refers to the ritual dimension at each of the first five stages. Oser and

Gmünder choose an entirely different course. Their treatment of rituals and of the cognitive processes related to them is influenced by their theory's grounding in the principles of epistemology outlined by Jean Piaget (1926, 1981). Against this backdrop, a preferential use of the concept of ritual in the sense of magical ritual appears plausible. In general, Oser and Gmünder seem to follow M. Weber's vision of the "disenchantment of the world," when they state: "Long ago, magic transferred its power into the symbolic forms of communicative expressions. Religious praxis occurs as self-authorization of people by themselves and for themselves" (Oser and Gmünder 1984, 81).

Thus, ritual behavior occurs only at two of the six stages of religious judgment: In one case, stage 2, it is explicitly affirmed and actively employed by the individual. In the other case, stage 3, it is criticized and rejected. At the second stage, characterized by the perspective of *do ut des,* the Ultimate, which is conceived of as beyond the subject, can be influenced by human action. The characteristic judgment for this level is: "if people conform to certain rules, perform certain rituals, are good to poor people, pray in a particular manner, etc., then the desired effect occurs" (Oser and Gmünder 1984, 81). Coupled with such a religious or fear-related, animistic action pattern is a particular concept of prayer.

Oser's and Gmünder's basis for the classification of magical rituals is, among other things, one of the polar dimensions that are constitutive of the religious judgment. This dimension is entitled "Opaqueness (Magic) versus Functional Transparency" (Oser and Gmünder 1984, 31, 41).

The hallmark of the development of religious judgment from stage 2 to stage 3, the stage characterized by the perspective of deism, consists chiefly in persons' cognitive ability to separate the Ultimate's transcendent sphere of influence from their own worldly domain of action and decision making. The "new-found" knowledge of an independent domain of human action and authority with its own inner-worldly set of causalities results almost directly in a "rejection of religious practices" (Oser and Gmünder 1984, 94) in the sense formulated above. Subsequently, and consistent with the postulated irreversible sequence of developmental stages, stages 4–6 do not make any mention of rituals in terms of magical or animistic actions or meanings.

In light of this description and categorization of ritual behavior in the developmental theory of religious judgment, the question arises whether such a limited view of ritual does justice to the breadth of human ritual behavior and to the various conceptions of ritual. This question points to the general problem of using a concept of development whose parameters might be too narrow and limited (see Heimbrock 1986a; Fetz and Bucher 1986). In this context, we can pursue this general issue only in relation to the ritual dimension.

Initially it is clear that, unlike other approaches, Oser and Gmünder's structural developmental theory is helpful in conceptualizing ritual behavior as a phenomenon that emerges during the course of human development rather than as a fact that surfaces suddenly. However, at the same time, the possibility of participating in rituals depends on certain cognitive capacities. This is true even in the case of a very narrow conception of ritual as magic. One essential ingredient, among others, that comes into play involves a certain role-taking ability.

It might be more prudent to address these issues within the context of a broader concept of ritual. Let us postpone the problem of how to interpret magical behavior and address instead the topic of language-based rituals of prayer. It seems unlikely that the linguistic ritual of prayer could be limited to a particular stage of religious judgment. Taking into account the richness of nonverbal ritual actions and elements in contemporary worship services as well as the diversity of religious rituals throughout history, one soon faces a whole set of different cognitive capacities that are at work in the individual: the imagination, an awareness of object permanence, the ability to structure time, a competence for role-taking, etc.

It seems fair to say that some of the conceptual authorities for the hypothetical construction of stage 6 (with its orientation to universal communication and solidarity) such as K. Rahner and E. Schillebeeckx, as well as Oser and Gmünder themselves, could be expected to display ritual behavior beyond stage 2 *do ut des* behavior or stage 3 deism. To assume that these persons regress to stage 2 whenever they take part in religious rituals strikes one as highly improbable. Rather, one may presuppose that these persons and many others employ quite mature and demanding cognitive operations when they engage in ritual practices that are relevant to them. For example, it takes a relatively advanced cognitive operation to comprehend that the Absolute cannot be depicted in the finite or to come to terms with a certain degree of flexibility in the rules that govern traditional religious rituals.

The questions and arguments above lead to the supposition that, from a developmental perspective, human ritual praxis is not limited to the cognitive stage 2 described by Oser and Gmünder but can also be found at other stages. As far as empirical research is concerned, this implies the task of searching, in more precise fashion, for specific cognitive presuppositions which underlie the diverse notions and practices of ritual.

II

In order to further theoretical discourse in the field of developmental psychology of religion, another important issue must be investigated: the function of ritualization in the service of cognitive development. Erik Erikson examined this issue in several publications (Erikson 1966, 1978; see also Kavanagh 1973). Erikson describes human development in the matrix of psychosocial and psychosexual stages of identity formation. Although religious rituals are not his central concern, Erikson's deliberations are helpful insofar as they open up additional aspects of the ritual dimension.

Erikson's concept of ritual is grounded in a particular concept of play. This includes the human capacity to play in all its varieties, from an infant playing with toys, to sporting competitions, to the power plays in the political arena. He is not so much interested in highly developed rituals, but rather in common phenomena of everyday ritualizations. He understands these to be expressions of a certain underlying capacity "that is grounded in the evolution of humanity . . . (i.e., the capacity) to use objects with a certain symbolic meaning in an imagined scenario within a clearly delimited sphere" (Erikson 1978, 35). One can clearly see how his psychosocial concept of ritual differs from Freud's approach (Freud 1907). It resembles more closely S. Langer's concept of ritual in the sense of "presentative symbolism" (Langer 1957).

In his work, Erikson took up and investigated further Langer's old supposition that presentative symbolism has its own characteristic development. He was able to show how, during the course of the developmental stages of his epigenetic life-cycle model, ritualizations serve to channel drives. Each developmental stage, with its fundamental psychosocial conflict, is linked to a specific element of ritualization. At each of the eight stages, amid the ambivalence of being flooded by drives and being subject to compulsory limits, individuals develop different aspects of ritual experience which shape the rest of their life story. The seeds of ritual experience are laid in infancy with the recurring mutuality of being known by the primary caretaker. Erikson calls this aspect the "numinous element" of ritualization. Each stage and each crisis add an additional element, up to that stage when individuals begin to perceive themselves as generators of rituals. However, at each stage there is a real danger that the ritual dimension becomes fixated in a particular form of individual or social pathology; be it as a compulsive clinging to certain visions, as anxious legalism and literalism, or as an obsession to be on center stage at all times and in all places.

It is important for our discussion to point out that Erikson repeatedly refers to the adaptive function of everyday ritualizations. At the first stage, this is the case in the highly ritualized, though highly individualized, care that infants receive from their mothers. The rituals of care serve two adaptive functions: they provide the mother with a balance between affection and aggression and stimulate the infant's cognitive capacities to identify the limits of other persons as well as her own. At the anal stage, the adaptive function of ritualization continues with the family-specific rituals which regulate the child's cleanliness. The daily-repeated definition of good and bad, "clean" and "unclean" also come to form a foundation for the moral conscience (see also Spitz 1966). When children reach school age, the school as a social institution ritualizes through the formalized routine of daily learning a formal aspect of human achievement. According to Erikson this serves to integrate growth in insight and knowledge into everyday, routine behavior. However, this assessment is probably too optimistic.

Instead of addressing the adaptive function of ritualization at each of the stages in detail, one more remarkable point made by Erikson needs to be amplified because of its importance for further theorizing about human development. Several times, Erikson voices the assumption that a certain correspondence may exist between the "stages of ritualization as described (by him) and the familiar stages of Piaget" (Erikson 1978, 69).

■

The possibility of such a correspondence has been examined further by others (Noam and Kegan 1982). Although an identity or convergence of the different theoretical models of developmental psychology was more asserted than conclusively proved, thus leaving a number of questions unanswered, the central concepts of "limit" and "externalization" appeared well chosen, considering Erikson's contributions to the psychic dynamic of ritual. The developmental model relying on the dialectic of "individuation" and "separation," "differentiation" and "integration" could easily be sharpened in regard to important elements in the concept of ritual at different stages.

The remarks on a different conceptualization of human development, that is, Erikson's model, depicted phenomena of ritualization from a different perspective. These phenomena were not relegated to a transitional stage of infantile animism. Instead, they were viewed as modifications of a specifically human capacity for play during the course of the developmental life journey and in constant interdependence with cognitive development. Thus, the question arises how—in principle, and ethological connections notwithstanding—the specific human capacity for the generation of rituals shall be properly understood and assessed. Obviously, the perspectives and evaluations of the researchers play a significant role—not just the "presentation" of so-called empirical data.

III

By coupling the ritual dimension with magic and animism, conceptualizations in developmental psychology reveal a low appreciation for the ritual dimension. This is neither an original nor a singular occurrence. Rather it reflects a cultural value pattern that, indeed, is "plausible" in modern societies. In earlier times, the field of history of religion passed similar judgments by employing references such as "primitive" or "semicivilized" for cultures in which magic rituals were discovered. Grave consequences resulted for the theoretical discussion in the social sciences as well as for the empirical sociology of religion when R. K. Merton formulated the pejorative concept of ritualism as meaningless behavior (Merton 1968). Such a loaded premise in the social sciences converged with the one in developmental psychology to shape what appears as the unquestionably valid evaluation: both ontogenetically and phylogenetically rituals ought to be viewed as archaic elements. In addition, in spite of Erikson's relevant warning (Erikson 1978, 93ff.), another presupposition comes into play either overtly or covertly: that mature adults as well as highly civilized cultures have already shed such elements. The view is widespread that ritual behavior constitutes an expression of a prerational world view; the further the capacities for language and reasoning are developed, the more goal-oriented individuals and cultures concentrate on rational behavior.

At the end of their book Oser and Gmünder cautiously formulate the following task: "the distinction between phylogenetics and ontogenetics must be clarified further with new and progressive research" (Oser and Gmünder 1984, 278). The following deliberations want to engage in that task by investigating whether the restrictive conception of ritual as magical and prerational, in the context of individual development, can be corrected by employing new theories on ritual behavior from the social sciences.

1. It is general sociological knowledge that rituals as deeply rooted patterns of behavior are extremely useful, even irreplaceable, for the maintenance of social systems, regardless of their stage of cultural development (Goffman 1986). A qualitative conceptual advance, however, seems to be the distinction between "social" and "cultural" systems introduced by sociology and social anthropology (Geertz 1973). This distinction reveals that one aspect of rituals, as roles, serves an action-guiding function and that their interpretative aspect is an element of society's process of providing symbolic meanings.

It is interesting that it is precisely in the context of such social-scientific considerations that the issue was addressed from a fresh angle: the issue of the proper understanding of magic as a test case for the proper understanding of strange rituals in general (Kippenberg and Luchesi 1978). It is impossible here to recapitulate the discussion in its complexity and the range of controversial positions. However, a few arguments relevant to the critique and construction of psychological theories of development will be introduced.

The discussion about the proper understanding of magic no longer deals with the old distinction between magic and ritual (Durkheim 1965). Neither does it center on a primarily functionalistic view of certain ritual behaviors as instrumental for preserving the social order or for coping with individuals' inner conflicts (Malinowski 1948). Rather, in connection with the sociology of knowledge (Weber 1922; Schütz 1932), the issue under discussion now concerns the meaning of ritual behavior. Thereby, however, the problem of ethnocentrism inevitably becomes part of the discussion.

As far as the question about the meaning of ritual behavior is concerned, a strong group of social anthropologists is pleading for an extension of the current perspective. According to them, ritual must not be evaluated primarily as a form of instrumental action, since then, almost by necessity, it will have to be evaluated as undeveloped, "pre-scientific," or "pseudo-scientific." Rather, ritual behavior ought to be viewed as a different mode of action: one that has its "purpose" in itself (Leach 1966).

Scientific rationality, in the conventional sense, analyzes the world in order to facilitate instrumental action. Ritual, however, as well as myth and art, belongs to the domain of expressive action. If one can even use the term in a meaningful way at all, the "purpose" of these forms of expression is the dramatization of experience, not its analysis. They fulfill their "purpose" also in those instances where certain ceremonial actions can be interpreted, on a secondary level, from the perspective of social and psychological functionality. However, we are dealing here with two different forms of reasoning: science analyzes experience; myth, magic, and ritual dramatize it. "The creators of myths . . . belong among the poets, not the scientists; while both groups discover order in apparent disorder, the types of order discovered are entirely different. In addition, they employ different means of investigation" (Beattie 1978, 203; see also Beattie 1966).

A caveat: the aforementioned distinction should not be misunderstood as a sequential ordering, that is, magic behavior followed by instrumental behavior. The evidence is to the contrary. Cultural anthropologists have encountered both types of action at the same time in so-called primitive as well as in highly civilized cultures. This, then, sheds some doubts on the popular assumption of a stagelike sequence from a ritual to a rational world view.

Such an assumption becomes even more questionable, if one begins to reflect on the hermeneutical issues at stake. This is a concern for both sociologists and psychologists. If one views rituals primarily as forms of expressive symbolism, the following questions surface: Who actually has to comprehend the symbolic meaning of an object or action? The actor? The observer? Or both? Here, research confronts certain limits that must be acknowledged. "Considerable confusion has been caused by the failure to be clear as to whether a certain act or object is symbolic for the actor, or for the observer or for both" (Goody 1961, 152). Thus, the interpretation of ritual behavior becomes even more problematic. Objective interpretations from the position of an outside or independent observer alone are inadmissible, since an adequate decoding of ritual symbolism needs to rely on context-bound criteria, in addition to rationality. These are "criteria which incorporate the specific worldview or the particular symbol-system of the culture under investigation" (Beattie 1978, 196).

2. New perspectives are emerging in cultural anthropology which address

the fundamental problem due to the grounding of the development of religious judgment in the development of communicative competence. By adapting the work of Habermas and Peukert in that domain, Oser and Gmünder imported the formal necessity to construct a developmental model that "is tied to and grounded in the fundamental structure of communicative action" (Oser and Gmünder 1984, 25). And the descriptions of stages 5 and 6 indicate clearly (Oser and Gmünder 1984, 53ff.) the value ascribed to communicative competence in the structurally most developed forms of religiosity.

In this context it seems appropriate to introduce the work of the social anthropologist Mary Douglas, which up to this point has not received much attention from developmental psychologists and religious educators (Douglas 1968/69, 1982, 1986). Employing a sociolinguistic instrument (Bernstein 1965, 1986), Douglas investigates the specific modality and performance of nonverbal communication in rituals in relation to the development of God images.

One of Douglas's intentions is to counter sociological as well as theological reductionism in the guise of secularization and ethics debates. She pushes back against such tendencies, when she states: "human experience is ordered by means of symbolic limits and boundaries. Non-verbal symbols constitute the basis of meaning-structures which enable individuals to relate to others in permanent ways and to discover for themselves fundamental life purposes" (Douglas 1986, 53).

Using ethnological comparisons of body rituals, Douglas develops the thesis that rituals ought by no means be viewed as underdeveloped or incomplete forms of communication which therefore need encoding in conceptual reasoning and moral judgment. Rather, rituals must be regarded as "restricted code." A sociolinguistic analysis is characterized by the synopsis of family structure and linguistic behavior. Assigned to the "positional" system of family structures, a "restricted code" is characterized by a more rigid ordering of linguistic patterns, a higher degree of particularity, contextuality, and a higher count of nonverbal elements. In terms of ideal types, a "restricted code" can be distinguished from an "elaborate code" which features a greater syntactical variety, a relative context independence of its semantics, plus other characteristics. This type is assigned to a family system designated as "personal."

According to Douglas, attempts at slanting the interpretation of rituals in favor of an ethically or dogmatically "purified" type of religiosity miss the significant connection between symbol system and social structure. The devaluing and even the elimination of rituals, typical for large segments of the middle class in Europe and the United States, has serious consequences. First, it robs families of the under class of an indigenous medium of communication. Second, the socialization of children takes a precarious direction.

This is so, because, on the one hand, the specific role and importance of rituals as part of the "restrictive code" are being overlooked. On the other hand, the one-sidedness of the "elaborate code" is being underestimated. For the assumption "that the rational, explicitly verbal and personal relation to God is more highly developed and better than its presumed opposite, i.e. formal, ritualistic conformity" is false (Douglas 1986, 15). Persons' abilities or inabilities to participate in communication via rituals is not causally related, as might be assumed, to the development of cognitive structures but rather to the structural transformations in the primary institutions of social-ization. For example, in the case of a so-called primitive culture with an anti-ritualistic spirit, the transformation of the social structures follows by no means the direction of a one-dimensional logic of development. Important for our line of reasoning is Douglas's skepticism concerning the alleged priority of the "elaborate code." The preference for an "elaborate code" leads to particular consequences. Stated briefly, in the context of a family struc-ture with a personal orientation, children "are raised for a social world which is continually changing" (Douglas 1986, 15). While this orientation produces better scholastic results and assures social advancement according to existing career development patterns, it also contains "seeds of alienation." These, then, make it difficult for individuals to "grasp their identity as a given part of their social context" (1986, 46).

Douglas's reference to the profound impact of changing patterns of sociali-zation and communication on the self-concepts and belief systems of indi-viduals is very useful. When rituals are critiqued in the context of "personal" patterns of family relations, the result is "a predisposition toward an 'ethical orientation.'"

> On the one hand, it unlocks the language of feelings. On the other hand, such a critical stance toward ritual destroys the faculty for perceiving and interpreting the forms and structures of social life. Persons reared in that manner cannot justify their existence through the keeping of existing rules. That means, they have to find justification via an engagement on behalf of the well-being of other people, or via achieving personal success, or both. (Douglas 1986, 57; for implications for religious education, see Fraas 1983)

Coupled with the loss of the ritual dimension is the loss of that dimension of religious communication which satisfies the life long need of persons to grasp things in nonverbal fashion as well as their recurring and by no means infantile yearning for an overcoming of the deeply ingrained boundaries between "interior" and "exterior" which they perceive in their everyday experiences.

The line of thought advanced by Douglas elicits several responses. For example, are there really only two modes of justifying human existence? Also, it would be fruitful to relate Douglas's analysis of the different theories about ritual behavior to psychoanalytic theories of socialization. In the context of our inquiry, her deliberations challenge any hierarchical value scale of communicative action—like the one that underlies the structural theory of religious judgment. When Douglas states "whoever derides . . . rituals actually adheres, in the name of reason, to a highly irrational concept of communication" (Douglas 1986, 74), she poses the critical question as to what degree "universal communication" may constitute an elitist structure of religious communication accessible only to a few and not even welcomed all around.

<h2 style="text-align:center">IV</h2>

The above psychological and social-anthropological considerations on the development of the capacity for ritualization as well as those on the culture dependency of its interpretation have several implications. On the one hand, they point out that theories of religious development need to pay more attention to this domain than previously has been done. On the other hand, our considerations critiqued developmental theories for maintaining an opposition between ritualized forms of expression and an enlightened reasoning process.

However, changes are under way. Deliberations in philosophy of science as well as those which take into account the praxis of everyday life have realized the problems inherent in such a one-dimensional perspective. It would be an anachronism if a psychology of religion that is grounded in the history of science were to retain the rare agreement between Freud and Piaget, who asserted that rituals will come to an end when people begin to reason "correctly."

Furthermore, developmental theories oriented toward the disappearance of rituals would have little persuasive power in the face of the recent, substantially increased participation in rituals in Western societies. Religious and pseudo-religious rituals of civil religion (Bellah 1968; Schieder 1987), the organization of group rituals by those who yearn for salvation, the increasing leanings among adolescents toward the occult and spiritualistic practices, the religious references of food rituals in the so-called bio-dynamic food movement, and others, all counter a one-dimensional view of individual and societal development according to M. Weber's phrase, "the disenchantment of the world." It seems unlikely that the aforementioned phenomena can all be explained with the conceptual scheme "magical versus instrumental." The danger is real that such forms of religiosity will become more attractive to the same degree that empirical research in religion ignores or simply dismisses them.

The implication for a theory of the human capacity for ritualization is that such a theory must be grounded in a broad concept of ritual lest it overlook important phenomena and connections. Thus it must not be prematurely blinded by a certain philosophy of history or by a theological critique of ritual to the fact that anthropological similarities do exist between elements of ritual in different religions and in different cultures. Such a theory would be most likely to do justice to the phenomena under consideration if it viewed human ritualization as noninstrumental, purpose-free expressive behavior cast into certain forms and patterns. Such a view facilitates, on the one hand, the taking into consideration of the ethological context of rituals. On the other hand, it enables a nonfunctional approach to the human capacity for ritualization.

It cannot be denied that, in the execution of rituals, persons actualize a certain "inner behavior," that they mobilize and act out feelings, and that they have a certain rational-cognitive cognizance of what they are doing at the time. However, it appears questionable whether one should rely on these elements for the construction of a developmental theory of ritualization. The psychodynamic and cognitive theories reviewed above lead us to fear that a theory of ritualization derived from those phenomena may constitute only an application of such theories, with all their strengths and weaknesses. It is particularly equivocal to what degree one can construct at all an unambiguous sequence of certain stages of a more or less "mature" or "developed" concept of ritual. Psychoanalytical theories and recent theories of social cognition (Noam and Kegan 1982) have introduced the (double) helix as an image for development. With this, they have advanced beyond the developmental image of a one-dimensional, irreversible sequence of stages. Therefore, it appears untenable today to assign the psychic dynamic of the Christian worship experience in its entirety to a certain developmental stage of narcissism (Herms 1977) or to classify, with Piaget (and Oser and Gmünder), the cognitive dimension only as prerational, noninstrumental magic. I suggest that any theoretical approach to rituals ought to identify and address certain fundamental dimensions. In my opinion, each of these dimensions would have to be studied separately and from a developmental perspective. They should be conceived of as ritual only in their joint interaction in the behavior of individuals or in the model available. The following short list of the dimensions of ritual praxis is preliminary and deserves further discussion. However, I suggest the dimensions of (a) time, (b) symbols, (c) dramaturgy.

a. In any ritual, individuals deal in a particular fashion with time, with the experience of existing temporally (Turner 1985). Rituals can order the experience of time according to different segments, such as days, years, the life cycle, cosmic time. Rituals have a particular structuring function for the biographic transitions from one stage of the life cycle to the next (Meyer 1981; cf. Gennep 1986). However, as Erikson's reference to the antiritualism of puberty documents, persons do not have the same access to rituals during the different phases of the life cycle. Among other things, one of the constitutive qualities of rituals is to provide a certain repetitiveness among the life changes, to reprise what is unique.

Such a structuring of time is manifest, for example, in the particular arrangement of the huge stones in Stonehenge (S. England), which only once a year, at the summer solstice, captures the light of the sun in a unique way. Another form of ritualization can be discerned in the recurring obsessive acts of neurotics who, in a veiled and thus unsatisfactory fashion, repeat again and again traumatic experiences from their past. A structuring of time of a different, though no less important, sort is constituted by the ritual described in Deuteronomy 6:2ff. and by the insertion of this narrative in the Jewish Passover liturgy. Here, three different levels of time are placed cotemporal: the level of the text, the Exodus event as its central ingredient, and the actual usage of the text. The dimension of time is depicted not just by means of a certain sequence of events, but also with the aid of spatial images. For example, the passing through a gate may represent the transition in status.

A theory of the human capacity for ritualization has to clarify the conditions that enable or hinder the person in gaining verbal and nonverbal access to the formal language of the dimension of time (v. Weizsäcker 1960). The cognitive competence to recognize sameness amid change (Piaget 1977) is but one such capacity. It must be noted that one of the specific conditions for the experience of time in our culture is the interruption and cessation of traditional patterns of timing and structuring of everyday life (e.g., shift work). This implies for practical theology's theorizing on worship and pastoral acts an awareness of relevant changes in persons' "feel for time," which may necessitate a reshaping of liturgy and ritual.

b. It was mentioned several times that ritual behavior or action must be understood as a symbolic form of expression in addition to, or in connection with, instrumental action. The uniqueness and the developmental conditions of symbolic functioning have already been studied in detail. It suffices here to refer to relevant works (Scharfenberg and Kämpfer 1980; Biehl 1984; Heimbrock 1986b). Fowler has connected religious development consistently with symbolic functioning (Fowler 1981). He adequately addresses the nonlinear element of the developmental trajectory of symbols when he suggests that the "mythic-literal" stage is followed first by a symbol-critical stage. The following stage, then, features a "post-critical return" to the concept and use of symbols (Moran 1983). For the future it seems important to pay more attention to rituals as nonverbal symbols. It is equally important to avoid an *a priori* view of verbal forms of communication as superior to nonverbal forms. The work of Mary Douglas yields new perspectives for the classification of God-concepts and images.

c. In addition to the aforementioned dimensions of time and symbols, a third one is introduced: the dimension of dramaturgy. Rituals in all religions dramatically enact and visibly convey certain everyday activities (Turner 1969; Laeuchli 1987). This symbolic reenactment does not occur just, or solely, linguistically. It takes place in certain locales, with certain behavior patterns, gestures, and with certain roles. In this respect, one of our cultural contradictions consists in the fact that we have emptied our worship services of this dramatic element, thereby degrading them to mere teaching events. At the same time, however, we conduct political rituals such as election campaigns and entertainment rituals like television shows with technological perfection and with the best of our instrumental repertoire for the maximization of effect.

If we assume that the symbolic dimension of rituals is closely related to the world views that are represented, then dramaturgy involves the construction of the rules for participation, the variety of inner and outer roles which participate in the "holy play." Previous attempts at explaining how the available roles are adopted by individuals range from simple theories of imitation to the concept of a temporary stage change (v.d. Lans 1984). In the context of pastoral-psychological considerations, J. Scharfenberg submitted the original proposal to make the symbolic dimension of the traditional order of worship transparent by employing the psychic dynamic of a pastoral counseling dialogue (Scharfenberg 1985, 101ff.). The imaginary dialogue presented in Scharfenberg's publication seems to be an excellent example of the multilayered quality of the concept of symbol in the sense of P. Ricoeur's "second naïveté": emphatic perception and critical interpretation go hand in hand with "magical" elements.

However, a theory that does not want to be blind to reality must inquire about those elements which sometimes lead to a compulsory adoption of roles or to a wholesale rejection of available liturgical roles, as is the case for those who no longer attend worship services. In addition, the analysis of psychological and political power plays an important and necessary role in the context of ritual behavior. An analysis of that sort is guided by an interest in the facilitation of participation in rituals which playfully or with a provocative imagination explode the existing constraints of everyday life.

Ritual praxis and its development, which is described with the aid of the three aforementioned dimensions, obviously cover a broad spectrum. Certainly, rituals are not classified from a narrow normative perspective and assigned to specific stages of religious development. And insofar as the tension between rituals and the praxis of everyday life is a constitutive element of the ritual praxis, more than just the few sanctioned ritual forms (or relics) of an official denomination is included.

A theory constructed along those lines seems indeed capable of addressing a twofold task. On the one hand, it can assist in examining the psychological

profile of ideal religious rituals. On the other hand, by relying on the aforementioned dimensions and their aspects, it can assist in studying more
closely and without bias concrete ritual practices of persons in particular
situations. While an investigation of rituals guided by the narrow paradigm
of functional rationality quickly reaches its explanatory limits, an inquiry
guided by questions concerning the dimensions of time, symbolism, and
dramaturgy can suggest new attempts at explanation. Such attempts will be
useful for a practical theology of rituals to the degree that they leave open
the issue of the truth of rituals in favor of a differentiated (and nonreduc-
tionistic) description of their effective elements.

V

New theoretical attempts about ritualization benefit religious education in
several ways. For example, while the developmental perspective of rituals
is logically connected to recent designs in the field of "symbol didactics"
(Feifel 1978; Biehl 1984; Heimbrock 1984, 176ff.), it can counter tendencies
of narrowly focusing on verbal symbols. It also suggests caution about a naïve
identification of "development" and "learning." Learning to participate in old
as well as new rituals is crucial in an age where persons on their developmental journey seem more to unlearn communication by means of rituals. Religious education in secular societies must not neglect to impact the religious
development of young persons in a constructive and critical manner. It must
take extra care to address the issues such as growth in maturity and eman-
cipation. Its grounding in the Christian notion of freedom will compel it to
attend to the possibility that both old and new rituals can function to create
free spaces as well as operate as mechanisms of manipulation. Finally, in the
interest of human and humane coexistence, religious education ought not
neglect to assist young persons in cultivating their capacities for noninstrumental, purpose-free forms of expression. This is particularly significant in
the context of functionalism and instrumentalism. Yet a curious question
remains: How can this task be accomplished successfully as long as educational institutions keep participating in the paradox of wanting to sponsor
persons toward more noninstrumental, purpose-free actions while attempting this within an educational organization that itself operates on purposive-
rational, instrumental principles?

Part 5

Faith Development
and Education
in Society and Church

12

Human Development and Capitalist Society

JOHN M. HULL

IN "EXTRACTS FROM THE REPORT of the Centenary Celebration of Grand Vizier Services," Michael Kidron and Ronald Segal satirize the attitudes of the entrepreneurs supplying services to their most wealthy clients. In his annual address, the president of the firm advises his senior management on how they can best take advantage of the strengths and weaknesses of the wealthy and describes the conditions, both political and psychological, that will do most to advance their own prosperity. He exhorts them:

> All of us, not only we the executives, but also the principals, if I may pursue a distinction, must train assiduously in the use of power. We must exercise it constantly, in a manner that is firm, fair and open. In this way we will satisfy the deepest inner needs of humankind, for without social order, without a planned sequence of attainable and spiritual goals for each person, there can be no self-fulfillment and no sense of security. Social harmony and our considerable advantages rest on our providing a framework, however modest it might be, within which that sense might flourish. (Kidron and Segal 1987, 143).

In this clever parody, Kidron and Segal make bare the connection between the "jargon of authenticity" and the purposes it serves. Government, including the internal government of the affairs of the company, must be both fair and open, but at the same time it must be "firm" because it constantly seeks to maintain and to extend the power of vested interests. The language of spirituality is particularly useful in this respect, since modern marketing methods explore and create intimate links between the inner, psychic world of the individual consumer and the product or service that is created in order to minister to (i.e., nurture rather than satisfy) those needs. The president of Grand Vizier Services shows himself sensitive to the spiritual needs of people today. He knows that it would be insensitive to speak of "mankind," for many of his clients are wealthy women, highly educated and well aware of patriarchal power. He understands that people need to experience "self-fulfillment" and that this is related to a "sense of security" without which the stock markets will become nervous and people will not be able to relax enough to enjoy the luxurious services the company offers. Without this inner harmony there can be no "social harmony," and without social harmony the social pyramid of power would be threatened. Above all, people need a "planned sequence of attainable and spiritual goals," so that, however complex and mystifying the external world might seem, there will always be an inner world of rationality, order, and control, which will impart a sense of purpose and planning to the lives of ordinary men and women. Because the world of business is international, and Grand Vizier Services is itself a multinational company, this "planned sequence" of spiritual stages must be available "for each person," and again we notice the sensitive use of inclusive language by our enlightened president. It is up to companies such as Grand Vizier Services to provide such frameworks for modern living and to encourage other people to do the same.

The links between capitalism and spirituality are both direct and indirect. At the direct level, we may consider the obvious intimacy between the electronic churches and modern capital, expressed in the increasingly familiar theology of success, while at the hidden level we may study the alienation and false consciousness of the middle-class spirituality of wealthy churches in a poverty stricken world. If religion is the opium of the people, severe addiction seems to be typical of wealthier people.

In their final chapter, Kidron and Segal take off the mask of satire and announce their own conclusions about the impact upon human values of the world of business and money: "Where it has not swept aside other ways of organizing and thinking, it has subverted and appropriated them. It has subjected or reduced all considerations—moral, aesthetic, intellectual, spiritual—to the material imperative" (Kidron and Segal 1987, 178).

In what follows we will be discussing some of the ways in which stage development theories might be thought of as products of modernity. We will not try to do this in comparison with other contemporary expressions of spirituality. It may be that some of the modern religious cults or aspects of the counseling movement and so on can also be considered as products of modernity, and this may be true of other approaches to the study of human behavior and experience today, such as behaviorism and psychoanalysis, but these remarks will be confined to stage development theories. We will also ask whether stage development theories are not only products of modernity but may become weapons against modernity. Insofar as they are a genuine response to problems created by modernity, they can be purged or detoxified, conscientized and redirected so as to become instruments for passing beyond modernity. Is it possible that next year's presidential address to the

management of Grand Vizier might be a little less certain about the safe
spirituality of the planned sequences of spiritual goals?

Stage Development Theories as Products of Modernity

Development in Capitalism and in Stage Theories

Gabriel Moran has pointed out that the word development is used mainly
by psychologists, economists, and photographers. "Are psychological
theories of development a justification for the status quo issued by the well-
to-do part of well-to-do countries?" (Moran 1983, 4). The distinctions
between developed, developing, and underdeveloped countries are clearly
made in the interests of business potential. Moran regards development as
a characteristic image in modernity, tracing it to the emerging historical consciousness of the nineteenth century, in which the way to understand things
was to stand back and watch them develop. He contrasts the ancient images
of the process of change, which often involved ideas of decay and suffering,
with this characteristically modern image, associated with growth, progress,
and improvement, noting that this cluster of ideas represents "more an
ideological doctrine than an incontestable fact" (Moran 1983, 17–20).

Studies of human development concentrated at first on infancy and childhood, under the influence of biology, especially embryology, and only in the
mid-1970s did the theories expand so as to catch the attention of the public
in adult development. It is in the last ten years that there has been a particularly noticeable impact on the lives of adults of the tremendous world-
wide expansion of competitive consumption and capital escalation. While it
is true that Erik H. Erikson made extensive use of the concept of the "life
cycle" to extend Freudian ego psychology from adolescence to old age, it will
be shown below that his theory ignores just those institutions of contemporary industrial growth which are having the most decisive impact on the
lives of adults. This aspect of the Eriksonian life cycle becomes apparent as
one gazes back on it in the light of the last ten years of developments in
modernity. In a word, the intensification of capital development is leading
not only to an intensification of interest in adult stage development theories
but also to a hermeneutical suspicion about the relationship between stage
theories and modernity itself (e.g., Broughton 1986, 90–114; Heimbrock
1986a, 150–54).

Modernity Itself as a Stage Development Theory

There is a second way in which stage development theories are closely related to modernity. Modernity itself is often understood as the contemporary

stage in a stage development theory of history. The foundations of this perspective were laid down by Hegel, and Kierkegaard's response to Hegel consisted partly in outlining a series of psychological or spiritual stages of inner transformation (the aesthetic, moral, and religious stages) in contrast to the world-historical-spiritual evolutionary theory of Hegel. The interpretation of modernity as a historical stage was used by Karl Marx to relativize industrial society by showing that it had certain origins and could be expected to have certain outcomes. Marxist socialism understands itself as pointing to a stage (communism) that lies beyond capitalist industrialization and will be its superior successor. Western theories of individual, internal stage development may be thought of as a psychological and spiritual (economic?) response to the historical and sociological interpretation of the stages of history offered by communism, a bit like Kierkegaard's response to Hegel. It is interesting to note that Kierkegaard became popular in Europe in the early years of the twentieth century, particularly after the First World War, and is one of the inspirations behind contemporary faith development theory. On the other hand, we may trace the impact of Kierkegaard, Martin Buber, and Karl Barth upon a writer such as Paulo Freire, where the existentialism results not in a theory of individual inner development but in a "dialogical education" within a Marxist framework as part of a humanistic societal and historical revolutionary program. If the existentialism of North America is strikingly different from that of South America, the political and economic conditions prevailing in the two continents of the new world cannot be entirely overlooked.

Not only is the concept of modernity itself the product of stage development theories, but there have been many attempts to interpret religious modernity in a similar manner. It should be noted that stage development theories of the history of religions coincide with stage development theories of the religious development of modern individuals. This helps us to see that religious stage development theories are a characteristic feature of religious modernity itself, and it also throws light on certain characteristics of the psychological theories of stage development.

As an example, we might take the well-known theory of Robert Bellah, in which a description is offered of the history of religion in structuralist, stage-developmentalist terms, postulating five stages: primitive religion, archaic religion, classical, early modern, and modern religion. The theory focuses on religion as the development of symbols which express and concern both cultural and individual identity, the structure of the symbol system undergoing transformations from stage to stage. The transformation from classical and early modern religion to the religion of modernity is characterized by a change from what Bellah calls "compact symbolism." The compact coherence of the specific religions and denominations with their self-conscious boundaries excluding one system from the other have given way during the modern period to a more free and fluent situation of symbolic complexity in which coherent content is less clearly defined, individuals being encouraged to formulate their own synthesis during the course of their own migration of faith, under the general auspices of a sponsoring denomination (Bellah 1970, chap. 2).

In other words, one of the distinctive features of any particular religion under the conditions of modernity is that it exists alongside other religions in a state of mutual competitiveness and intermingling and is at the same time undergoing internal pluralization, not so much in the sense in which Protestantism had a tendency to break into innumerable sects (early modern religion) but in the sense that each religious believer contains within his or her own subjectivity a range of possible religious identities. The sociological interpretation of this phenomenon offered by Robert Bellah may be compared to the theological interpretation offered by H. Richard Niebuhr in his use of the term "polytheism" to describe the modern individual who exists within several worlds, and "henotheism" to describe the modern individual who in order to maintain internal coherence rejects plurality for the sake of an internal totalitarianism. Polytheism and henotheism are contrasted by Niebuhr with monotheism, which refers to the modern individual who has overcome both inner and outer pluralization in loyalty to universal being itself (Niebuhr 1960). It is hardly necessary to remind readers of this study that H. Richard Niebuhr is one of the major theological influences upon the faith development movement.

In stage development theory, content is replaced by form. The author of the Letter to the Hebrews identified immature Christians by the religious topics with which they were concerned, whereas to be mature they should have been concerned with a different range of religious and theological subjects (Heb 6:1f.). We may regard this as a content-based understanding of spiritual maturity. This understanding of religious development will work only during the period of compact symbolism, when the intellectual and emotional system of religion can itself be arranged in a hierarchy so as to provide a rationale for progressive improvement. When the systems are fragmented and relativized by intersystemic collision and internal proliferation, to say nothing of the effects upon religious faith of secularization, the most satisfying alternative is simply to abandon content altogether as a criterion of spiritual maturity. Its place can be taken by form, and if the forms can be distinguished from each other by structures and related to each other as a sequential hierarchy, then we have classical religion reconstituted with a sort of antiradiation defense kit which will enable the survivors to pick their way safely through the life of heretical imperative which Peter Berger has described so well (Berger 1979). We may contemplate the work of Rudolph Bultmann and that of the stage developmentalists as offering different models of demythologization under the impact of modernity. Whereas

Bultmann demythologizes the content in a historical reductionist approach, stage development theory demythologizes content by a category shift from content into structure. The result of Bultmann's approach is a renegotiation of content. The result of the stage development approach is to substitute form for content. There is no doubt that both approaches are extremely powerful to religious believers made sensitive to modernity, and it is interesting to notice a certain seepage between the two approaches, which occurs when a categorization that purports to be structural slips into a sort of theological classification, where content is arranged in ascending order of superiority as it becomes more highly demythologized in the Bultmannian sense. In the work of the English stage developmentalist Ronald Goldman we may note such a conflation of Piaget and Bultmann (McGrady 1983, 126–33; Slee 1986, 84–93). It is also important to notice that contemporary representatives of stage developmental theories are much more theologically sensitive than those of twenty years ago. Theological concerns have always been much more overt in the faith development movement, and it is noticeable that theology is becoming increasingly important in recent faith development literature. If we contrast Ronald Goldman with James Fowler, we see a liberal Bultmannian rationalism which was mainly unconscious and which must therefore be regarded as being ideological, in contrast to a much more self-conscious representative of American radical social transcendence in which theology is actually distorting (or liberating) the elements of the stage developmental theory itself (Goldman 1964; Fowler 1984a, 1987a) insofar as it could be thought of as a product of modernity. In other words, the later work of Fowler points beyond modernity, whereas the work of Goldman was enclosed within modernity. Stage development theory is developing rather nicely.

Reason and Fantasy

We now come to a third way in which the stage development theories may be thought of as being products of modernity. It was Max Weber who did most to interpret modernity as a form of rationality. Reason becomes rationalization, the efficient calculation of ways and means in order to maximize profitable production as measured by economic statistics (see Marcuse 1986, chap. 6; Wellmer 1985, 35ff.). The rational society becomes immanent in its most characteristic class, the bureaucracy. Several contemporary studies of modernity have concentrated on bureaucracy as being the characteristic form of modern political life, whether in the East or the West (Lefort 1986; Berger, Berger, and Kellner 1973, chap. 2). This rationality of the efficient institution has its analogue in the rational ego,[1] and it is interesting to notice that the search for the rational ego emerged out of the quest for the irrational id in the early and middle 1930s,[2] the period when the rationality of modern industrialization had collapsed in the irrationality of the Nazi state. The experience of social irrationality was accompanied by a quest for ego rationality and for ways of relating ego and society.[3] One of the results was the psychosocial theory of life cycle development in eight stages associated with Erikson.[4]

Sigmund Freud's theory of sexual development was an attempt to understand certain aspects of irrational adult behavior, that is, the neuroses. In a somewhat similar way, although perhaps less self-consciously, stage development theory seeks to bring moral order out of the moral relativity and conflict of modernity by transforming moral dilemmas into diagnostic procedures (Kohlberg,) transforming the bewildering anonymity of contemporary institutions from a source of *anomie* leading to suicide (Durkheim) into a sequence of nurturing institutions giving intergenerational strength arranged in the form of a repetitive cycle (Erikson), turning the breakdown of traditional life patterns into a series of predictable crises (Sheehy 1976) and the bewildering range of faith options into a coherent and stable series of successive faith structures (Fowler).

It is important to realize that modernity has two sides. There is the rational side expressed in the ideals of the eighteenth-century Enlightenment, and there is the insidious way in which this was subverted into the rationalization of the industrial process under the pressure of growing capitalism until it resulted in a rationality that was no longer rational (Horkheimer 1973; Horkheimer and Adorno 1975). At this point, the true and the false reason had to be linked together in order to maintain credibility, and this could only be done by fantasy. It is extremely important to understand the role of fantasy, both in modernity itself and in the stage development theories as an

---

[1] Note the idea of the "institutional self" in Kegan 1982. The self is described as a bureaucracy, through the metaphors of administration and management.

[2] The foundations of ego psychology were laid down by A. Freud (1936/1968) and Hartmann (1937/1960). For the earlier evolution of Sigmund Freud's own theory of the ego, see Hartmann 1950/1972, chap. 6 ("Psychoanalysis and Developmental Psychology"). Erikson notes the significance of the fact that in an increasingly mechanical age the ego was now being seen in mechanical metaphors (1980, 47).

[3] In his 1944 paper "Psychoanalysis and Sociology," Hartmann finds the link between older psychoanalytic theory and the study of social structures to lie in the development of psychoanalytic object-relations theory. "We are therefore primarily concerned with the question in what manner and to what degree does a given social structure bring to the surface, provoke or reinforce certain instinctual tendencies . . ." (Hartmann 1950/1972, 28).

[4] The antecedents of Erikson's psychosocial theory lie in Freud's investigations of the intimate relationship between the personality structure and the social structure and in Hartmann's development of this work (see Hartmann 1950/1972).

expression of modernity (Horkheimer 1967, 106; Horkheimer and Adorno 1975, chap. 4; Castoriadis 1984; Haug 1986, chap. 1, sec. 6, and chap. 2, sec. 2; Hull 1987). On the face of it, modernity looks like the triumph of rationality. Many of its most sensitive critics (e.g., the nineteenth-century French poet Baudelaire and the German novelist and art critic Walter Benjamin) have emphasized that modernity is essentially the fleeting moment, that which is transitory, the perennially new, the whimsical, and the novel. This is why they tried to catch the spirit of modernity in the scraps and tatters of culture, in the fads and fashions of the shops, in cigarette ends, newspaper cuttings, and junk (Frisby 1985). In the stage development theories the radically new comes into being but is transitory. It passes away into what succeeds it, which is again qualitatively new (Haug 1986, chap. 1, sec. 7). Moreover, although stage development theory (especially in Piaget and Kohlberg) seems to be so powerfully rational, it is surprising how vulnerable it becomes to criticism of its imagery (e.g., Gilligan 1982; Moran 1983). The rational side is turned over, and underneath is a mass of symbols and images with which our life today is being interpreted. Rationality and fantasy blend in the stage development theories just as they do in modernity itself.

Structuralism

Structuralism provides a fourth link between the stage development theories and modernity. One of the main criticisms of the structuralist approach is that although at first sight what is new in history and society seems to be permitted to emerge as one structure succeeds the next, closer examination reveals that "the possibility of the emergence of something genuinely new, of real history, seems negated from the start. Change can only be a relatively new reorganization of the elements within an already established structure of relationships" (Bonino 1986, 83). The result of this attempt to reduce human experience to its essential structures, and so to make it universal, can lead to a suppression of the historically unique, and so when the bottom line is reached structuralism becomes a legitimization of the status quo.

Let us take an example from the work of Ronald Goldman. The story of Moses and the burning bush was used by Goldman to determine the developmental stage of children and young people in Piagetian terms, that is, intuitive, concrete, and abstract stages. In the form of the story that Goldman used, however, the following words were left out. "The people of Israel groaned under their bondage and cried out for help, and their cry under bondage came up to God, and God heard their groaning, and God remembered His covenant, and God saw the people of Israel, and God knew their condition" (Exod 2:23). These words are an essential introduction to the burning bush, since they set the theophany in the context of the liberating intention of God. Moreover, Goldman's version of the story ended before God had a chance to tell Moses *why* he had appeared in the burning bush. "Then the Lord said, 'I have seen the affliction of my people who are in Egypt and have heard their cry because of their task-masters. I know their suffering, and I have come down to deliver them'" (Exod 3:7). The result was a story that was no longer about radical historical change leading to a realignment of power on the part of the oppressed, but one that had already passed through the structuralist process, a story that was already prepared for the structuralist interpretation of what the children would say, and which also prepared the children to find in the story a problem of cause-and-effect rationality within a matter-of-fact "scientific" world (Goldman 1964, 253).

It is at this point that the social imaginary becomes visible (Castoriadis 1984, 83). The theological language is neutralized by the reification of such "invisible institutions" as "the concrete" and "the abstract." This is an example of what Cornelius Castoriadis meant when he spoke of "the prejudice that believes it is possible to describe a thing as it is without prejudice," pointing out that this prejudice "is itself only the skin of a certain historical institution of the project of theory" (Castoriadis 1984, 130). In other words, the things which we think we are describing so fairly and with such objectivity are the visible outcrops of the larger formations that are actually invisible to us, because they lie far beneath and are the basic support for our whole way of perceiving and speaking. The intention to discover in the children's minds the progressive unfolding of reason in a sequence of structured stages is the visible outcrop of the entire project of an enlightenment that seeks to discover in history and especially in our own history the unfolding and the culmination of progressive reason. This becomes visible only when an alternative mass is encountered. This is what happens when Goldman's version of the story is put back into its original biblical context. We then discover what I have elsewhere described as "an ideological crack" (Hull 1985, 85).

In commenting on the use of structuralism in psychoanalysis, Castoriadis remarks: "there is no reference to the concrete, historical life of the patients in society in which they have developed. The patient . . . is regarded as being merely the expression of a number of impersonal structures. Behind the emptiness of the personal life of the patient, everything is forever the same" (Castoriadis 1984, 46ff.). So, when the cognitive stage developmentalist looks for the way in which such abstractions as "the concrete" and "the abstract" may reveal themselves in the persons being studied, the investigator is under the power of "the social imaginary."

Structuralism is a variety of essentialism, in which the essence of human thought is sought in certain structural *a priori* categories. It is easy for this emphasis on essence, with its universality and its timelessness, to lead to an arrangement of ordered hierarchies. "This is part of the annunciation of the ideology of the monopoly capitalist period in which domination by the most powerful economic groups is effected by means of the delegation of power to prototypical leadership personalities, and in which the interests of these groups are concealed by means of the image of an essentially personal order of values, leadership and followings, status, order, racial elite and so forth. The intuition of essence helps to set up essentialist hierarchies in which the material and vital values of human life occupy the lowest rank, while the types of the saint, the genius and the hero take the first place (Marcuse 1968, 63).[5]

Power to the Powerless: Stage Theory and the Unconscious

One final link between the stage development theories and modernity must be noted. This has to do with these theories as examples of ego psychology. In its idealist antecedents (Kant), as also in the work of Freud and the structuralists proper of the middle years of this century, the structures remain unconscious. They order the conscious mind but are not themselves an object of consciousness. This becomes a problem for those versions of stage development theory which emphasize the formation and evolution of personal meaning in life, since if a more coherent meaning is to become a project of the ego it cannot remain at the preconscious or subconscious levels. It is in recognition of this that recent developments of this kind of stage development theory are compelled to speak of the structuring power of content, rather than the structuring power of the actual structures.

If we leave on one side the idea about the structuring power of content, because it does not seem reconcilable with the idea that it is the structures themselves that have structuring power, we are left with a problem in stage development theory concerning the relationship of the conscious and the unconscious. There is, as stage development theory affirms, a difference between the manifest content of the speech and that which is hidden beneath the surface of the content, that structure of which the speech is a symptom, that meaning for which the researcher seeks. From the point of view of ego psychology, this is a perfectly legitimate inquiry into the adaptation processes of the ego, the relationship between the manifest and the latent being sought in the "conflict-free areas of the ego."

By restricting the relationship between the manifest and the latent to these areas, and by "naturalizing" the manifest/latent relationship under the perspectives of universalizing structuralism, stage development theory encourages a neglect of the kind of relationships between the manifest and

---

[5] For further comments on the relationship between structuralism and stage development theory, see Heywood 1986, 72–78; Broughton 1981.

the latent that are potentially more explosive and more liberating. Particularly in the case of religious language, one has to reckon with "false consciousness" and with the barriers of resistance which prevent the latent meaning from breaking through the disguise of the open surface of thought. In stage development theory there is little notion of the manifest as occupying a dominating role over the deeper and potentially liberating hidden meanings. The manifest is not conceived of as having a repressive function but is made impersonal, inevitable, and natural by means of structuralism. Stage development theories certainly point out inconsistencies in the manifest content, but these are regarded as symptomatic of stage residence or stage transition, for the theory does not permit an arousal of hermeneutical suspicion which might suggest that the inconsistencies are the result of deeper, repressed disturbances originating in the history of the individual rather than in universal structures and precluding complete interpretation without recourse to ethics. In other words, the repressed relationship of the latent to the manifest requires understanding, sympathy, reconciliation, forgiveness, and renewal.

The result of this limitation is that stage development theory gives power to the teacher rather than to the pupil. It would not make much difference to the pupils if they knew they were in the concrete stage, but it would help the teacher to teach better. It is all too common that in the teacher–pupil relationship, too much power lies in the hands of the teacher, and the best pedagogies seek to transfer power from the teacher to the pupil. It seems to lie beyond the scope of stage development theory to do this, and this is why it remains, for the most part, an instrument of diagnosis and not a weapon of liberation. This feature of stage development theory is in itself sufficient to arouse the hermeneutical suspicion of those who study it with the interests of the powerless in mind. This is why stage development theory often seems to have but little potential for the renewal of the religious life today. It seeks to understand what is, rather than to create what is not.

Let us consider for a moment the case of Erik H. Erikson. It is likely that Erikson would agree with much of what has been said about the impact of modernity in its capitalistic form upon the life cycle. For example, he remarks that the ideology characteristic of our own time advocates "complete pragmatic abandon to the processes of production," because "unceasing production seems to be the thread which holds present and future together" (Erikson 1980, 170ff.). Often Erikson's attitudes toward the industrialized society are quite favorable. He explains that during the third stage of childhood, when the characteristic balance is between initiative and guilt, there is a need to instill into the child a spirit of free enterprise, continuing "the word 'enterprise' was deliberately chosen, for a comparative view of child-training suggests that it is the prevalent economic ideal . . .

which is transmitted to the child at a time when in identification with his parents he applies the dreams of early childhood to the as yet dim goals of an active adult life" (Erikson 1980, 86). Similarly, we note that the characteristic balance of the next stage, the stage of schooling, is *industry* versus inferiority. At other times, Erikson seems to be more alarmed about the consequences for psychic health of the ideology of a competitive, industrial world. Our language and our customs have begun to standardize the modern person, "so that he may become a reliable mechanism, prepared to adjust to the competitive exploitation of the machine world" (Erikson 1980, 47).

Erik Erikson and Capitalist Society

In view of his undoubted sensitivity to the economic and political context of the socialization process, it is surprising that Erikson did not include a wider range of institutions in his theory, in which the characteristic conflict or problem of one stage of individual life is met by an institution in which the strengths of many generations have been collected for the very answering of that need. So, for example, the religious institutions enable individuals throughout their entire life cycle to relive the basic infantile conflict between trust and mistrust. Erikson also includes the legal institutions, the theater, the school, the ideologies, the conventional expressions of friendship and solidarity, and marriage. There are, however, some significant omissions from his list. Erikson does not pay sufficient attention to the state itself or to the institutions of political life, the media, and the armed forces. While he sees the importance of industry up to a point, he does not include the giant industrial corporation among the formative institutions, and in spite of his wonderfully sensitive work on toys, he seems unaware of the significance of the commodity upon the shaping of the inner life of persons today. It is true that he does consider the double-edged nature of each institution, being aware, for example, of the way in which religion can become both a source of renewed hope and a rigid defense against wider loyalties, and it is also true that in compiling his list of relevant institutions he is looking for sources of ego strength or virtue, and so would naturally select institutions that are generally regarded as being beneficial. Nevertheless, the result is an emasculated series of social institutions in which the profound impact of the power of organized money and big business is generally ignored. So serious is this defect in a stage theory that is specifically psycho*social*, that the theory can only retain its usefulness if it is purged by a much more critical approach to the identity-shaping influence of contemporary structures of social power. To put it in the language of Jürgen Habermas, we might say that the structures of the life world must show far greater sensitivity to the colonizing power of the systems if they are to have any chance at all of reasserting their dignity and creativity over against the systems.[6]

Stage Theories as Pointing beyond Modernity

Let us close by briefly suggesting some of the ways in which stage development theories, even if they are vulnerable to the sort of ideological criticism we have been suggesting, may also point beyond modernity.

First, there seems to be a growing tendency to interpret the significance of the stage development theories in the light of interpretation theory itself. There is an increasing interest in the significance of the images which are suggested in the theories for the unfolding of human lives. This does not necessarily mean that the character of the stage theories as offering genuine knowledge of how and why human lives do in fact develop will be imperiled;[7] it does, however, suggest a more flexible way of understanding the knowledge, as a series of models and metaphors rather than as something springing from impersonal and unchanging essences.

Second, it is noticeable that theology is being increasingly used to provide alternative models and to offer sources of impetus both across the stages and for conversions within each stage. The somewhat ambiguous role of stage 6 in faith development theory is an interesting case. This could be interpreted as a "kingdom of God" intrusion that could, in principle, occur to people within any stage of development. There seems to be little remaining reason, in the light of the more recent developments in the theory, to retain stage 6 at the end of a hierarchal sequence. It is possible that faith development theory might move toward the Eriksonian idea of seeing within each crisis an outcome that leads to greater strength alongside an alternative possibility that would lead to increased weakness. So, within each stage, people may develop along lines that will encourage a self-grounded position or may become more open toward a "kingdom of God" situation. Faith development, the theory is coming close to saying, is not enough if it remains nearly normal. The autonomy of self-subsistence must be broken at each stage if human vocation is to be fulfilled.[8]

[6] For recent statements of his views, see the contributions by Jürgen Habermas in Bernstein 1985.

[7] For a discussion of the difference between the objective knowledge content of a social theory and its character as formed by ideological corruption, see Moskvichev 1986.

[8] These reflections arise from chap. 3 ("Faith Development Theory and the Human Vocation") of Fowler 1984a. On p. 128 the word "detoxification" occurs in a context that refers to the possibility of ideological contamination of the work of a teacher. This seems to mark a deepened sensitivity on the part of Fowler to these issues. On the other hand, he refers with approval to the work of Daniel Bell (pp. 77ff., 97ff.), who is regarded by Habermas as typical

Third, the idea that institutions have an optimal sponsoring level is applied to church congregations by James Fowler in his most recent book. There seems to be no reason why this could not be applied to other institutions, and it would be interesting to reflect, in the light of faith development theory, on the pastoral care of persons in film and television, waged and un-waged situations, the institutions that care for the disabled and the sick, and especially in the great financial institutions of today.

What is the relationship between Fowler's more recent ideas about pastoral care and the concept of "culture creation" in recent theories of industrial management (Huczynski 1987)? How do the various ways in which institutions may be changed correspond to the changes which people experience in the passage from one stage to another? What would a "king-dom of God" alternative be for each institution in each kind of institutional transformation?

Finally, the power that the stage development theories generate must be put into the hands of the powerless. An interesting move in this direction is found in the "tapestry of life" worksheet at the end of Fowler's most recent book, although faith development theory seems to have played only a minor part in its composition (Fowler 1987a, 118). At this point, a courageous attempt must be made to overcome the impersonal implications of the sub-liminal nature of structural residents by introducing the methods of ideo-logical critique and other forms of critical theory. It ought to be possible for adults to be helped to recognize elements of intuitive-projective thinking in their lives and to value and to criticize these. The faith development diag-nosis could be used for helping people to identify and to evaluate positively and negatively elements of mythic literalism in their thoughts. Moreover, more should be done to adumbrate the ways in which the later stages appear as seeds in the earlier stages. It should be possible for young children in stages 1 or 2 to be helped to recognize features of later stages present within their own thinking already and to make use of these to proliferate childlike imagery. In the Christian nurture process, this can be turned into a variety of techniques of theological conversation with young children. Whether with children or adults, one stage can be used to critique another stage. In other words, can the elements of stage development theory, and especially faith development, be turned into a pedagogy of the oppressed?

In his study of the hermeneutics of revelation, Paul Ricoeur has distin-guished the revelatory significance of a number of different kinds of biblical speech (Ricoeur 1981, 73ff.). In a somewhat similar manner, may we not interpret faith development theory as offering a kind of hermeneutic of the contemporary religious life? There are various kinds of religious speech,

---

of the American conservative culture critics who form a major threat to the liberation of human life systems.

each of which expresses some perspective on the religious life, and each of which needs to be purged both internally by the "kingdom of God" perspective and externally by the negotiation of one style of speech against another. The vital thing is to prevent the colonization of the religious consciousness by one form of religious speech. Without entirely abandoning its sequential or cumulative character, the stage development theories can develop into pedagogical manifolds for mutual emancipation.

13

The Influence of Societal and Political Factors on Religious Development and Education in the United States

GLORIA DURKA

Three Interpretations of U.S. Social and Political Experience

SOCIAL CRITICS such as Gregory Baum (1986) use three politicophilosophical approaches to interpret contemporary U.S. society. The first one is often euphemistically called *neoconservative*. It represents a peculiar union between monetarism and militarism. The neoconservative political philosophy regards the free market as the essential principle of society, assuring economic growth, personal freedom, and the relative justice of equal opportunity.

The second political philosophy in the United States represents the *liberal* tradition. It is critical of monetarism and militarism, and it proposes reform. According to this liberal philosophy, what has gone wrong in society is the decline of morals. People in the United States have become selfish, narcissistic, and concerned only with themselves and their self-promotion. Gone are the traditional spirit of social responsibility and the ideal of the citizen imbued with loyalty to the community. The classical expression of the liberals' lament is Robert Bellah's work, *Habits of the Heart* (1985). According to this study, all that is left in the United States is expressive individualism, which manifests itself on a purely material level as the search for self-fulfillment. If healing and reform are to come to the U.S. republic, Bellah and his associates think it will have to come through a cultural conversion to the secular and religious traditions that are bearers of community values.

There is a third approach to U.S. society, which has been called the *radical* approach. Here social evils, fragmentation of community, and indifference toward third-world nations are seen as the consequences of a politico-economic order created by the rich and powerful to enhance and protect their own privileges. If this analysis is correct, then the liberal social philosophy turns out to be an ideology designed to legitimate existing power structures. A striking and rather recent example of this radical approach has come from a small group of somewhat influential pastoral leaders. In their pastoral letter on the economy (1987), the U.S. Catholic bishops have a clear sense that the problems of personal spirituality, personal ethics, and personal well-being cannot be understood and overcome without an analysis of the material factors of domination and a historical commitment to eman-cipation. They call for bold proposals for what they term "a new American experiment" which will allow for an economy that is to be by the people and for the people. To achieve this, the bishops recommend structural changes for which there exist no precedents in the history of capitalism (Pastoral Letter on Catholic Social Teaching and the U.S. Economy, paragraphs 283, 285).

While this approach exists as a minority trend among U.S. theologians, it is of no small significance that a strong impetus for such an approach comes from women theologians who situate the struggle of women in a movement critical of all forms of domination. The work of these women theologians reflects what many consider to be the most revolutionary movement of our times—feminism, with its radical critique of all forms of personal and social reality. It is through this feminist lens that some of the most cogent aspects of U.S. societal and political experience are revealed as having impact on religious development and education. The most pivotal of these, in the view of many, converge at the feminist critique of women's reality.

The Social and Religious Construction of Women's Reality: Some Feminist Perspectives

Some years ago, I suggested that the linking of mutually exclusive dualisms with the distinction between male and female has produced ideol-ogies and social structures that oppress women and have been the source of stress for women who challenge these prevailing myths by their personal and/or professional lives (Durka 1982). There is a genuine sense in which feminists already know that human experience is always interpreted experi-ence, for to be a feminist is to be aware of the power of cultural images of women and theories about the nature of women to twist their own experi-ences and understanding of themselves into hurtful and hateful shapes. On the other hand, feminists also realize that it is far more difficult to transcend the limits placed by social and cultural conditioning than we Western rationalists have long thought. When women recognize this fact and struggle to express who they really are and what they hope for, they become aware that all thinking, including feminist thinking, takes place within a network of unconscious and semiconscious presuppositions about the wider context within which all experience occurs. Ultimately this network constitutes an implicit metaphysics whose premises are embedded in our institutions, in the structure and lexicon of our language, and in the unquestioned deliverances of "common sense." These premises, although not obviously patriarchal, nevertheless shape and are shaped by patriarchal structures and modes of thought. They are also the source of inadequate models of anthropology which have prevented women from gaining access to power and leadership in society and in the church.[1]

Models of Anthropology

Even the briefest inquiry into the two prevailing models of anthropology used to describe women's experience is enough to reveal their basic inadequacies. In the Catholic Church, the first model is reflected in official arguments against the ordination of women. Simply put, the first model is that of a *dual-nature anthropology* in which a complementary duality between the sexes is seen as inherent in nature and, therefore, part of the divine plan. This duality "is the ordering principle for complementary roles, functions, and activities of women and men" (Research Report, Catholic Theological Society of America, 1978). It emphasizes the unchanging structure of nature, and it views revelation, tradition, theology, and ethics as past-oriented: What is has been given and must not be changed. New knowledge of the human person derived from the human sciences is irrelevant to theological discussion since the goal of the latter is to preserve the past order as natural, as the order of creation, and as revealed.

---

[1] Feminist philosophers and theologians have observed that throughout its history Western culture has been pervaded by a series of mutually exclusive dualisms or dichotomies. These include, for example, creator and creature, humanity and nature, mind and body, reason and emotion, self and other, subject and object, individuality and relatedness, life and death. Each of these dichotomies has in some way been correlated with the dualism of male and female. Furthermore, each has exhibited a pattern of dominance and subordination. The paradigm of dualism and domination and linking of these various dualisms with the distinction between male and female have produced ideologies and social structures that oppress women. The assumptions on which these ideologies and structures are based are metaphysical in the last analysis. They are concretely embedded in our languages and institutions and engraved in our deepest feelings. These ideas are explored in an essay by Valerie Saiving entitled "Feminism and Process Philosophy: A Feminist Appropriation of Whitehead's Thought," delivered as a Dudleian Lecture at Harvard University in 1977.

The *single-nature anthropology* is radically opposite. Besides its negation of rigidly defined roles for women or men beyond the biological, this anthropology puts emphasis on history and the data of experience rather than on nature. It affirms the importance of the human sciences for theological reflection. Greater scope is given to human freedom and responsibility since past social patterns are likely to be construed as human products rather than as God-given permanent structures. The emphasis is on history, whose changing patterns are seen as the responsibility of human agency. This approach entails views of revelation, tradition, theology, and ethics as grounded in present experience as well as in the past.

While for the most part there are no longer assertions of the inferiority of women in U.S. ecclesiastical or theological discourse, recent official documents of the Roman Catholic Church, for example, affirm a dual anthropology, the complementary "different but equal" status of men and women as inherent in nature and, therefore, part of the divine plan. This is the basis from which the complementary roles and functions of the sexes derive. Beyond the biologically determined psychological and sociological characteristics and the limited scope of human freedom already noted, this view finds a central analogy between nature and the economy of salvation.

A third vision is struggling into existence today, a *"transformative," person-centered model*. This view regards both the dual and single anthropologies as inadequate because they place the impetus for change on individual efforts. The new transformative model is both personal and public; it seeks to transform the old gender stereotypes at the same time as it aims to transform the social and cultural structures, which are their inseparable context in human life. This transformative model received its impetus from changes that have begun in society and from the Christian faith, which calls all persons to likeness to the God of Jesus in love, compassion, mercy, peace, service, care, and community. Both women and men are called to this likeness, not to the half-personhood of complementarity that often is a hidden form of domination.

The difference in the transformative model from the other two lies in its explicit acknowledgment that anthropological models are not merely formal, individualistic concepts, but they are embedded in particular social contexts. Thus the dual anthropology corresponds to a hierarchic-elitist model of society. It is a model present in its clearest form since the rise of the state and the development of political ruling classes, although it was broken in principle by the English, American, and French revolutions. On the other hand, the one-nature model corresponds to the "one-dimensional" society, a product of the modern period, and associated with the revolutions' ideals of freedom, equality, brotherhood, and democracy. Despite the inspiring ideals of this vision, experience has proved that "under the cloak of democracy, the real ruling groups have been hidden (Buckley 1979). In the United

States, for example, blacks, Native Americans, newly arrived immigrants, and women must struggle to have a voice. The upper elite is really the paradigm for all people, and thus women and minorities must conform to the single (male, white, Protestant) norm.

While societal situations may severely limit human freedom in its self-determination, political and liberation theologians have stressed even further the depth of societal conditioning on freedom and responsibility, the very basis of human response to God.[2] These themes are helpful in appraising the variety of views of human nature or the nature of women especially as they indicate past, present, and future perspectives. While the dual anthropology conforms at least partially to the past experience of women, the single anthropology corresponds in part to their present experience and aspiration. The dual anthropology, though adequate to the historical past, clearly proves inadequate to the experience and aspiration of women (and many men), and to the gospel message of equality today. The single anthropology is more adequate, but fails if it capitulates to an individualistic, or single male or female model; all the virtues of the gospel are needed by all persons. The transformative model indicates especially the future hopes of women for both individual and social dimensions of human life. It also indicates the element of radical human freedom in determining what human nature will become: Humanity will choose whatever future human beings will be. The transformative model is more adequate to a fully social vision of the future if it preserves awareness of the historical conditioning of the past and the struggle for equality (if not transformation) on the part of women in the present (Carr 1980).

Women's Voice and Place in U.S. Society

Historically the Christian churches in the United States have emphasized the religious education of children. In the Roman Catholic tradition, for example, the greater part of available resources were earmarked for that

---

[2] Nature/culture polarity can readily be transposed to biblical and theological ideas of human creaturehood and freedom, immanence and transcendence. Both are dimensions of human personhood, experience, and action. While Christian churches focus their critique on societal forms that fail to reverence both poles (natural life and human agency), the feminist critique must be heard in the churches as well, with its insistence that neither pole is more fully embodied in either sex. Nature and culture are the responsibility of both men and women as human beings. The full integration of this biblical and theological anthropology would be truly revolutionary in both church and society, changing the gender-based character of private and public life as we know it. The gospel vision of the integrity of human creatureliness and transcendence has something important to teach the culture, and women. But the feminist experience has something to teach the churches as well. For further development of these ideas, see Carr 1980.

purpose, that is, a separate school system for the young, sacramental preparation programs, in-service education for teachers of the young. Recently, religious development theory has helped broaden the scope of religious education to extend across the whole life cycle. But it has also generated new questions about "feminine" and "masculine" characteristics of religious experience and reminded us that any method, any theory of interpretation, any argument can aid conversation. But none can replace it. Those who have been absent from the conversation need a voice in it. Women represent the largest segment of the human population that has been absent from educational conversation. It is not so curious then that researchers concerned with the development of women have found that women repeatedly used the metaphor of voice to depict their intellectual and ethical development; and that the development of a sense of voice, mind, and self were inextricably intertwined (Belenky 1986).

The lack of voice, on the other hand, has deleterious personal and political effects, as researchers have also shown.[3] For example, studies have repeatedly revealed violent families, whether rich or poor, to be characterized by high levels of social isolation, poor communication, rigid sex-role stereotyping, and extreme inequalities in the distribution of power among family members. These characteristics are consistently noted, whether the studies are of wife battering, child abuse, or abuse of the elderly, and they occur at all levels of the social class structure (Finkelhor 1983). The research raises serious questions for religious educators and pastoral ministers/theologians who have the courage to face the history of their own religious tradition's attitude of condoning and tolerating violence within the family structure. What role have the Christian churches played in supporting wife beating, for example? And have such attitudes been passed down uncritically so as to find expression in teaching and preaching even to this day?[4] And more specifically to

---

[3] Being denied a voice is what Gustavo Gutierrez calls "cultural death," the taking away of all those things that give unity and strength to the dispossessed of the world (1983). Many thinkers have dealt with the connection between violence and silence but the following assessment by Thomas Merton will suffice here: "Violence is essentially wordless, and it can begin only where thought and rational communication have broken down. Any society which is geared for violent action is by that very fact systematically unreasonable and inarticulate. Thought is not encouraged, and the exchange of ideas eschewed as filled with all manner of risk. Words are kept at a minimum, at least as far as their variety and content may be concerned, though they may pour over the armed multitude in cataracts; they are simply organized and inarticulate noise destined to arrest thought and release violence, inhibiting all desire to communicate with the enemy in any other way than by destructive impact" (1965).

[4] From the misogyny of Church Fathers such as Augustine, Jerome, and Tertullian to recent statements about the complementary role of women in the family, churches have continued to play an ambivalent role regarding the abuse of women, at times supporting wife beating and at other times suggesting moderation. In the fifteenth-century *Rules of Marriage* by Friar Cherubino of Siena is found the following advice: "When you see your wife commit an offense

the topic of this essay, has the women's movement been successful in making a real difference in women's place in U.S. society?

The Myth of Women's Liberation in the United States

Greater Opportunity for the Few

Two ramifications of the women's movement are quite apparent for the middle class elite. First, women's life-course changes in recent years reflect changes in their relationships with two social institutions: the labor force and the family. Recent studies have documented the rapid transformation of the U.S. woman from dependent, family-centered individual—one who makes life-course decisions (school, marriage, work, children, etc.) in terms of someone else's objectives (parents, husband, children)—to primary individual, one who makes these decisions in terms of her personal objectives. This is the young woman of the 1980s. All aspects of her life course—where and with whom she lives, when she marries, when she works, and when she has children—are now much less determined by her family role and are much more a function of personal choice.

A second ramification that emerges from the research is that these changes in women's demographic behavior are actually returns to trends established in the first half of this century. By several key measurers, today's

---

... scold her sharply, bully and terrify her. And if this still doesn't work ... take up a stick and beat her soundly, for it is better to punish the body and correct the soul. ... Readily beat her, not in rage but out of charity ... so that the beating will redound to your merit and her good" (in Okun 1986, 3). Bernard of Siena, a predecessor of Cherubino, exhorted his parishioners to exercise more compassion for their wives, by treating them with as much mercy as they would their hens and pigs. The Reformation brought no great changes to the patriarchal structure for women. Martin Luther also believed that women are subject to men as punishment for sin: "The rule remains with the husband, and the wife is compelled to obey him by God's command" (Lectures on Genesis, 2:18.) Nor did the views of the Calvinist John Knox hold out any promise for women. Reviewing the Bible and the ideas of the earlier Church Fathers, Knox reiterated the natural and irrefutable inferiority of women's character, their sole place in the family, and their rightful subordination to their husbands, and God's decree that it be so.

The sixteenth to eighteenth centuries were known as the "great age of flogging" which was used as a way of controlling the powerless, that is, children, women, and the lower classes. Wife beating, in spite of the theologians' use of the moral order and fear of damnation to win compliance, remained widespread. Community tolerance of such behavior was great, as long as physical force was suitable. It was the moderate use of physical punishment that separated the reasonable husband from the brute. It was only in the latter part of the nineteenth century that reforms in the treatment of women and wives began in both England and America. By the end of that century wife beating had been made illegal. According to Okun (1986), however, though the laws of chastisement ended de jure, they continue to live on de facto in the attitudes that prevail in the daily lives of people, in continuing sexist bias in our society, in an inability to see that wife abuse continues, or in an unwillingness to consider it a serious problem.

young women appear more similar to their grandmothers than to their mothers. The characteristics of women's life course mentioned above are believed to be long-term patterns that provide a better benchmark for projecting women's behavior than the aberrant behavior of the 1950s (McLaughlin and Melber 1986). The only current change with no historic precedent is the rapid entry of women into the labor force in recent years. From 1890 to 1940, the proportion of women in the labor force grew from 18.2 percent to 25.8 percent.[5] By 1966 more than 40 percent of women were employed, and by 1978 half of all women were employed. Although there is no precedent for the rapid entry of women into the labor force, a larger historical perspective casts light on the phenomenon. Participation in the labor force can be viewed as post–industrial revolution participation in the production of goods and services. When the United States was primarily an agricultural society, the family served as a focus for both production and consumption, and women played a large role in the former. With industrialization and urbanization, production shifted outside the family, and men assumed primary responsibility for that function. The family became the unit of consumption, and women, though they continued to work in the home, ceased to produce goods and services. Seen in this light, the recent trend toward participation in the labor force in a wider range of occupations represents the reinstitution of women's central role in production (McLaughlin and Melber 1986). In sum, the rise of elite middle-class women as primary individuals is concomitant with a decline in the significance of marriage and family as *the* controlling institutions around which women organize their lives.[6] Although an oversimplification, it also can be said that the relationship of women to both institutions has become like that of men. This convergence of male and female attitudes is due primarily to changes in the attitudes of women regarding work; male attitudes have changed much less. Researchers see this dissonance as a pressure wave moving

---

[5] During World War II, women's labor force participation reached its apex in 1944, at 36.3 percent. The proportion dropped to 30.8 percent after the war and then continued to rise, with some fluctuation related to the economy, at a rate far greater than in prewar years, exceeding wartime levels by 1956 (McLaughlin and Melber 1986).

[6] These changes, however, did not affect one important constant: women continue to place a high value on marriage and family, even as marriage rates fall, divorce rates remain high, and the family exerts less control over their lives (McLaughlin and Melber 1986). This is confirmed by the research on changing structures of family life conducted under my direction at Fordham University. Over the last eight years, with the help of thirty research assistants and over sixty graduate students, more than eight hundred randomly selected families have been interviewed to obtain information on various dimensions of family life. In addition to these structured interviews, participant families completed the Moos Family Environment Scale, an empirical instrument that is recognized for its high degree of validity and reliability. Results of some of these studies are reported in *Changing Patterns of Catholic Family Life*, ed. G. Durka (Bronx, NY: Fordham University Graduate School of Religion and Religious Education, 1978).

through the workplace and the home as women struggle to manage both career and family. Women pay a heavy price in trying to balance the competing demands of the family and the workplace, both of which are presently organized around traditional assumptions concerning women's roles. These assumptions are now invalid, and new formats for the worker-mother are being invented.[7] Public policy has not, however, addressed the issue of structural tension for employed mothers and for fathers who do not have full-time helpmates at home. In effect, today's woman is acting on her own to reduce the impact of the family on her life course.

A Lesser Life for the Many

Closer analysis of the effect of the women's movement on the wider society exposes some disturbing myths. Today 45 percent of working women are single, divorced, separated, or widowed, and have no option but to take prime economic responsibility for themselves and their children. The low earning power of women helps explain why 35 percent of single mothers fall below the poverty line. Only 7 percent of employed women in the United States work in managerial positions, and only 10 percent earn more than $20,000 a year. Three quarters of U.S. working women continue to be employed in traditional "women's jobs." Most are badly paid.[8] In 1984, one out of every four women earned less than $10,000 a year working full time. In addition, the United States is the only industrialized country that has no statutory maternity leave. One hundred and seventeen countries (including every industrial nation and many developing countries) guarantee a woman the following rights: leave from employment for childbirth, job protection while she is on leave, and the provision of a cash benefit to replace all or most of her earnings (Hewlett 1986).

Why hasn't the women's movement succeeded in upgrading the economic conditions of women's lives? Why has the experience of European women been so very different from that of women in the United States? Part of the

---

[7] Sharing child care is on the rise among working parents. Research also indicates that most young men and most young women agree that both husband and wife should share in household work. Today's men, however, have not been devoting more time to household chores than men did in the past. The extent to which men do share the work has not been measured.

[8] "Society therefore has been rather hypocritical in the praise it has lavished upon feminine caring. The 59 cents female dollar is inconceivable apart from such hypocrisy, as is the exclusion of feminine care from the boardrooms of power. . . . None of the major institutions that one sees when surveying the cultural landscape has adopted androgynous, let alone feminist paradigms. The praise of feminine care that wafts through religion, education, medicine, or government is quite tainted, and more than vulnerable to the charge of being proffered in bad faith" (Carmody, 1984, 150).

explanation lies in the goals and objectives of feminism in Europe and the United States. The U.S. movement has defined the problem of womankind as that of acquiring a full set of legal, political, and economic rights, and achieving control over one's body. The assumption is that once women possess the same rights as men and can choose not to have children, they achieve true equality of opportunity and are able to attain power, status, and money on the same terms as men. In Europe social feminists have conceived of the problem differently. For them, it is not woman's lack of legal rights that constitutes her main handicap or even her lack of reproductive freedom. Rather, it is her dual burden—in the home and in the work force—that leads to second-class citizenship. The goal of the social feminists has, therefore, become one of lightening this load by instituting family support systems. The conviction is that because women are wives and mothers as well as workers and citizens, they need special compensatory policies if they are to accomplish as much as men in the world beyond the home. Equal rights are seen as only part of the struggle. If such is the dilemma, what is its import for those who fashion theories of religious development and education?

The Impact of the Women's Movement on Religious Development and Education

Women's recent reflection on their own experience in all its variety and their attempt to develop corresponding models of humanity are important developments in theological anthropology. Religious development theorists need to pay critical attention to the changes in human nature that are occurring through the experience of women today. Far from a merely speculative enterprise, it is a necessary exploration of past and present experience which has become focused on the question of the future: What will humankind become? For if human persons have the power to determine, in part at least, what the human future will be, then indeed, the experience of women must be heeded. The uniqueness of feminist theology is the fact that women claim the principle of full humanity for themselves. Women name themselves as subjects of authentic and full humanity (Ruether 1983). How then will the perspectives of the gospel, with its message of sin and liberation in Christ, be integrated into that future for women?

While recognizing that society has always imaged women through the metaphor of *be-ing*, religious educators have the obligation to propose *do-ing* as an appropriate metaphor for conceptualizing the world of women. Religious educators dare not minimize the very real historical power of women to be architects of what is most authentically human. On the one hand, close analysis of women's history will reveal that anyone who has lived in "women's place" in human history has had to come to terms with the responsibility of being a reciprocal agent. Women's lives literally have been shaped by the power not only to bear human life at the biological level but to nurture life; this is a social and cultural power. Though much of contemporary culture has come to disvalue women's role and, with it, to disvalue nurturance, genuine nurturance is a formidable power. Insofar as it has taken place in human history, it has been largely through women's action (Harrison 1981). But on the other hand, religious educators cannot deny the restrictions of women's be-ing and do-ing that still oppress women.[9] Rather, the critical act of education requires that women be made aware of how their notions of reality are shaped by patriarchal structures and modes of thought. Otherwise, so long as the forces that shape women's reality remain unconscious, they threaten to vitiate all attempts to understand and express women's own emerging vision of reality. Women themselves must bring more fully into consciousness and criticize their unexamined notions about the nature of things.

Will women respond to "consciousness raising" about their own religious lives, much less that of women in the larger global world? The answer, I believe, is already being traced even on the basis of the limited research done so far on the inner life of women. The theme of increased self-esteem (expressed as increased interest in the self as a person) is distributed across the whole age range studied.[10] Moreover, it is in no way limited to women who have raised children; thus it cannot be explained by children's increasing independence and the need for a new focus as the nest empties. Nor is this theme limited to women who were married. And women who were employed and those who were not are equally likely to express it. "Interest" is defined as attention, curiosity, concern, and having the *power* of exciting these attitudes. Perhaps a new sense of power in the self is implied by the responses of the women interviewed for these studies. What shape this new sense of power can take could provide religious educators with a new agenda for women. For example, the work done by Belenky et al. (1986) suggests that connected knowing comes more easily to many women than does separate knowing. This was borne out by Gilligan (1982) and Lyons (1983), who demonstrated that an ethic of responsibility may be more natural to most women than an ethic of rights. Just as Freire claims that if the banking model is abandoned in favor of the problem-solving model "the power of oppression" will be undermined (Freire 1971, 62), so too if the separate model

---

[9] The critique of the distorted social systems in which we live is an arduous task which calls for courage, knowledge, independence, initiative, and responsibility, the ability to challenge and to struggle — qualities traditionally associated with male humanity. Thus "feminine" and "masculine" qualities are needed by both women and men (Buckley 1979). And in religious terms, repentance and conversion are needed not only by individuals, but also at the institutional levels of church and society, as that is where the personal and public dimensions of experience are joined.

[10] See, e.g., Baruch and Barnett 1979; Belenky 1986; Durka 1982, 163–78; Gilligan 1982; Neugarten 1979; Rubin 1979; Sheehy 1981.

of knowing is replaced with the connected model, women can be spared the alienation, repression, and division their schooling currently confers on them (Jacobus 1979). Education that emphasizes connection over separation, understanding and acceptance over assessment, and collaboration over debate would help women toward community, power, and integrity. Such an education could facilitate the development of women's minds and spirits rather than, as in so many cases reported in the research, arresting or even reversing their growth.

In sum, the religious development of women is an important phenomenon deserving more research. In undertaking such research and in teaching to its implications, religious educators should be aware that interpretation of its findings depends on who is designing and evaluating the work. This entails being wary of the biases introduced by a too-easy acceptance of conventional categories and models. A feminist appropriation of any theory will be creative, that is, active, critical, and imaginative. It will be open to new ways of thinking but will take nothing on authority; and it will insist on testing every hypothesis by reference to the immediate experience of women.

Some Possible Uses of Religious Development Theory: An Educational Perspective

There is no intellectual, cultural, political, or religious tradition of interpretation that does not ultimately live by the quality of its conversation; there is also no tradition that does not eventually have to acknowledge its own plurality and ambiguity (Tracy 1987). Conversations such as the present volume promote a working paradigm of the human situation drawn from a sufficiently large sample of experience that can eventually stimulate dialogue and lead yet to a further synthesis. This task has already begun (e.g., Dykstra and Parks 1986). Other people must create other paradigms and make different syntheses of various cultural-religious traditions. In addition, other possible uses of religious development theory include the following:

— Each theory presents its own common language which makes conversation possible and allows experience to be shared, validated, and questioned.

— A feminist critique of theories of religious development uncovers incipient patriarchal ideology, thus destroying its normative character. Further, if the prophetic norm is asserted to be central to biblical faith and feminists appropriate this norm for women, then patriarchy will no longer be maintained as authoritative. Prophetic faith denounces religious ideologies and systems that function to justify and sanctify the dominant, unjust social order, especially but not exclusively in the basic unit of society, the family.

— Finally, current theories illustrate that there is no final and definitive theory of development, no final synthesis that encompasses all human experience, criticizes what is oppressive, and appropriates what is usable in all religious traditions. This reminds us of the reconstructive nature of theory building itself, which is faithful to the quest for greater adequacy and appropriateness, to use Tracy's terms (Tracy 1975).

Questions for Further Consideration

What are some of the educational questions that arise when religious development is viewed through the lens of emerging social and political factors? In my view an open exploration of educational questions requires several specific features: (a) appreciating that the prime task of educational scholarship is not merely to convey understanding of educational practices but to reflectively understand these relationships as social constructions and to initiate an awareness that these patterns are objects of choice and possible candidates for change; (b) identifying discrepancies between dominant versions of reality promulgated in formal institutions and the lived experience of subordinate groups in relation to such institutions; (c) taking the vantage point of the subordinated and remaining engaged in collective dialogue with people more fully immersed in oppressive social relationships; (d) extending the dialogue of critical pedagogy beyond narrow educational concerns focused only on the schools to facilitate efforts to make sense of the entirety of everyday life; and (e) recognizing that it is through subordinated peoples' own appropriation of cultural power that more nonelitist democratic forms of education are most likely to be generated and sustained. With this background in mind, the following questions are proposed:

— Can any theory of religious development, as presently construed, help expose the dynamics of cultural power and enable popular engagement in creating alternative futures?

—What do current theories of religious development have to contribute to the empowerment of subordinate groups through shared understanding of the social construction of reality?

—What new insights will the life-course perspective in the study of social change yield for educators and/or ministers?

— How will religious education help women adjust to their changing family responsibilities and the consequent series of changes in their life course? What will be the impact of these changes on the social environment?

— For women, unable to communicate with the God of patriarchy, imprisoned in a night of unbroken symbols, how is the image of God to undergo transformation? Can a theory of religious development be a crucible in which God-images and language will be transformed?

—What image of authentic human life does religious development theory present to women, and to the whole Christian community, about women?

— How can any theory of religious development help to break the silence of those who are victims in society, nurture the religious imagination of the spiritually impoverished, bind the alienated in communities of hope, free the dominant to surrender privilege, empower families to nurture transfamilial loyalties which reach out to the world?

Conclusion

One of the unanticipated rewards of bringing others into the conversation (especially women, as this essay seeks to highlight) is that the study and education of the other enable us to see all of religious education differently. A strategy for this difficult dialogue has been named "an analogical imagination" (Tracy 1981).

As a heuristic and pluralistic strategy it may prove useful for the conversation among different theorists of religious development. The phrase can remind conversation partners that difference and otherness once interpreted as other and as different are thereby acknowledged as in some way possible, and, in the end, analogous. Anyone who can converse can learn to appropriate another possibility. Between person and person, as well as between person and theory, there exists in every authentic conversation an openness to mutual transformation. Our conversations can become what they in fact always were: limited, fragile, necessary exercises in reaching relatively adequate knowledge. Such religious education conversation, to use Jane Rowland Martin's words, ". . . will also enable us to discern ways to bring educational practice into tune with the full range of people's lives and with the present perils to life on earth" (J. R. Martin 1985).

Bibliography

Achermann, M.
  1981   *Kognitive Argumentationsfiguren des religiösen Urteils bei Atheisten.*
          Lizentiatsarbeit. Prepublication draft. Fribourg: Pädagogisches Institut.
Althof, W., and F. Oser
  1986   "Der moralische Kontext als 'Sumpfbeet' möglicher Entwicklung:
          Erziehung angesichts der Individuum-Umwelt-Verschränkung." In
          Gesellschaftlicher Zwang und moralische Autonomie, edited by H.
          Bertram. Frankfurt: Suhrkamp.
Ames, E. S.
  1910   *The Psychology of Religious Experience.* London: Constable.
Andree, T. G. I. M.
  1983   *Gelovig word je niet vanzelf: Godsdienstige opvoeding van r.k. jongeren
          tussen 12 en 20 jaar.* Nijmegen: Dekker & van de Vegt.
  1984   "Zeg me wie je ouders zijn." In *Godsdienstige opvoeding in het geding,*
          edited by W. Ytsma and D. Brokerhof. Kampen: Kok.
Arlès, P.
  1965   *Centuries of Childhood: A Social History of Family Life.* Translated by R.
          Baldick. New York: Random House.
Asheim, I.
  1901   *Glaube und Erziehung bei Luther: Ein Beitrag zur Geschichte des Ver-
          hältnisses von Theologie und Pädagogik.* Heidelberg: Quelle & Meyer.
Baker-Fletcher, G.
  1987   "Faith Development Theory and Black Male Experience in America."
          Unpublished paper, Harvard Divinity School.
Baker-Fletcher, K.
  1987   "Faith Development Theory and Biographies of Afro-American
          Women." Unpublished paper, Harvard Divinity School.
Bargel, T.
  1979   "Überlegungen und Materialien zu Wertdisparitäten und Wertwandel
          in der BRD." In H. Klages and P. Kmieciak, *Wertwandel und gesell-
          schaftlicher Wandel.* Frankfurt: Campus Verlag.
Barnes, E.
  1892   "Theological Life of a California Child." *Pedagogical Seminary* 2.
Baruch, G., and R. Barnett
  1979   *If the Study of Midlife Had Begun with Women.* Working Paper no. 38.
          Wellesley College Center for Research on Women.

Baum, G.
　1986　　"The Social Context of American Theology." *Catholic Theological Society of America Proceedings* 41.
Bayer, O.
　1980　　"Wer bin ich? Gott als Autor meiner Lebensgeschichte: Zum 250 Geburtstag von Johann Georg Hamann." *Theologische Beiträge* 11.
Beattie, J. H. M.
　1966　　"Ritual and Social Change." *Man* 1.
　1978　　"Über das Verstehen von Ritualen." In Kippenberg and Luchesi 1978.
Beck, U.
　1983　　"Jenseits von Stand und Klasse?" *Soziale Welt* 2.
Becker, E.
　1973　　*The Denial of Death.* New York: Free Press.
Becker, U.
　1987　　"Ökumenisches Lernen: Überlegungen zur Geschichte des Begriffs, seiner Vorstellungen und seiner Rezeption in der westdeutschen Religionspädagogik." In *Glaube im Dialog: 30 Jahre religionspädagogische Reform,* edited by K. Gossmann. Gütersloh: Mohn.
Beechick, R. A.
　1974　　"Children's Understanding of Parables: A Developmental Study." Ed.D. dissertation, Arizona State University.
Belenky, M. F., B. M. Clinchy, N. R. Goldberger, and J. M. Turule
　1986　　*Women's Ways of Knowing: The Development of Mind, Voice, and Self.* New York: Basic Books.
Bell, J.
　1985　　Review of Fowler 1984a. *Christian Century* 102.
Bellah, R. N.
　1968　　"Civil Religion in America." In *Religion in America,* edited by W. G. McLoughlin and R. Bellah. Boston: Houghton Mifflin.
　1970　　*Beyond Belief: Essays on Religion in a Post-Traditional World.* New York: Harper & Row.
Bellah, R. N., R. Madsen, W. M. Sullivan, A. Swidler, and S. M. Tipton
　1985　　*Habits of the Heart.* Berkeley: University of California Press.
Berger, P. L.
　1970　　*Auf den Spuren der Engel.* Frankfurt: Fischer.
　1979　　*The Heretical Imperative: Contemporary Possibilities of Religious Affirmation.* Garden City, NY: Doubleday, Anchor.
　1980　　*Der Zwang zur Häresie: Religion in der pluralistischen Gesellschaft.* Frankfurt: S. Fischer.
Berger, P. L., B. Berger, and H. Kellner
　1973　　*The Homeless Mind: Modernization and Consciousness.* New York: Random House.
　1975　　*Das Unbehagen in der Modernität.* Frankfurt: Campus.
Berkowitz, M. W., F. Oser, and W. Althof
　1987　　"The Development of Socio-moral Discourse." In *Social Interaction through Sociomoral Development,* edited by W. Kurtines and J. Gewirtz. New York: Wiley.

Bernstein, B.
1965   "A Socio-Linguistic Approach to Social Learning." In *Penguin Survey of the Social Sciences,* edited by J. Gould. Baltimore: Penguin Books.
1986   "A Social-Linguistic Approach to Socialisation." In *Directions in Socio-Linguistics,* edited by J. Gumperz and D. Hymes. New York: Basil Blackwell.

Bernstein, R. J., ed.
1985   *Habermas and Modernity.* Cambridge: Polity Press.

Biehl, P.
1984   "Symbol und Metapher." In *Jahrbuch der Religionspädagogik,* edited by P. Biehl et al., vol. 1. Neukirchen-Vluyn: Neukirchener Verlag.

Betz, O.
1987   "Fest und Ritual." In *Handbuch Religiöser Erziehung,* edited by W. Böcker, H. G. Heimbrock, and E. Kerkhoff. Düsseldorf: Schwann.

Bittner, G.
1974   *Das andere Ich: Rekonstruktionen zu Freud.* Munich: R. Piper.
1977   *Tarnungen des Ich: Studien zu einer subjektorientierten.* Abwehrlehre. Stuttgart: A. Bonz.
1988   *Das Unbewußte—ein Mensch im Menschen, erscheint.* Würzburg: Königshausen & Newman.

Bogt, T. ter
1987   *Opgroeien in Groenlo. Jongeren, zingeving en levensbeschouwing.* Amersfoort u.a. (Acco).

Bonino, J. M.
1986   *Christians and Marxists: The Mutual Challenge to Revolution.* Grand Rapids: Eerdmans.

Bose, R. S.
1929   "Religious Concepts of Children." *Religious Education* 24.

Bowden, J. S.
1958   "An Enquiry in Religious Education in the West Midland Counties." Ph.D. dissertation, University of Birmingham.

Bregman, L.
1986   *Through the Landscape of Faith.* Philadelphia: Westminster.

Broughton, J. M.
1981   "Piaget's Structural Developmental Psychology." *Human Development* 24.
1984   "Not Beyond Formal Operations but Beyond Piaget." In Commons, Richards, and Armon 1984.
1986   "The Political Psychology of Faith Development Theory." In Dykstra and Parks 1986.
1988   "Ego and Ideology: A Critical Review of Loevinger's Theory." In *Self, Ego and Identity: Integrative Approaches,* edited by D. Lapsley and C. Power. New York: Springer.

Brown, A. W.
1892   "Some Records of the Thoughts and Reasonings of Children." *Pedagogical Seminary* 2.

Brown, L. B.
  1966   "Egocentric Thought in Petitionary Prayer: A Cross-cultural Study. *Journal of Social Psychology* 68.
  1968   "Some Attitudes Underlying Petitionary Prayer." In *From Cry to Word*, edited by A. Godin. Brussels: Lumen Vitae Press.
Browning, D. S.
  1983   Review of Fowler 1981. *Anglican Theological Review* 65.
Browning, R. L., and R. A. Reed
  1985   *The Sacraments in Religious Education and Liturgy*. Birmingham, AL: Religious Education Press.
Brumlik, M.
  1985   "Die religiöse Entwicklung von Martin Buber." Prepublication draft. Fribourg: Pädagogisches Institut, No. 43.
Buchanan, C. H.
  1987   "The Fall of Icarus: Gender, Religion, and the Aging Society." In *Shaping New Vision: Gender and Values in American Culture*. Ann Arbor, MI: UMI Research Press.
Bucher, A.
  1985a   *Die religiöse Entwicklung des Dichters Rainer Maria Rilke*. Prepublication draft. Fribourg: Pädagogisches Institut, No. 52.
  1985b   "Wenn zwei das gleiche Gleichnis hören, so ist es nicht das gleiche." Prepublication draft. Fribourg: Pädagogisches Institut.
  1987a   *Wenn zwei das gleiche Gleichnis hören, so ist es nicht das gleiche*. Strukturgenetische Untersuchung zur Rezeption dreier synoptischer Parabeln. Prepublication draft. Fribourg: Pädagogisches Institut.
  1987b   "Gleichnisse: Schon in der Grundschule? Ein kognitiv-entwicklungspsychologischer Beitrag zur Frage der altersgerechten Behandlung biblischer Gleichnisse." *Katechetische Blätter* 112.
Bucher, A., and F. Oser
  1987a   "Haupströmungen in der Religions-psychologie." In *Angewandte Psychologie: Ergebnisse und Perspektiven*, edited by D. Frey, C. Graf Hoyoz, and D. Stahlberg. Munich: Urban & Schwarzenberg.
  1987b   "Wenn zwei das gleiche Gleichnis hören . . . Theoretische und empirische Aspekte einer struktur-genetischen Religionsdidaktik." *Zeitschrift für Pädagogik* 33.
Buckley, M.
  1979   "The Rising of the Woman is the Rising of the Race." *Catholic Theological Society of America Proceedings* 34.
Cairns, R. B.
  1983   "The Emergence of Developmental Psychology." In *Handbook of Child Psychology*, Vol. 1, *History, Theory, and Methods*, edited by P. H. Mussen. New York: Wiley.
Caldwell, J. A., and M. W. Berkowitz
  1987   "Die Entwicklung religiösen und moralischen Denkens in einem Programm zum Religionsunterricht." *Unterrichtswissenschaft* 15.

Campbell, R. L., and M. H. Bickhard
  1986   "Knowing Levels and Developmental Stages." *Contributions to Human Development*, No. 16. Basel: Karger.

Carmody, D. L.
  1984   "Feminist Spirituality as Self-transcendence." In *Rising from History*, edited by R. J. Daly. College Theology Society 30. New York: University Press of America.

Carr, A.
  1980   "Theological Anthropology and the Experience of Women." *Chicago Studies* 19.

Case, A.
  1921   "Children's Ideas of God." *Religious Education* 16.

Castoriadis, C.
  1984   *Crossroads in the Labyrinth*. Brighton: Harvester Press.

Chirban, J.
  1980   "Intrinsic and Extrinsic Motivation in Faith Development." Th.D. dissertation, Harvard University, 1980.

Cobb, J.
  1982   *Beyond Dialogue: Toward Mutual Transformation of Christianity and Buddhism*. Philadelphia: Fortress.

Cohen, T.
  1977   "Ästhetisch/nicht-äesthetisch und der Begriff des Geschmacks." In *Das ästhetische*, edited by R. Bittner and P. Pfaff. Cologne: Kiepenheuer & Witoch.

Colby, A.
  1978   "Evolution of a Moral-developmental Theory." In *New Directions for Child Development II: Moral Development*, edited by W. Damon. San Francisco: Josey-Bass.

Coleman, J. A.
  1987   "The Substance and Forms of American Religion and Culture." *New Catholic World* 230.

Comenius, J. A.
  1965   *Pampaedia*. Edited by D. Tschizewskij et al. Heidelberg: Quelle & Meyer.

Commons, M. L., F. A. Richards, and C. Armon, eds.
  1984   *Beyond Formal Operations: Late Adolescent and Adult Cognitive Development*. New York: Praeger.

Conn, W. E.
  1981   "Affectivity in Kohlberg and Fowler." *Religious Education* 76.
  1986   *Christian Conversion: A Developmental Interpretation of Autonomy and Surrender*. New York: Paulist.

Conrad, R.
  1982   Review of Fowler 1981. *Currents in Theology and Mission* 9.
  1985   Review of Fowler 1984a. *Currents in Theology and Mission* 12.

Crossin, J. W.
  1981   Review of Fowler 1981. *Theological Studies* 42.

1985   Review of Fowler 1984a. *Theological Studies* 46.

Damon, W.

1977   *The Social World of the Child.* San Francisco: Josey-Bass.

d'Aquili, E.

1983   "The Myth-Ritual-Complex: A Biogenetic Structural Analysis." *Zygon* 18.

Dawes, R. S.

1954   "The Concepts of God among Secondary School Children." M.A. dissertation, University of London.

Dawson, G. E.

1900   "Children's Interest in the Bible." *Journal of Genetic Psychology* 7.

Deconchy, J. P.

1965   "The Idea of God: Its Emergence Between 7 and 16 Years." In *From Religious Experience to a Religious Attitude,* edited by A. Godin. Chicago: Loyola University Press.

Dekker, G.

1987   *Godsdienst en samenleving: Inleiding tot de studie van de godsdienstsociologie.* Kampen: Kok.

de Moor, R.

1984   "Waarden en normen in Europa." In *Symposium over Verschuiving van waarden en normen in Nederland.* Heerlen: Hogeschool voor Theologie en Pastoraat.

DeNicola, K.

1990a   *Directory of Researchers in Faith Development.* Atlanta, GA: Center for Research in Faith and Moral Development.

1990b   *Faith Development Bibliography.* Atlanta, GA: Center for Research in Faith and Moral Development.

Dessoir, M.

1890   *Das Doppel-Ich.* Leipzig: E. Gunther.

Dick, A.

1982   *Drei transkulturelle Erhebungen des religiösen Urteils.* Eine Pilotstudie. Lizentiatsarbeit. Prepublication draft. Fribourg: Pädagogisches Institut.

Dobash, R. E., and P. D. Russell.

1979   *Violence against Wives.* New York: Free Press.

Döbert, R.

1984   "Religiöse Erfahrung und Religionsbegriff." *Religionspädagogische Beiträge* 14.

1986   "Wider die Verhachlässigung des 'Inhalts' in den Moraltheorien von Kohlberg und Habermas." In *Zur Bestimmung der Moral,* edited by W. Edelstein and G. Nunner-Winkler. Frankfurt: Suhrkamp.

1987   "Horizonte der an Kohlberg Orientierten Moralforschung." *Zeitschrift für Pädagogik* 35.

Döbert, R., and G. Nunner-Winkler

1984   "Die Bewältigung von Selbstmordimpulsen im Jugendalter." In *Soziale Interaktion und soziales Verstehen,* edited by W. Edelstein and J. Habermas. Frankfurt: Suhrkamp.

Donaldson, M.
  1978   *Children's Minds.* New York: Norton.
Douglas, M.
  1968/69 "The Contempt of Ritual." *New Blackfriars* 49.
  1982   *In the Active Voice.* Boston: Routledge & Kegan Paul.
  1986   *Ritual, Tabu, und Körpersymbolik.* Frankfurt: Fischer Wissenschaft.
Downing, F. L.
  1986   *To See the Promised Land: M. L. King's Pilgrimage of Faith.* Macon, GA:
          Mercer University Press.
Durka, G.
  1982   "The Religious Journey of Women: The Educational Task." *Religious
          Education* 77.
Durkheim, E.
  1965   *The Elementary Forms of the Religious Life.* New York: Macmillan.
Dykstra, C.
  1982a   "Theological Table-Talk: Transformation in Faith and Morals." *Theology
          Today* 39.
  1982b   Unpublished response, Conference on Faith Development, Auburn
          Theological Seminary, March.
  1986a   "What is Faith?: An Experiment in the Hypothetical Mode." In Dykstra
          and Parks 1986.
  1986b   "Youth and the Language of Faith." *Religious Education* 81.
Dykstra, C., and S. Parks, eds.
  1986   *Faith Development and Fowler.* Birmingham, AL: Religious Education
          Press.
Ebert, K.
  1981   "Theorien zur Entwicklung des religiösen Bewusstseins." *Der Evange-
          lische Erzieher* 6.
Egan, H.
  1982   Review of Fowler 1981. *Horizons* 9.
Eibl-Eibesfeld, I.
  1985   *Liebe und Haß: Zur Naturgeschichte elementarer Verhaltensweisen.*
          Munich: Piper.
Elbow, P.
  1986   *Embracing Contraries.* New York: Oxford University Press.
Elkind, D.
  1961   "The Child's Conception of His Religious Denomination I: The Jewish
          Child." *Journal of Genetic Psychology* 99.
  1962   "The Child's Conception of His Religious Denomination II: The
          Catholic Child." *Journal of Genetic Psychology* 101.
  1963   "The Child's Conception of His Religious Denomination III: The Protes-
          tant Child." *Journal of Genetic Psychology* 103.
Englert, R.
  1985   *Glaubensgeschichte und Bildungsprozess: Versuch einer religionspädago-
          gischen Kairologie.* Munich: Kösel.

1986 "Vor einer neuen Phase materialkerygmatischer Erneuerung." *Katechetische Blätter* 111.

Erikson, E.
1963 "Childhood and Society." *Toys and Reasons.* 2nd ed. New York: Norton.
1966 "Ontogeny of Ritualization in Man." In *Philosophical Transactions of the Royal Society of London,* "A Discussion on Ritualization of Behaviour in Animals and Man." Ser. B., Vol. 251.
1977 *Toys and Reasons: Stages in the Ritualization of Experience.* New York: Norton.
1978 *Kinderspiel und politische Phantasie: Stufen der Ritualisierung in der Realität.* Frankfurt: Suhrkamp.
1980 *Identity and the Life Cycle.* New York: W. W. Norton.

Fasick, F. A.
1984 "Parents, Peers, Youth Culture and Autonomy in Adolescence." *Adolescence* 19.

Feifel, E.
1978 "Symbolerziehung durch Ritualisierung." *Lebendige Seelsorge.* Fribourg: Seelsorge-Verlag.

Feige, A.
1982 *Erfahrungen mit der Kirche: Daten und Analysen einer empirischen Untersuchung über Beziehungen und Einstellungen Junger Erwachsener zur Kirche.* 2nd ed. Hannover: Luth. Verlagshaus.

Felling, A., J. Peters, and O. Schreuder
1986 *Geloven en leven: Een nationaal onderzoek naar de invloed van religieuze overtuigingen.* Zeist: Kerckebosch.

Fernhout, J. H.
1986 "Where is Faith? Searching for the Core of the Cube." In Dykstra and Parks 1986.

Fetz, R. L.
Fetz, R. L.
1984 "Was steht hinter dem religiösen Urteil? Eine grundsätzliche Problemstellung im Zusammenhang mit der Weltbildentwicklung." Fribourg: Pädagogisches Institut.
1985 "Zur Entwicklung der Himmelssymbolik in Menschheitsgeschichte und individueller Entwicklung: Ein Beitrag zu einer genetischen Semiologie." In *Schriften zur Symbolforschung, Band 2,* edited by A. Zweig. Bern: Peter Lang.
1986 "Was steht hinter dem religiösen Urteil? Eine grundsätzliche Problemstellung im Zusammenhang mit der Weltbildentwicklung." Prepublication draft. Fribourg: Pädagogisches Institut.

Fetz, R. L., and A. Bucher
1986 "Stufen der religiösen Entwicklung? Eine rekonstruktive Kritik der von F. Oser und P. Gmünder vorgelegten Theorie des religiösen Urteils." In *Jahrbuch für Religionspädagogik,* edited by P. Biehl et al., vol. 3.

Fetz, R. L., and F. Oser
1985 "Weltbildentwicklung und religiöses Urteil." Beitrag zur zweiten

Ringbergkonferenz. Prepublication draft. Fribourg: Pädagogisches Institut, No. 47. Shortened version in *Zur Bestimmung der Moral*, edited by W. Edelstein and G. Nunner-Winkler. Frankfurt: Suhrkamp, 1986.

Finkelhor, D., R. J. Gelles, G. T. Hortaling, and M. A. Strauss, eds.
1983   *The Dark Side of Families: Current Family Violence Research*. New York: Sage.

Firet, J.
1986   *Dynamics in Pastoring*. Grand Rapids: Eerdmans.

Fischer, K., and L. Silvern
1985   "Stages and Individual Differences in Cognitive Development." *Annual Review of Psychology* 36.

Flavell, J. H.
1963   *The Developmental Psychology of Jean Piaget*. Princeton, NJ: Van Nostrand.

Fleischer, R.
1984   "Verständnisbedingungen religiöser Symbole am Beispiel von Tauf-ritualen." Theology dissertation, Universität Mainz.

Ford-Grabowsky, M.
1987   "Flaws in Faith Development Theory." *Religious Education* 82.

Foster, C. R.
1982   "Three Big Books in Christian Education." [Review of Fowler 1981.] *Quarterly Review* 2.

Fowler, J. W.
1974a   "Toward a Developmental Perspective on Faith." *Religious Education* 69.
1974b   *To See the Kingdom: The Theological Vision of H. Richard Niebuhr*. Nashville: Abingdon; Lanham, MD: University Press of America.
1976a   "Stages in Faith: The Structural-Developmental Approach." In *Values and Moral Development*, edited by T. C. Hennessy. New York: Paulist.
1976b   "Faith Development Theory and the Aims of Religious Socialization." In *Emerging Issues in Religious Education*, edited by G. Durka and A. Smith. New York: Paulist.
1978   "Life/Faith Patterns: Structures of Trust and Loyalty." In *Life Maps: Conversations on the Journey of Faith*, edited by J. Berryman. Waco, TX: Word.
1980a   "Faith and the Structuring of Meaning." In *Toward Moral and Religious Maturity*, edited by J. Fowler et al. Morristown: Silver Burdett.
1980b   "Moral Stages and the Development of Faith." In *Kohlberg and Moral Education*, edited by B. M. Mapel. Notre Dame: Religious Education Press.
1981   *Stages of Faith: The Psychology of Human Development and the Quest for Meaning*. San Francisco: Harper & Row.
1982a   "Stages of Faith and Adults' Life Cycles." In *Faith Development in the Adult Life Cycle*, edited by K. Stokes. New York: W. H. Sadlier.
1982b   Review Symposium. *Horizons* 9.

1983   "Practical Theology and the Shaping of Christian Lives." In *Practical Theology: The Emerging Field in Theology, Church, and World*, edited by D. S. Browning. San Francisco: Harper & Row.

1984a   *Becoming Adult, Becoming Christian: Adult Development and Christian Faith*. San Francisco: Harper & Row, 1984a.

1984b   "Pluralism, Particularity, and Paideia." *Journal of Law and Religion* 2.

1984c   "Critique and Future Directions of Study of Faith Development Theory." Unpublished lecture, Harvard Divinity School.

1985   "Practical Theology and Theological Education: Some Models and Questions." *Theology Today* 42.

1986a   "Faith and the Structuring of Meaning." In Dykstra and Parks 1986.

1986b   "Dialogue Toward a Future in Faith Development Studies." In Dykstra and Parks 1986.

1987a   *Faith Development and Pastoral Care*. Philadelphia: Fortress.

1987b   "Commonalities of Faith in Religious Pluralism: An Encounter with Wilfred Cantwell Smith." Unpublished paper.

1987c   "The Teaching Power of Worship and Sacraments." Unpublished paper.

1989   "Strength for the Journey: Early Childhood Development in Selfhood and Faith." In *Faith Development in Early Childhood*, edited by D. Blazer. New York: Sheed & Ward.

1990   "Faith Development Through the Family Life Cycle." In *Catholic Families: Growing and Sharing Faith*. New Rochelle, NY: Don Bosco Multi Media.

1991   *Weaving the New Creation: Stages of Faith and the Public Church*. San Francisco: Harper & Row.

Fowler, J. W., D. Jarvis, and R. M. Moseley
1986   *Manual for Faith Development Research*. Atlanta: Center for Research in Faith and Moral Development, Emory University.

Fowler, J. W., and S. Keen
1978   *Life Maps: Conversations on the Journey of Faith*. Edited by J. Berryman. Waco, TX: Word Books.

Fowler, J. W., R. W. Lovin, et al.
1980   *Trajectories in Faith: Five Life Stories*. Nashville: Abingdon.

Fraas, H.-J.
1983   *Glaube und Identität*. Göttingen: Vandenhoeck & Ruprecht.

1984   "Der Schüler: Religiöse Sozialisation—Religiöse Erziehung." In *Religionspädagogisches Kompendium*, edited by G. Adam and R. Lachmann. Göttingen: Vandenhoeck & Ruprecht.

Fraas, H.-J., and H.-G. Heimbrock, eds.
1986   "Religiöse Erziehung und Glaubensentwicklung: Zur Auseinandersetzung mit der kognitiven Psychologie." International Conference on "Religionspädagogik und Religionspsychologie," held in Göttingen. Unpublished.

Fraenkel, J. R.
1978   "The Kohlbergian Paradigm: Some Reservations." In *Readings in Moral Education*, edited by P. Scharf. Minneapolis: Winston.

Francis, L. J.
1979   "Research and the Development of Religious Thinking." *Educational Studies* 5.
1984a   *Teenagers and the Church: A Profile of Church-going Youth in the 1980s.* London: Collins.
1984b   *Rural Anglicanism: A Future for Young Christians?* London: Collins.
Francke, A. H.
1957   In *Pädagogische Schriften,* edited by H. Lorenzen. 2nd ed. Paderborn: Schoningh.
Frankena, W.
1973   *Ethics.* 2nd ed. Englewood Cliffs, NJ: Prentice Hall.
Freire, P.
1971   *Pedagogy of the Oppressed.* New York: Seaview.
Freud, A.
1936/1968   *The Ego and the Mechanisms of Defense.* London: Hogarth Press.
Freud, S.
1907/1976   "Zwangshandlungen und Religionsübungen." In *Gesammelte Werke Bd. VII,* 127–139. Frankfurt: S. Fischer.
1909/1976   "Analyse der Phobie eines fünfjährigen Knaben." In *GW VII.* Frankfurt: Fischer.
1928/1976   "Ein religiöses Erlebnis." In *GW XIV.* Frankfurt: Fischer.
1930/1976   *Das Unbehagen in der Kultur.* In *GW XIV.* Frankfurt: Fischer.
1927/1976   *Die Zukunft einer Illusion.* In *GW XIV.* Frankfurt a.M.
Friedman, E. H.
1985   *Generation to Generation: Family Process in Church and Synagogue.* New York: Guilford.
Frisby, D.
1985   *Fragments of Modernity: Theories of Modernity in the Work of Simmel, Kracauer and Benjamin.* Cambridge: Polity Press.
Fromm, E.
1979   *Psychoanalyse und Religion.* Munich: Goldmann.
Garz, D.
1987   "Theorie der Moral und gerechten Praxis." Habilitationsschrift [Inaugural Dissertation]. Oldenburg, Universität.
Gates, B.
1976   "Religion in the Developing World of Children and Young People." Ph.D. dissertation, University of Lancaster.
1986   "ME + RE = Kohlberg with a difference." In *Kohlberg: Consensus and Controversy,* edited by S. Modgil and C. Modgil. London: Falmer.
Geertz, C.
1973   "Religion as a Cultural System." In Geertz, *The Interpretation of Cultures.* New York: Basic Books.
Gibbs, J. C.
1977   "Kohlberg's Stages of Moral Judgment: A Constructive Critique." *Harvard Educational Review* 47.

1979   "Kohlberg's Moral Stage Theory: A Piagetian Revision." *Human Development* 22.

Gilligan, C.
1982   *In a Different Voice: Psychological Theory and Women's Development.* Cambridge, MA: Harvard University Press.

Giunti, L.
1984   "God Doesn't Like People Who Lie to Him: A Study of the Relationship between Moral and Religious Thinking." Unpublished paper, University of Notre Dame.

Godin, A.
1968   "Genetic Development and the Symbolic Function: Meaning and Limits of the Work of R. Goldman." *Religious Education* 63.

Godin, A., and S. Marthe
1960   "Magic Mentality and Sacramental Life." *Lumen Vitae* 15.

Godin, A., and B. van Roey
1959   "Immanent Justice and Divine Protection in Children of 6 to 14 Years." *Lumen Vitae* 14.

Goffman, E.
1982   *Interaction Ritual.* New York: Pantheon Books.
1986   *Interaktionsrituale.* Frankfurt.

Going, C. M.
1982   Review of Fowler 1981. *Horizons* 9.

Goldman, R. J.
1962   "Some Aspects of Religious Thinking in Childhood and Adolescence." Ph.D. dissertation, University of Birmingham.
1964   *Religious Thinking from Childhood to Adolescence.* London: Routledge & Kegan Paul.
1970   *Readiness for Religion.* New York: Winston-Seabury/Harper & Row.
1972   *Vorfelder des Glaubens: Kindgemäße religiöse Unterweisung.* Neukirchen-Vluyn: Neukirchener Verlag.

Goody, J.
1961   "Religion and Ritual: The Definitional Problem." *British Journal of Sociology* 12.

Gorman, M.
1982   Review of Fowler 1981. *Horizons* 9.

Greenacre, I.
1971   "The Response of Young People to Religious Allegory." Dip.Ed. dissertation, University of Birmingham.

Greer, J. E.
1980   "Stages in the Development of Religious Thinking." *British Journal of Religious Education* 3.
1981   "Religious Attitudes and Thinking in Belfast Pupils." *Educational Review* 23.
1983   "A Critical Study of 'Thinking About the Bible.'" *British Journal of Religious Education* 5.

Grom, B.
1981   *Religionspädagogische Psychologie des Kleinking-, Schul-, und Jugend-alters.* Göttingen: Vandenhoeck & Ruprecht.
1986   Review of F. Oser and P. Gmünder 1984. *Christlich-pädagogische Blätter* 1.
Grunberger, B.
1987   "Don Quijote - Narziß: Sein Kampf und sein Scheitern." *Forum der Psychoanalyse* 3.
Gustafson, P. M.
1986   Review of Fowler 1984a. *Review of Religious Research* 27.
Gutierrez, G.
1983   *We drink from our own wells.* New York: Orbis.
Habermas, J.
1976   *Zur Rekonstruktion des Historischen Materialismus.* Frankfurt: Suhrkamp.
Hager, F. P.
1987   "Stufen der religiösen Entwicklung bei Pestalozzi." Prepublication draft. Fribourg: Pädagogisches Institut.
Hall, G. S.
1891   "The Contents of Children's Minds on Entering School." *Pedagogical Seminary* 1.
Hanselmann, J., H. Hild, and E. Lohse, eds.
1985   *Was wird aus der Kirche.* 3rd ed. Gütersloh: Mohn.
Harms, E.
1944   "The Development of Religious Experience in Children." *American Journal of Sociology* 50.
Harris, M.
1986   "Completion and Faith Development." In Dykstra and Parks 1986.
Harrison, B. W.
1981   "The Power of Anger in the Work of Love." *Union Seminary Quarterly Review* 36.
Hartmann, H.
1937/1960 *Ego Psychology and the Problem of Adaptation.* Translated by David Rapaport. New York: International Universities Press.
1950/1972 *Essays on Ego Psychology: Selected Problems of Psychoanalytic Theory.* New York: International Universities Press.
Haug, W. F.
1986   *Critique of Commodity Aesthetics, Appearance, Sexuality and Advertising in Capitalist Society.* Cambridge: Polity Press.
Hayden, D.
1981   *The Grand Domestic Revolution.* Cambridge, MA: MIT Press.
Heimbrock, H.-G.
1984   *Lern-Wege religiöser Erziehung.* Göttingen: Vandenhoeck & Ruprecht.
1985   "Entwicklung und Erziehung: Zum Forschungsstand der religionspäda-gogischen Psychologie." *Jahrbuch für Religionspädagogik* 1.

1986a   "The Development of Symbols as a Key to the Developmental Psychol-
         ogy of Religion." In *Current Issues in the Psychology of Religion*, edited
         by J. A. van Belzen and J. M. van der Lans. Amsterdam: Rodopi. Also
         in *British Journal of Religious Education* 8.
1986b   "Intellektuelle Problembewältigung oder verstehendes Erschließen?" In
         Fraas and Heimbrock 1986.
Herms, E.
1977   "Gottesdienst und Religionsausübung." In *Gottesdienst und öffentliche
         Meinung*, edited by M. Seitz and L. Mohaupt. Stuttgart and Fribourg:
         Calwer Verlag.
Herrmann, U.
1982   "Pädagogische Anthropologie und die 'Entdeckung' des Kindes im Zeit-
         alter der Aufklärung—Kindheit und Jugendalter im Werk Joachim
         Heinrich Campes." In *Die Bildung des Bürgers: Die Formierung der
         bürgerlichen Gesellschaft und die Gebildeten im 18. Jahrhundert*, edited
         by H. Herrmann. Weinheim and Basel: Beltz.
Hewlett, S. A.
1986   *A Lesser Life: The Myth of Women's Liberation in America*. New York:
         William Morrow.
Heywood, D.
1986   "Piaget and Faith Development: A True Marriage of Minds?" *British
         Journal of Religious Education* 8.
Hilliard, F. H.
1959   "Ideas of God among Secondary School Children." *Religion in Education*
         27.
Hinder, E.
1986   "Grundlagenprobleme bei der Messung des sozial-moralischen Urteils."
         Dissertation, Fribourg University.
Hoehn, R. A.
1983   Review of Fowler 1981. *Review of Religious Research* 25.
Hoffman, M. L.
1986   "The Contribution of Empathy to Justice and Moral Judgment." In
         Empathy and Its Development, edited by N. Eisenberg and J. Strayer.
         New York: Cambridge University Press.
Hoge, D. R., and G. H. Petrillo
1978   "Development of Religious Thinking in Adolescence: A Test of Gold-
         man's Theories." *Journal for the Scientific Study of Religion* 17.
Horkheimer, M.
1967   *Zur Kritik der instrumentellen Vernunft*. Frankfurt: S. Fischer.
1968   "Autorität und Familie." In *Kritische Theorie: Eine Dokumentation*,
         edited by M. Horkheimer and A. Schmidt, vol. 1. Frankfurt: S. Fischer.
1973   *Eclipse of Reason*. New York: Continuum.
Horkheimer, M., and T. W. Adorno
1972   *Critical Theory: Selected Essays*. New York: Seabury.
1975   *Dialectic of Enlightenment*, trans. J. Cumming. New York: Continuum.

Huczynski, A.
    1987   *Encyclopedia of Organizational Change Methods.* Aldershot: Gower.

Huebner, D.
    1982a   "From Theory to Practice: Curriculum." *Religious Education* 77.
    1982b   Unpublished response to papers, Conference on Faith Development, Auburn Theological Seminary, March.
    1986   "Christian Growth in Faith." *Religious Education* 81.

Hull, J. M.
    1985   *What Prevents Christian Adults from Learning?* London: SCM Press.
    1987   Editorial on fantasy. *British Journal of Religious Education* 10.

Hunter, R. J.
    1982   Review of Fowler 1981. *Pastoral Psychology* 31.

Hyde, K. E.
    1984   "Twenty Years after Goldman's Research." *British Journal of Religious Education,* 7.

Inglehart, R.
    1977   *The Silent Revolution.* Princeton: Princeton University Press.

Institute of Christian Education, ed.
    1957   *Religious Education in Schools.* London: Institute of Christian Education.

Ivy, S. S.
    1982   Review of Fowler 1981. *Journal of Pastoral Care* 26.

Jacobus, M., ed.
    1979   *Women Writing about Women.* New York: Harper & Row.

Jetter, W.
    1978   *Symbol und Ritual: Anthropologische Elemente im Gottesdienst.* Göttingen: Vandenhoeck & Ruprecht.

Johnson, J. E.
    1955   "An Enquiry into Some of the Religious Ideas of Six-Year-Old Children." Dip.Ed. dissertation, University of Birmingham.

Johnson, K. L.
    1982   Review of Fowler 1981. *Word and World* 2.

Josuttis, M.
    1982   "Der Gottesdienst als Ritual." In *Praktische Theologie,* edited by F. Wintzer et al. Neukirchen-Vluyn: Neukirchener Verlag.

Jüngel, E.
    1980   *Entsprechungen: Gott—Wahrheit—Mensch.* Munich: Kaiser.

Jung, C. G.
    1977   "Über Konflikte der kindlichen Seele." In *GW* 17. Olten and Fribourg: Walter.

Kalam, T. P.
    1981   "The Myth of Stages and Sequence in Moral and Religious Development." Ph.D. diss., University of Lancaster.

Kant, I.
    1922   "Kritik der Urteilskraft." In *Werke* Bd. 5. Berlin: B. Cassirer.

254 BIBLIOGRAPHY

Kaufmann, F. X.
1984   "Nutzen und Vergeblichkeit empirischer Forschung in der Religions-soziologie." In *Religion und gesellschaftlicher Wandel,* edited by H. May. Loccumer Protokolle.
Kavanagh, A.
1973   "The Role of Ritual in Personal Development." In *The Roots of Ritual,* edited by J. D. Shaughnessy. Grand Rapids: Eerdmans.
Kay, W. K.
1981   "Religious Thinking: Attitudes and Personality Amongst Secondary Pupils in England and Ireland: A Study with Particular Reference to Religious Education." Ph.D. dissertation, University of Reading.
Kegan, R. E.
1980   "There the Dance Is." In *Toward Moral & Religious Maturity,* edited by J. Fowler et al. Morristown, NJ: Silver Burdett.
1982   *The Evolving Self: Problem and Process in Human Development.* Cambridge, MA: Harvard University Press.
Keller, M.
1982   "Die soziale Konstitution sozialen Verstehens: Universelle und differentielle Aspekte." In *Perspektivität und Interpretation,* edited by W. Edelstein and M. Keller. Frankfurt: Suhrkamp.
Kidron, M., and R. Segal
1987   *The Book of Business Money and Power.* London: Pan Books.
Kippenberg, H. G., and M. Luchesi, eds.
1978   *Magie: Die Sozialwissenschaftliche Kontroverse über das Verstehen Fremden Denkens.* Frankfurt: Suhrkamp.
Kirchenamt der Evangelischen Kirche in Deutschland, ed.
1985   *Ökumenisches Lernen: Grundlagen und Impulse.* Gütersloh: Mohn.
Klaghofer, R., and F. Oser.
1987   "Dimensionen und Erfassung des religiösen Familienklimas." *Unterrichtswissenschaft* 2.
Kohlberg, L.
1958   "The Development of Modes of Thinking and Choices in Years 10 to 16." Ph.D. dissertation, University of Chicago.
1973a   "Stages and Aging in Moral Development: Some Speculations." *Gerontologist* 13.
1974   *Zur kognitiven Entwicklung des Kindes.* Frankfurt.
1978   "Revisions in the Theory and Practice of Moral Development." In *New Directions for Child Development II: Moral Development,* edited by W. Damon. San Francisco: Josey-Bass.
1981a   *Essays on Moral Development,* Vol. 1, *The Philosophy of Moral Development.* San Francisco: Harper & Row.
1981b   "Moral Development, Religious Thinking and the Question of a Seventh Stage." In Kohlberg 1981a.
1984   *Essays on Moral Development,* Vol. 2, *The Psychology of Moral Development.* San Francisco: Harper & Row.

1986   "A Current Statement on Some Theoretical Issues." In *Lawrence Kohl-*
        berg: Consensus and Controversy, edited by A. Modgil and C. Modgil.
        Philadelphia: Falmer.
Kohlberg, L., and C. Armon
1984   "Three Types of Stage Models Used in the Study of Adult Development."
        In Commons, Richards, and Armon 1984.
Kohlberg, L., D. R. Boyd, and C. Levine
1986   "Die Wiederkehr der sechsten Stufe: Gerechtigkeit, Wohlwollen und
        der Standpunkt der Moral." In *Zur Bestimmung der Moral,* edited by W.
        Edelstein and G. Nunner-Winkler. Frankfurt: Suhrkamp.
Kohlberg, L., and A. Higgins
1984   "Continuities and Discontinuities in Childhood and Adult Development
        Revisited—Again." In Kohlberg 1984.
Kohlberg, L., and R. Kramer
1969   "Continuities and Discontinuities in Children and Adult Moral Develop-
        ment." *Human Development* 12.
Kohlberg, L., C. Levine, and A. Hewer
1983   *Moral Stages: A Current Formulation and Response to Critics.* Basel:
        Karger.
1984a   "The Current Formulation of the Theory." In Kohlberg 1984.
1984b   "Synopsis and Detailed Reply to Critics." In Kohlberg 1984.
Kohlberg, L., and C. Power
1981   "Moral Development, Religious Development and the Question of a
        Seventh Stage." *Zygon* 16.
Kohut, H.
1978   "Forms and Transformations of Narcissism." In *The Search for the Self:*
        Selected Writings of Heinz Kohut, 1950–1978, ed. Paul Ornstein. New
        York: International Universities Press.
1979   *Die Heilung des Selbst.* Frankfurt: Suhrkamp.
Kürzdörfer, K.
1987   "Von Kohlberg zu Fowler—ein pädagogischer Fortschritt?" Anmerk-
        ungen zur pädagogischen Diskussion in den U.S.A. Manuskript
        Würzburg.
Kuiper, F. H.
1985   "Can Research Challenge and Foster Religious Education." *Religious*
        Education 80.
1987   "Zal een gelovig mens zelfstandig zijn?" In F. H. Kuiper, J. J. van Nijen,
        and J. C. Schreuder, *Zelfstandig geloven: Studies voor Jaap Firet.*
        Kampen: Kok.
Laeuchli, S.
1987   *Das Spiel vor dem dunklen Gott. "Mimesis"—Ein Beitrag zur Entwicklung*
        des Bibliodramas. Neukirchen-Vluyn: Neukirchener Verlag.
Laeyenddecker-Thung, M. A.
1984   "Religion und Wertwandel in empirischen Untersuchungen der Nieder-
        lande." In *Religion und gesellschaftlicher Wandel,* edited by H. May. Loc-
        cumer Protokolle.

Langdon, A. A.
    1969   "A Critical Examination of Dr. Goldman's Research Study on Religious Thinking from Childhood to Adolescence." *Journal of Christian Education* 12.

Langer, S.
    1942   *Philosophy in a New Key: A Study in the Symbolism of Reason, Rite and Art.* Cambridge, MA: Harvard University Press.
    1957   *Philosophy in a New Key: A Study in the Symbolism of Reason, Rite and Art.* 3d ed. Cambridge, MA: Harvard University Press.

Lawrence, P. J.
    1965   "Children's Thinking about Religion: A Study of Concrete Operational Thinking." *Religious Education* 60.

Leach, E. R.
    1966   "Ritualization in Man in Relation to Conceptual and Social Development." *Philosophical Transactions of the Royal Society of London.* Ser. B, Vol. 251.
    1968   "Ritual." In *International Encyclopedia of Social Sciences,* edited by D. L. Sills, vol. 13. New York: Macmillan.

Lefort, C.
    1986   *The Political Forms of Modern Society: Bureaucracy, Democracy, Totalitarianism.* Cambridge: Polity Press.

Leuba, J. H.
    1917   "Children's Conceptions of God and Religious Education." *Religious Education* 12.

Link, C.
    1987   "Schöpfung ohne Schöpfer? Chancen und Risiken der ökologischen Theologie," *Ev. Erzieher* 39.

Livingstone, D. W.
    1987   *Critical Pedagogy and Cultural Power.* South Hadley, MA: Bergin and Garvey.

Locke, J.
    1823   "Some Thoughts Concerning Education." In *The Works of John Locke.* Vol. IX. London: Davidson.

Loder, J. E., and J. W. Fowler
    1982   "Conversations on Fowler's *Stages of Faith* and Loder's *The Transforming Moment.*" *Religious Education* 77.

Loevinger, J.
    1976   *Ego Development: Conceptions and Theories.* San Francisco: Josey-Bass.

Long, D., D. Elkind, and B. Spilka
    1967   "The Child's Conception of Prayer." *Journal for the Scientific Study of Religion* 6.

Loomba, R. M.
    1942   "The Religious Development of the Child." *Indian Journal of Psychology* 17.

Lorenz, K.
1966   "Evolution of Ritualization in the Biological and Cultural Spheres." *Philosophical Transactions of the Royal Society of London*, Ser. B, Vol. 251.
Lorenzer, A.
1981   *Das Konzil der Buchhalter: Die Zerstörung der Sinnlichkeit. Eine Religionskritik.* Frankfurt: Europäische Verlagsanstalt.
Luckmann, T.
1967   *The Invisible Religion.* New York: Macmillan.
Luhmann, N.
1977   *Funktion der Religion.* Frankfurt: Suhrkamp.
Luther, M.
1520/1977 "Sermon von den guten Werken." In *Calwer Luther-Ausgabe.* Bd. III. Munich: Siebenstern Taschenbuch Verlag.
1969a   *Pädagogische Schriften.* Edited by H. Lorenzen. Paderborn: Schoningh.
1526/1969b *Deutsche Messe und Ordnung des Gottesdienstes.* In Luther 1969a.
1530/1969c *Eine Predigt, daß man Kinder zur Schulen halten solle.* In Luther 1969a.
1530   *Der große Katechismus.* In Luther 1969a.
1966   *Works.* American Edition. Vol. 44. Philadelphia: Fortress.
Lyons, N.
1983   "Two Perspectives on Self, Relationships, and Morality." *Harvard Educational Review* 53.
Maas, R.
1986   "Biblical Catechesis and Religious Development: The Goldman Project Twenty Years Later." *Living Light* 22.
MacLean, A. H.
1930   *The Idea of God in Protestant Religious Education.* New York: Teachers College Contributions to Education, Columbia University.
Makarenko, A. S.
1959   "Ein pädagogisches Poem (Der Weg ins Leben)." In *Werke* 1. Band. Berlin: Volk und Wissen.
Malinowski, B.
1948/1984 *Magic, Science and Religion.* New York: Greenwood.
Marcuse, H.
1965   "Industrialisierung und Kapitalismus im Werk Max Webers." In Marcuse, *Kultur und Gesellschaft.* Bd. 2. Frankfurt: Suhrkamp.
1968   "Zum Begriff des Wesens." In Marcuse, *Schriften.* Bd. 3. Aufsätze aus der Zeitschrift für Sozialforschung 1934–1941. Frankfurt: Suhrkamp.
Marstin, R.
1979   *Beyond Our Tribal Gods: The Maturing of Faith.* Maryknoll, NY: Orbis.
Martin, G. M.
1987   "Speil." In *Handbuch religiöser Erziehung.* Bd. 1, edited by W. Böker et al. Düsseldorf: Schwann.
Martin, J. R.
1985   *Reclaiming a Conversation: The Ideal of the Educated Woman.* New Haven: Yale University Press.

Martinsson, S.
1968   *Religionsundervisning och mognad.* [Religious Education and Readiness.] Stockholm: Stockholm School of Education.
Mathias, W. D.
1943   *Ideas of God and Conduct.* New York: Teachers College Contributions to Education, Columbia University.
McDargh, J.
1983   Review of Fowler 1981. *Journal of the American Academy of Religion* 51.
McDowell, J. B.
1952   *The Development of the Idea of God in the Catholic Child.* Washington: Catholic University of American Press.
McGrady, A.
1983   "Teaching the Bible: Research from a Piagetian Perspective." *British Journal of Religious Education* 5.
1987   "A Metaphor and Model Paradigm of Religious Thinking." *British Journal of Religious Education* 9.
McLaughlin, S. D., and B. D. Melber
1986   *The Cosmopolitan Report: The Changing Life Course of American Women.* Vol. 2. New York: Hearst.
McLean, S. D.
1986   "H. Richard Niebuhr's Influence on Faith Development Theory." In Dykstra and Parks 1986.
Meadow, M., and R. Kahoe, eds.
1984   *The Psychology of Religion: Religion in Individual Lives.* New York: Harper & Row.
Meissner, W. W.
1987   *Life and Faith: Psychological Perspectives on Religious Experience.* Washington, DC: Georgetown University Press.
Merton, R. K.
1968   *Social Theory and Social Structure.* New York: Free Press.
Merton, T.
1965   *Gandhi on Non-violence.* New York: New Directions.
Mette, N.
1983   *Voraussetzungen christlicher Elementarerziehung: Vorbereitende Studien zu einer Religionspädagogik des Kleinkindalters.* Düsseldorf: Patmos.
Metz, J. B.
1977/1984 *Glaube in Geschichte und Gesellschaft.* Mainz: M. Grünewald.
1980   *Faith in History and Society.* New York: Crossroad.
Meulemann, H.
1984   "Religion und Wertwandel in empirischen Untersuchungen der Bundesrepublik Deutschland." In *Religion und gesellschaftlicher Wandel,* edited by H. May. Loccumer protokolle.
Meyer, H.
1981   "Zeit und Gottesdienst: Anthropologische Bemerkungen zur liturgischen Zeit." *Liturgisches Jahrbuch* 31.

Miles, G. B.
  1971   "A Study of Logical Thinking and Moral Judgments in GCE Bible Knowledge Candidates." M.Ed. dissertation, University of Leeds.
Miller, K. L.
  1976   "The Relationship of Stages of Development in Children's Moral and Religious Thinking." Ed.D. dissertation, Arizona State University.
Mischey, E. J.
  1976   "Faith Development and Its Relationship to Moral Reasoning and Identity Status in Young Adults." Ph.D. dissertation, University of Toronto.
Mokrosch, R.
  1987   "Wertwandel des Wertwandels?" In *Christliche Werterziehung angesichts des Wertwandels,* edited by R. Mokrosch. Osnabrück: Universität Osnabrück.
Moltmann, J.
  1971   *Mensch: Christliche Anthropologie in den Konflikten der Gegenwart.* Stuttgart and Berlin: Kreuz-Verlag.
Moltmann-Wendel, E.
  1986   *A Land Flowing with Milk and Honey.* New York: Crossroad.
Moran, G.
  1983   *Religious Education Development: Images for the Future.* Minneapolis: Winston.
  1987   *No Ladder to the Sky: Education and Morality.* San Francisco: Harper & Row.
Morley, H. C.
  1975   "Religious Concepts of Slow Learners: An Application of the Findings of Ronald Goldman." *Learning for Living* 14.
Moseley, R. M., and K. Brockenbrough
  1988   "Faith Development in the Pre-School Years." In *Handbook of Preschool Religious Education,* edited by D. Ratcliff. Birmingham, AL: Religious Education Press.
Moseley, R., D. Jarvis, and J. W. Fowler
  1986   *Manual for Faith Development Research.* Atlanta: Center for Faith Development, Emory University.
Moskvichev, L. N.
  1986   "The Formation of Sociological Theory." In *Developments in Marxist Sociological Theory,* edited by A. G. Zrdravonyslov. London: Sage.
Murphy, R. J. L.
  1977a   "The Development of Religious Thinking in Three Easy Stages?" *Learning for Living* 17.
  1977b   "Does Children's Understanding of Parables Develop in Stages?" *Learning for Living* 16.
  1978   "A New Approach to the Study of the Development of Religious Thinking in Children." *Educational Studies,* 4.
  1979   "An Investigation into Some Aspects of the Development of Religious Thinking in Children Aged Between Six and Eleven Years." Ph.D. dissertation, University of St. Andrews.

Musgrove, F.
1965   *Youth and the Social Order.* Bloomington, IN: Wiley Interscience.
Nagle, U.
1934   *An Empirical Study of the Development of Religious Thinking in Boys from 12 to 16 Years Old.* New York: Catholic University Press of America.
Nagy, M.
1948   "The Child's View of Death." *Journal of Genetic Psychology* 73.
Nelson, C. Ellis, and D. Aleshire
1986   "Research in Faith Development." In Dykstra and Parks 1986.
Neuenzeit, P.
1985   Review of Oser and Gmünder 1984. *Religionsunterricht an höheren Schulen* 28.
Neugarten, B.
1979   "Time, Age and the Life Cycle." *American Journal of Psychiatry* 136.
Newman, J. H.
1870/1985   *An Essay in Aid of a Grammar of Assent.* New York: Oxford University Press.
Niebuhr, H. R.
1941   *The Meaning of Revelation.* New York: Macmillan.
1957   *Faith on Earth.* Unpublished manuscript, Niebuhr Archives.
1960   *Radical Monotheism and Western Culture, with Supplementary Essays.* London: Harper & Brothers.
1989   *Faith on Earth.* New Haven: Yale University Press.
Niggli, A.
1987a   *Familie und religiöse Erziehung in unserer Zeit: Eine empirische Studie über perzipierte religiöse Erziehungspraktiken als Kodetermanten religiöser Merkmale bei Erzogenen.* Dissertation, Pädagogisches Institut der Universität, Freiburg. Bern: Peter Lang. In 1988 a shortened version was written with the same main title.
1987b   "Untersuchung über Zusammenhänge zwischen dem religiösen Erziehungsstil der Eltern und religiösen Entwicklungsstufen ihrer Kinder." *Unterrichtswissenschaft* 2.
Nipkow, K. E.
1975/1984   *Grundfragen der Religionspädagogik,* Vols. 1, 2. Gütersloh: Mohn.
1982/1988   *Grundfragen der Religionspädagogik,* Vol. 3. Gütersloh: Mohn.
1983a   "Wachstum des Glaubens — Stufen des Glaubens. Zu James W. Fowlers Konzept der Strukturstufen des Glaubens auf reformatorischem Hintergrund." In *Reformation und Praktische Theologie,* edited by H. M. Müller and D. Rössler. Festschrift Werner Jetter zum 70. Geburtstag. Göttingen: Vandenhoeck & Ruprecht.
1983b   "Elementary Encounters with the Bible." *British Journal of Religious Education* 5.
1985   "Education's Responsibility for Morality and Faith in a Rapidly Changing World." *Religious Education* 80.

1986 "Elementarisierung als Kern der Lehrplanung und Unterrichtsvorbereitung am Beispiel der Eliaüberlieferung." *Braunschweiger Beiträge* 37(3).

1987a *Erwachsenwerden ohne Gott? Gotteserfahrung im Lebenslauf. (2d ed., 1988).* Munich.

1987b "Lebensgeschichte und religiöse Lebenslinie: Zur Bedeutung der Dimension des Lebenslaufs in der praktischen Theologie und Religionspädagogik." In *Jahrbuch der Religionspädagogik*, vol. 3, edited by P. Biehl et al. Neukirchen-Vluyn: Neukirchener Verlag.

1987c "Entwicklungspsychologie und Religionsdidaktik." *Zeitschrift für Pädagogik* 33(3).

1988 "Religiöse Denkformen in Glaubenskrisen und kirchlichen Konflikten: Zur Bedeutung postformaler dialektisch-paradoxaler und komplementärer Denkstrukturen. *Religionspädagogie.* Beiträge, 21.

Nipkow, K. E., and F. Schweitzer

1988 "Theorien der Glaubensentwicklung und des religiösen Urteils auf dem Prüfstand." In *Jahrbuch der Religionspädagogik*, vol. 4, edited by P. Biehl et al. Neukirchen-Vluyn: Neukirchener Verlag.

Nipkow, K. E., F. Schweitzer, and J. Fowler, eds.

1988 *Glaubensentwicklung und Erziehung.* [This is the German version of the current volume.] Gütersloh: Mohn.

Noam, G., and R. Kegan

1982 "Social Cognition and Psychodynamics: Towards a Clinical-Developmental Psychology." German trans. in *Perspektivität und Interpretation,* edited by W. Edelstein and M. Keller. Frankfurt: Suhrkamp.

O'Brien-Steinfels, M.

1987 "Women and Work." *New Catholic World* 230:140–43.

Ochs, C.

1983 *Women and Spirituality.* Totowa, NJ: Rowman & Allanheld.

Ogden, S.

1966 *The Reality of God.* New York: Harper & Row.

Okun, L.

1986 *Women Abuse: Facts Replacing Myths.* Albany: State University of New York Press.

Oser, F.

1980 "Stages of Religious Judgment." In *Toward Moral and Religious Maturity,* edited by J. Fowler et al., 277–315. Morristown, NJ: Silver Burdett.

1981 *Moralisches Urteil in Gruppen: Soziales Handeln, Verteilungsgerechtigkeit.* Frankfurt: Suhrkamp.

1985 "Religious Dilemmas: The Development of Religious Judgment." In *Philosophical and Psychological Issues in the Development of Moral Reasoning,* 175–90. Chicago: Precedent Publishing.

1987 "Toward a Logic of Religious Development: A Reply to My Critics." Paper presented at the Blaubeuren symposium on "Religious Development and Education," June 12–17, 1987.

1988   *Wieviel Religion braucht der Mensch?* Studien zur religiösen Autonomie. Gütersloh: Mohn.

Oser, F., W. Althof, and M. W. Berkowitz

1986   "Lo sviluppo della logica argomentativa nei dialoghi tra pari." *Età evolutiva: Rivista di Scienze dello sviluppo* 24:76–85.

Oser, F., W. Althof, and A. Bucher

1986   "Wisdom and Religious Development." Paper presented to the Symposium "Meaning of Life, Wisdom, Values and Religion: Aspects of Cognitive Development in Adulthood." Second European Conference on Developmental Psychology, Rome, 1986.

Oser, F., and A. Bucher

1985   "Wie beten Kinder und Jugendliche? Entwicklungs-stufen und Lernhilfen." *Lebendige Katechese.* Beiheft zu lebendige Seelsorge, 7:163–71.

1987   "Die Entwicklung des religiösen Urteils: Ein Forschungsprogramm." *Unterrichtswissenschaft* 2:132–56.

Oser, F., and P. Gmünder

1984   *Der Mensch: Stufen seiner religiösen Entwicklung: Ein strukturgenetischer Ansatz.* Zurich and Cologne: Benziger (2nd ed., 1988). Gütersloh: Mohn.

Oser, F. K., and K. H. Reich.

1987a   "The Challenge of Competing Explanations: The Development of Thinking in Terms of Complementarity of 'Theories.'" *Human Development* 30:178–86. Longer version: "Zur Entwicklung von Denken in Komplementarität." Prepublication draft. Fribourg: Pädagogisches Institut, No. 53.

1987b   "Moral Judgment, Religious Judgment, World Views: Their Relationship Considered Conceptually and as Supported by Empirical Data." *Berichte Zur Erziehungswissenschaft,* 61. Fribourg. Paper originally presented at the Biennial Meeting of the SRCD, Baltimore, Maryland, April 23–26, 1987.

Osmer, R.

1985   "Practical Theology and Contemporary Religious Education: An Historical and Constructive Analysis." Doctoral dissertation, Emory University.

Otto, R.

1963   *Das Heilige: Ueber das Irrationale in der Idee des Göttlichen und sein Verhältnis zum Rationalen.* Munich: Piper.

Palmer, C.

1844   *Evangelische Katechetik.* Stuttgart: Verlag der J. F. Steinkopf'schen Buchhandlung.

Paloutzian, R. F.

1983   *Invitation to the Psychology of Religion.* Glenview: Scott, Foresman.

Pannenberg, W.

1971   *Theologie und Reich Gottes.* Gütersloh: Mohn.

1973   *Wissenschaftstheorie und Theologie.* Frankfurt: Suhrkamp.

1976   *Theology and the Kingdom of God.* Philadelphia: Westminster.

Parks, S. L.
1980   "Faith Development and Imagination in the Context of Higher Education." Th.D. dissertation, Harvard University.
1986a   "Imagination and Spirit in Faith Development: A Way Past the Structure-Content Dichotomy." In Dykstra and Parks 1986, 137–56.
1986b   *The Critical Years: The Young Adult Search for a Faith to Live By*. San Francisco: Harper & Row.
1987   "Home and Pilgrimage: Spirituality as Nurture Toward a Vision of Our Planet as a Dwelling for the Whole Human Family." Presentation to the Ecumenical Institute of Spirituality, January 1987.
Patton, J.
1983   *Pastoral Counseling: A Ministry of the Church*. Nashville: Abingdon.
Paul, J.
1963   *Levana oder Erziehlehre*. Edited by K. G. Fischer. Paderborn: Schoningh.
Peatling, J. H.
1973   "The Incidence of Concrete and Abstract Religious Thinking in the Interpretation of Three Bible Stories by Pupils Enrolled in Grades Four Through Twelve in Selected Schools in the Episcopal Church in the United States of America." Ph.D. dissertation, University of New York.
1974   "Cognitive Development in Pupils in Grades Four Through Twelve: The Incidence of Concrete and Abstract Religious Thinking." *Character Potential* 7:52–61.
1977a   "Cognitive Development: Religious Thinking in Children, Youth and Adults." *Character Potential* 8:100–115.
1977b   "On Beyond Goldman: Religious Thinking and the 1970s." *Learning for Living*, 16:99–108.
Peatling, J. H., and C. W. Laabs
1975   "Cognitive Development of Pupils in Grades Four Through Twelve: A Comparative Study of Lutheran and Episcopalian Children and Youth." *Character Potential* 7:107–17.
Peatling, J. H., C. W. Laabs, and T. B. Newton.
1975   "Cognitive Development: A Three Sample Comparison of Means on the Peatling Scale of Religious Thinking." *Character Potential* 7:159–62.
Peck, M. S.
1978   *The Road Less Traveled*. New York: Simon & Shuster. German version 1986.
Perry, W. H.
1968   *Forms of Intellectual and Ethical Development in the College Years*. New York: Holt, Rinehart & Winston.
Pestalozzi, J. H.
1932   "Wie Gertrud ihre Kinder lehrt." In *J. H. Pestalozzi: Sämtliche Werke*, edited by A. Buchenau et al., 13. Berlin and Leipzig: de Gruyter.
1938   "Meine Nachforschungen über den Gang der Natur in der Entwicklung des Menschengeschlechts." In *J. H. Pestalozzi: Sämtliche Werke*. Berlin: de Gruyter.

Philbert, P. J.
   1982   Review Symposium. Review of Fowler 1981. *Horizons* 9(1):104–26.
   1985   Review of Fowler 1984a. *Horizons* 12(2):411–12.
Piaget, J.
   1929   *La représentation du monde chez l'enfant.* Paris: Presses universitaires de
             France. *The Child's Conception of the World.* London: Routledge &
             Kegan Paul.
   1947   *Psychologie der Intelligenz.* Zurich: Rascher.
   1954/1973 *Das moralische Urteil beim Kinde.* Zurich.
   1962   *The Moral Judgment of the Child.* New York: Collier.
   1970a   "Piaget's Theory." In *Carmichael's Manual of Child Psychology,* ed.
             Paul H. Mussen. 3d ed. Vol. 1. New York: Wiley.
   1970b   *The Child's Conception of Time,* trans. A. J. Pomerans. New York: Basic
             Books.
   1983   "Piaget's Theory." In *Handbook of Child Psychology,* Vol. 1, edited by
             P. H. Mussen. 4th ed. New York: Wiley.
Power, C., A. Higgins, and L. Kohlberg
   1988   "Moral Education, Community and Justice: A Study of Three Demo-
             cratic High Schools." Unpublished manuscript.
Power, C., and L. Kohlberg
   1980   "Religion, Morality, and Ego Development." In *Toward Moral and Reli-
             gious Maturity,* edited by J. Fowler et al. Morristown, NJ: Silver Burdett.
Powers, B. P.
   1985   Review of Fowler 1984a. *Faith and Mission* 3(1):105–6.
Priestley, J. G.
   1981   "Religious Story and the Literary Imagination." *British Journal of
             Religious Education* 4:17–24.
Proctor, R. A.
   1981   Review of Fowler 1981. *Review and Expositor* 78(4):612–13.
Rang, M.
   1959   *Rousseaus Lehre vom Menschen.* Göttingen: Vandenhoeck & Ruprecht.
Regan, T.
   1983   *The Case for Animal Rights.* Berkeley: University of California Press.
Reich, K. H.
   1987   "Children and Adolescents Between Religious and Scientific World
             Views: The Role of Thinking in Terms of Complementarity."
             Prepublication draft. Fribourg: Pädagogisches Institut, No. 63.
   1988   "Religiöse und naturwissenschaftliche Weltbilder: Entwicklung einer
             komplementären Betrachtungsweise in der Adoleszenz." *Unterrichts-
             wissenschaft* 3:332–41.
Rest, J. R.
   1983   "Morality." In *Cognitive Development,* edited by J. H. Flavell and E. M.
             Markman [*Manual of Child Psychology,* 4th ed., ed. P. H. Mussen, vol.
             3], 556–29. New York: Wiley.

Riccards, M. P.
1978 "The Structure of Religious Development: Empirical Evidence for a Stage Theory." *Lumen Vitae* 33:97–123.

Richmond, R. C.
1972 "Maturity of Religious Judgements and Differences of Religious Attitudes Between Ages of 13 and 16 years." *Education Review* 24:225–36.

Ricoeur, P.
1981 *Essays on Biblical Interpretation.* London: SPCK.

Riemann, F.
1961 *Grundformen der Angst.* Munich: Reinhardt.

Ringel, E., and A. Kirchmayer
1985 *Religionsverlust durch religiöse Erziehung: Tiefenpsychologische Ursachen und Folgerungen.* Vienna: Herder.

Rizzuto, A. M.
1979 *The Birth of the Living God.* Chicago: University of Chicago Press.
1980 "The Psychological Foundations of Belief in God." In *Toward Moral and Religious Maturity,* edited by J. Fowler et al., 115–35. Morristown, NJ: Silver Burdett.

Robertson, R.
1973 *Einführung in die Religionssoziologie.* Munich: Kaiser-Grünewald.

Rössler, D.
1986 *Grundriß der Praktischen Theologie.* Berlin and New York: Walter de Gruyter.

Rousseau, J.-J.
1981 *Emil oder Über die Erziehung.* Translated by L. Schmidts. Paderborn: Schoningh.

Rowe, A. J.
1981 "Children's Thinking and the Bible." *Journal of Christian Education* 70:18–32.

Roy, P. R.
1979 "Applications of Piaget's Theory of Cognitive Development to Religious Thinking with Special Reference to the Work of Dr. R. J. Goldman." M.Ed. dissertation, University of Liverpool.

Royce, J.
1908 *The Philosophy of Loyalty.* New York: Macmillan.
1912 *The Sources of Religious Insight.* New York: Charles Scribner's Sons.

Rubin, L.
1979 *Women of a Certain Age.* New York: Harper & Row.

Ruether, R.
1983 *Sexism and God-talk: Toward a Feminist Theology.* Boston: Beacon Press.

Salzmann, C. G.
1897 "Über die wirksamsten Mittel, Kindern Religion beizubringen." In *C. G. Salzmann: Ausgewählte Schriften,* edited by E. Ackermann. Langensalza.

Sawicki, M.
1986 Review of Fowler 1984a. *Lexington Theological Quarterly* 21(1):31–32.

Scharfenberg, J.
1976   "Kommunikation in der Kirche als symbolische Interaktion." In *Seel-sorgeausbildung*, edited by W. Becher. Göttingen: Vandenhoeck & Ruprecht.
1985   *Einführung in die Pastoralpsychologie.* Göttingen: Vandenhoeck & Ruprecht.
Scharfenberg, J., and H. Kämpfer
1980   *Mit Symbolen leben.* Olten: Walter.
Schelling, F.
1985   *Of Human Freedom*, trans. James Gutmann. Preu, IL: Open Court.
Schieder, R.
1987   *Civil Religion: Die religiöse Dimension der politischen Kultur.* Gütersloh: Mohn.
Schildknecht, M.
1984   "Entwicklungen von Argumentationsstrategien in moralischen und religiösen Diskussionen." Prepublication draft. Fribourg: Pädagogisches Institut.
Schillebeeckx, E.
1987   *On Christian Faith: The Spiritual, Ethical, and Political Dimensions.* New York: Crossroad.
Schleiermacher, F.
1966   *Pädagogische Schriften.* Edited by E. Weniger and T. Schulze. 2nd ed. Düsseldorf and Munich.
1967   "Über die Religion." In *Reden an die Gebildeten unter ihren Verächtern.* 6th ed. Göttingen: Perthes.
Schmidt, H.
1984   "Religionsdidaktik, Ziele, Inhalte und Methoden religiöser Erziehung in Unterricht und Schule." *Theologische Wissenschaft* 16(2). Teilband: Der Unterricht in Klasse 1–13. Stuttgart: Kohlhammer.
Schmidtchen, G.
1979   *Was den Deutschen heilig ist.* Munich: Kösel.
Schmidtchen, G., and M. Seitz.
1973   *Gottesdienst in einer rationalen Welt.* Stuttgart: Herder.
Schüssler Fiorenza, E.
1981   "Sexism and Conversion." *Network* May-June.
Schütz, A.
1932   *Der Sinnhafte Aufbau der sozialen Welt.* Vienna: Springer.
Schweder, R.
1982   Review of Kohlberg 1981a. *Contemporary Psychology* June, 421–24.
Schweitzer, F.
1985   "Religion und Entwicklung: Bemerkungen zur kognitiv-strukturellen Religionspsychologie." *Wege zum Menschen* 37:316–25.
1986a   Besprechung von Fraas and Heimbrock 1986. *Der Evang. Erzieher* 38:610–13.

1986b   "Soziales Verstehen und moralisches Urteil - Kognitive Entwicklungs-theorien und ihre pädagogische Bedeutung." *Sozialwissenschaftliche Literaturrundschau* 9(12):5–19.

1986c   "Moralisches Lernen—Überlegungen zur didaktischen Erschließung moralischer Inhalte." *Der Evang. Erzieher* 38:420–34.

1987a   *Lebensgeschichte und Religion: Religiöse Entwicklung und Erziehung im Kindes- und Jugendalter.* Munich: Kaiser.

1987b   "Progress, Continuity and Change: Three Approaches to the Language Problem in Religious Education." *British Journal of Religious Education* 9:70–77.

Selman, R. L.
1980   *The Growth of Interpersonal Understanding: Developmental and Clinical Analyses.* New York: Academic Press.

Seyfarth, C.
1984   "Religionssoziologische Aspekte der Wertwandelsproblematik." In *Religion und gesellschaftlicher Wandel,* ed. H. May. Loccumer Protokolle.

Sheehy, G.
1976   *Passages: Predictable Crises of Adult Life.* New York: E. P. Dutton.
1981   *Pathfinders.* New York: Morrow.

Shulik, R. M.
1979   "Faith Development, Moral Development and Old Age: An Assessment of Fowler's Faith Development Paradigm." Ph.D. dissertation. University of Chicago.

Simmons, H.
1982   Review of Fowler 1981. *Religious Education* 77(1):112–13.

Simpson, E. L.
1974   "Moral Development Research: A Case Study of Scientific Cultural Bias." *Human Development* 17:81–106.

Singer, R. E.
1959   "A Study of the God Concept of Children in Three Suburban Religious Schools Using the Osgood-Suci-Tannenbaum Semantic Differential Technique." Ph.D. dissertation, Northwestern University.

Slee, N.
1983   "Parable Teaching: Exploring New Worlds." *British Journal of Religious Education* 5:134–38.

1986a   "Goldman Yet Again: An Overview and Critique of His Contribution to Research." *British Journal of Religious Education* 8:84–93.

1986b   "A Note on Goldman's Methods of Data Analysis with Special Reference to Scalogram Analysis." *British Journal of Religious Education* 8:168–75.

1987

     "The Development of Religious Thinking: Some Linguistic Considerations." *British Journal of Religious Education* 9:60–69.

Smith, M. E.
1980   "Obedient Sonship." *British Journal of Religious Education* 2:85–98.
1981   "I did not speak about bread." *The Month* 14:48–52.

1983 "Developments in Faith." *The Month* 16:222–25.
1986a "Answers to Some Questions About Faith Development." *British Journal of Religious Education* 8:79–83.
1986b "Progress in Faith Development." *The Month* 19:93–95.
1986c "Vocation and Maturity of Faith." *The Month* 19:131–33.

Smith, M. E., and B. Miller
1984 "Symbol and the Faith Process." *The Month* 17:328–32.

Smith, W. C.
1962 *The Meaning and End of Religion.* New York: Macmillan.
1977 *Belief and History.* Charlottesville: University Press of Virginia.
1979 *Faith and Belief.* Princeton: Princeton University Press.

Snapper, M. J.
1982 Review of Fowler 1981. *Calvin Theological Journal* 17(1):105–7.

Snarey, J.
1990 "Faith Development, Moral Development, and Nontheistic Judaism: A Construct Validity Study." In *Handbook of Moral Behavior and Development,* Vol. 2, *Research,* edited by W. Kurtines and J. Gewirtz. Hillsdale, NJ: Erlbaum.

Sölle, D.
1975 *Suffering.* Philadelphia: Fortress.

Spilka, B.
1982 "Morality and Faith: Growing Up Together." [Review of Fowler 1981]. *Journal of Psychology and Theology* 10(2):150–54.

Spitz, R.
1957 *No and Yes: On the Genesis of Human Communication.* New York: International University Press.
1966 *No and Yes: On the Genesis of Human Communication.* Independence, MO: International University Press.

Spranger, E.
1960 *Psychologie des Jugendalters.* Heidelberg: Quelle & Meyer.

Steckel, C. J.
1987 "The Emergence of Morality and Faith in Stages: A Theological Critique of Developmental Theories." In *Changing Views of the Human Condition,* edited by Paul Pruyser. Macon, GA: Mercer University Press.

Stevenson-Moessner, J.
1985 Review of Fowler 1984a. *Religious Education* 30(3):491–92.

Stoffels, H. C., and G. Dekker
1987 *Geloven van huis uit.* Een onderzoek naar godsdienstige veranderingen bij studenten van de Vrije Universiteit. Kampen: Kok.

Stern, D. N.
1985 *The Interpersonal World of the Infant.* New York: Basic Books.

Stone, C.
1972 *Should Trees Have Standing?* Los Angeles: William Kaufman.

Streeter, H. C.
1981 "The Place of Religious Education in the Curriculum of Young Children." M.Ed. dissertation, Roehampton Institute of Higher Education.

Strommen, M. P., ed.
1971   *Research on Religious Development: A Comprehensive Handbook*. New York: Hawthorn.
Studzinski, R.
1986   Review of Fowler 1984a. *Worship* 60(3):276–78.
Sullivan, E.
1977   "A Study of Kohlberg's Structural Theory of Moral Development: A Critique of Liberal Social Science Ideology." *Human Development* 20:325–76.
Sully, J.
1908   *Studies of Childhood*. New York: Appleton.
Tamminen, K.
1976   "Research Concerning the Development of Religious Thinking in Finnish Students." *Character Potential* 7:206–19.
1987   "Religion und Jugend in der finnischen Forschung." In *Jugend und Religion in Europa*, edited by U. Nembach, 305–37. *Forschungen zur Prakt. Theologie* vol. 2.
Tanaka, J.
1985   "The Role of Religious Education in Preventing Sexual and Domestic Violence." In *Women's Issues in Religious Education*, edited by Fern M. Giltner. Birmingham, AL: Religious Education Press.
Tanner, A. E.
1906   "Children's Religious Ideas." *Pedagogical Seminary* 13:511–13.
ter Bogt, T.
1987   *Opgroeien in Groenlo*. Amersfoort: Acco.
Theissen, G.
1984   *Biblischer Glaube aus evolutionarer Sicht*. Munich: Kaiser.
Thouless, R., and L. Brown
1965   "Petitionary Prayer: Belief in Its Appropriateness and Causal Efficacy among Adolescent Girls." In *From Religious Experience to a Religious Attitude*, ed. A. Godin. Chicago: Loyola University Press.
Tillich, P.
1957   Dynamics of Faith. New York: Harper & Row.
1958   *Die verlorene Dimension*. In (1980): *Tillich-Auswahl*, Band 2. Gütersloh: GTB.
Toulmin, S.
1950   *An Examination of the Place of Reason in Ethics*. Cambridge: University Press.
Tracy, D.
1975   *Blessed Rage for Order*. New York: Crossroad/Seabury.
1981   *The Analogical Imagination*. New York: Crossroad.
1983   "The Foundations of Practical Theology." In *Practical Theology*, edited by D. S. Browning, 61–82. San Francisco: Harper & Row.
1987   *Plurality and Ambiguity*. San Francisco: Harper & Row.

Turner, E. B.
1978a   "Religious Language: Some Reflections of Cognitive Functioning."
         Catholic Education Today 12:20–24.
1978b   "Towards a Standardised Test of Religious Language Comprehension."
         British Journal of Religious Education 1:14–21.
1980   "Intellectual Ability and the Comprehension of Religious Language."
         Irish Journal of Psychology 4:182–90.
Turner, V.
1961   "Ritual Symbolism, Morality and Social Structure among the Nedembu."
         Rhodes-Livingstone Journal 30.
1964   "Symbols in Ndembu Ritual." In *Closed Systems and Open Minds*, edited
         by M. Gluckman. Chicago: Aldine.
1969   *The Ritual Process: Structure and Anti-Structure*. Hawthorne, NY: Aldine
         de Gruyter.
1985   "Images of Anti-Temporality: An Essay in the Anthropology of
         Experience." In *On the Edge of the Bush*, edited by V. Turner, 227–46.
         Tucson: University of Arizona Press.
University of Sheffield Institute of Education
1961   *Religious Education in Secondary Schools*. London: Nelson.
van den Daele, W.
1985   *Mensch nach Maß?* Munich: Beck.
van der Lans, J.
1984   "De functie van het symbool in de liturgie Theoretische preambule ten
         behoeve van een empirisch onderzoek." In *Spiritualiteit: Social-
         setenschappelijke en theologische beschouwingen*. Baarn: Ambo.
van der Leeuw, G.
1933   *Phänomenologie der Religion*. Tübingen: J. C. B. Mohr.
van der Ploeg, P.
1985   *Het lege testament: Een onderzoek onder jonge Kerkverlaters*. Franeker:
         Wever.
van Gennep, A.
1909   *Les Rites de Passage*. Paris: E. Nourry.
1909/1986 *Übergangsriten*. Frankfurt: Campus.
van der Ven, J. A.
1988   "Auf dem Weg zu einer empirischen Theodizee." *Religionspädegogie*.
         Beiträge, 21:139–56.
Vergouwen, L., and J. van der Lans
1986   "Wie gelóóft er nou zoiets? Geloofshoudingen bij jongeren." In *Een
         komende generatie gelovigen . . .* , edited by F. H. Kuiper and H. J. M.
         Vossen. Zwolle: Waanders.
Vine, I.
1986   "Moral Maturity in Socio-cultural Perspective: Are Kohlberg's Stages
         Universal?" In *Lawrence Kohlberg: Consensus and Controversy*, edited
         by A. Modgil and C. Modgil. Philadelphia: Falmer.

von Brachel, H. U., and F. Oser
  1984   *Kritische Lebensereignisse und religiöse Strukturentransformationen.*
          Prepublication draft. Fribourg: Pädagogisches Institut, No. 43.
Vygotsky, L. S.
  1962   *Thought and Language.* Cambridge, MA: MIT Press.
Walker, L.
  1980   "Cognitive and Perspective-Taking Prerequisites for Moral Develop-
          ment." *Child Development* 51:131–40.
Wallwork, E.
  1980   "Morality, Religion, and Kohlberg's Theory." In *Moral Development,
          Moral Education, and Kohlberg,* edited by B. Munsey. Birmingham, AL:
          Religious Education Press.

  1982   "Religious Development." In *Cognitive Developmental Psychology of
          James Mark Baldwin,* edited by J. Broughton, 335–87. Norwood, NJ:
          Ablex Publishing.
Way, P. A.
  1982   "Pastoral Care and Pastoral Theology: Responses to Faith Development
          Theory." Unpublished paper presented at the Conference on Faith
          Development, Auburn Theological Seminary, March.
Weber, H. R.
  1979   *Jesus and the Children.* Geneva: World Council of Churches.
Weber, M.
  1922   *Wirtschaft und Gesellschaft.* Tübingen: Mohr-Siebeck.
Webster, D. H.
  1984   "James Fowler's Theory of Faith Development." *British Journal of
          Religious Education* 7:14–18,
Weizsäcker, V. v.
  1960   *Gestalt und Zeit.* 2nd ed. Göttingen: Vandenhoeck & Ruprecht.
Wellmer, A.
  1985   "Reason, Utopia and the Dialectic of Enlightenment." In R. J. Bernstein
          1985.
Westerhoff, J. H., and W. H. Willimon
  1980   *Liturgy and Learning through the Life Cycle.* New York: Seabury.
White, L.
  1968   *Machina Ex Deo: Essays in the Dynamism of Western Culture.*
          Cambridge, MA: MIT Press.
Whitehouse, E.
  1972   "Children's Reactions to the Zacchaeus Story." *Learning for Living*
          11(4):19–24.
Wygotski, L. S.
  1964   *Denken und Sprechen.* Stuttgart: S. Fischer.
Yankelovich, D.
  1982   *New Rules: Searching for Self-Fulfillment in a World Turned Upside
          Down.* New York: Random.

Youniss, J.
   1982   "Die Entwicklung und Funktion von Freundschaftsbeziehungen." In
           Perspektivität und Interpretation, edited by W. Edelstein and M. Keller,
           78–109. Frankfurt: Suhrkamp.
Ziller, T.
   1884   *Grundlegung zur Lehre vom erziehenden Unterricht.* Edited by T. Vogt.
           Leipzig: Veit & Comp.
   1886   *Materialien zur speziellen Pädagogik.* Edited by M. Bergner. Dresden.

Contributors

Günther Bittner, University of Würzburg, Germany
Sharon L. Daloz Parks, Weston School of Theology, USA
Reiner Döbert, Free University of Berlin, Germany
Gloria Durka, Fordham University, USA
James W. Fowler, Emory University, USA
Hans-Günther Heimbrock, Gröningen University, Netherlands
John M. Hull, University of Birmingham, England
Gabriel Moran, New York University, USA
Karl Ernst Nipkow, Tübingen University, Germany
Fritz K. Oser, Fribourg University, Switzerland
F. Clark Power, University of Notre Dame, USA
Friedrich Schweitzer, Tübingen University, Germany
Nicola Slee, Rochampton Institute, Whitelands College, England

Index